Jo ... Tas... joys of teaching, she has spent 40 years in Sydney schools, the last 23 as principal, first at St Catherine's School, Waverley and then at St Lucy's School, Wahroonga. Now retired from paid work, she devotes her time to education and supporting families who have children with disabilities as well as assisting a women's co-operative in a South African township and visiting her grandchildren in the USA. In Sydney she lives surrounded by native bush and rose-fancying wallabies and is kept abreast of the urban and cool by a 14 year old grandson.

ABOUT THE ILLUSTRATOR

A former St Catherine's student, Robyn Chadwick studied at the National Art School, Sydney and now works from her studio at home. Drawing – in pen and ink and in watercolour – is her passion. She exhibits her watercolours in public galleries as well as creating whimsical cards and book illustrations. Her watercolours on fabric are sold all over the world.

To children everywhere who live life at the
edge of the bell curve and their parents and teachers

Brace yourself for an intensely emotional journey. Jo Karaolis's story of her transition from principal of an 'establishment' girls school to become the head of a primary school for children with severe disabilities will not only engross and inspire you; it will challenge you to rethink some of your own attitudes towards disability, cultural difference, compassion, tolerance, acceptance ... and the awesome power of love in education.

Hugh Mackay AO

As part of my duties as chair of the panel reviewing funding for schooling for the federal government I visited many schools. One of these was St Lucy's School for children with disabilities.

Even though it is now five years ago I remember perfectly ... What I saw there was absolutely remarkable. I met teachers who were devoted to their students. I was introduced to students with severe disabilities who (even though some could not talk) made me welcome and endeared themselves to me so that many of them come to my mind so many years later as I write this preface. The spirit in the school was strong and friendly and the parents that I met were totally committed.

It was to say the least a joyful experience and influenced me way beyond just the issues we were dealing with on school funding.

One of the most wonderful treats of the visit was to meet Jo Karaolis. I have always admired people who are 'on top of their game'. Jo undoubtedly was. In our discussions she displayed a wonderful modesty, an ambition for the school and its students and a patience and wish to contribute. To describe Jo as a star is probably a misstatement. The stars of the school undoubtedly were the students but Jo and her staff were 'up there'.

Reading With Enough Love *has brought back many of the memories and views that I felt and experienced in my visit that day.*

I confess to visibly smiling at times and developing a tear at others as I read the chapters that Jo has put together from her work with children who, yes, have disabilities but often have a spirit and make a contribution to one's inner self way beyond that given to one by able-bodied people.

This is a book worth reading but I warn it will make you wonder what your contribution is and question how does one bump into people of the quality of Jo who quietly make a contribution way beyond what the rest of us are able to achieve.

David Gonski AC

Jo Karaolis has been an inspiration in my life ever since I first encountered her approach to leadership as the Principal of St Catherine's School, Waverley. Jo's honest appraisal of her own prejudices and short comings and her willingness to challenge herself and to constantly search for solutions, for individual children and for the school, are at the heart of this story. The intrinsic value of the person shines through in her accounts of individual children and how much each of them teaches us about what is important in life. It is a very appropriate book to be launching in the first year of the full implementation of the National Disability Insurance Scheme.

Professor Mary Foley AM,
former Secretary of Health, NSW

During her time as principal, Jo introduced a curriculum that was heavily influenced by Reggio Emilia and centred on the Arts and creativity. The children's responses to and achievements through this approach were stunning and clearly demonstrate the transformative potential of the Arts in learning.

Robyn Ewing AM,
Professor of Teacher Education and the Arts,
The University of Sydney

This story ... is a powerful account of transformation and change ... (and) of how a school moves from an instructional and control focus to a learning-centred community where spiritual values are implemented in creative and practical ways. Love is not a common term in the daily lexicon of educators but in this volume its force is manifest. Moreover it motivates risk taking and demonstrates that remarkable outcomes occur when its power is unleashed.

Gordon Stanley,
Honorary Professor of Education,
The University of Sydney

First published in 2016 by Jo Karaolis

Text copyright © Jo Karaolis 2016
Illustrations copyright © Robyn Chadwick 2016

The moral right of the author has been asserted.

All rights reserved. No part of this book may be reproduced or transmitted by any persons or entity, including internet search engines or retailers, in any form or by any means, electronic or mechanical, including photocopying (except under the statutory exceptions provisions of the Australian Copyright Act 1968), recording, scanning or by any information storage and retrieval systems without the prior written permission of the author.

National Library of Australia Cataloguing-in-Publication entry

    Karaolis, Jo, author.

    With enough love : my ten years as principal of a very special school / Jo Karaolis.

    978-0-9945552-2-9 With Enough Love (print)
    978-0-9945552-3-6 With Enough Love (Createspace)
    978-0-9945552-4-3 With Enough Love (mobi)

    Subjects: School principals--Australia--Biography.
    Teachers--Australia--Attitudes.
    Educational change--Australia.

371.20092

Cover painting by Clare Hooper.

Custom book publishing by Captain Honey Pty Ltd.
Front cover and internal design by Natalie Winter.
www.captainhoney.com.au

5 4 3 2 1   16 17 18 19 20

With Enough Love

My ten years as principal of a very special school

JO KARAOLIS

CONTENTS

Foreword	xi
Note to Reader	xv
First Day	1
Meeting the Parents	20
Feeling My Way	41
At a Crossroad	62
Vision	78
Tasha Wins Through	93
Thinking Creatively	112
Inclusion	135
Finding Enough Love	157
Community	175
Marching on Canberra	196
Going Outback	215
Harry	233
Moment of Truth	253
High School	273
Final Year	292
Goodbye	309
Acknowledgments	315

FOREWORD

by Professor The Honourable Dame Marie Bashir AD C VO

With Enough Love is a moving account of an epic journey undertaken by a skilled and compassionate teacher during her years of responsibility leading a school, which was designed to improve the quality of life for children living with disabilities. A graduate in psychological studies, as well as in education, her insight into the effect of such disability was further enriched.

Whilst the author shares with us factual aspects of the many dimensions of her role, it is apparent that her considerable empathy with the children and her pragmatic, though also caring interaction with the parents, never faltered. Indeed these qualities contributed significantly to successful outcomes.

Having had fulfilling and successful appointments within two prestigious education facilities, the author subsequently undertook, with considerable hope, the challenge of enhancing the skills and confidence of children with disability, at a school established for such education and development. A few of the children were enduring complete visual loss – blindness. Many others had been identified with a diagnosis of autistic disorder, Down syndrome, Prader-Willi, Fragile X and a range of causes of developmental delay.

With Enough Love provides an inspirational account of the effect of a sensitively directed educational experience on these children, one which illuminated the potential and positive aspects of the individual child and their future ability.

Revealing the initial weight of personal responsibility involved, thc author shares her joy in observing the progress of so many of the children, and also in her capacity to act as a positive buffer between the difficulties of the children and the escalating frustration on the part of one or both parents.

Indeed, individual accounts of these experiences and interactions sensitise the reader to appreciate not only the priceless value to child and family of targeted, positive intervention. One also develops an awareness of the powerful preventive aspect of this skilled work. It is preventive in actively reducing the risk of such children, whether in childhood or in the coming years, of falling prey and victim to those who yearn to take destructive advantage, whether physical or psychological, of vulnerability in childhood or across the years of adolescence.

Those who work in various fields with young people will find that the author has provided not only fact, but also wisdom, which can be readily applied in working with this important population.

In particular, one is alerted to the difficulties experienced by some of the young people in their transition to a mainstream school after time spent in a very personal and supportive scholastic environment.

Not unexpectedly, one learns of the fight against cuts to government funding, a fight to ensure continuity of the program as well as efforts to extend its availability beyond the city, through creative use of Skype whereby one can share information across distances in positive and creative discourse.

And with the inclusion of Aboriginal young people and their families from rural regions, the importance of cultural understanding is stressed.

With Enough Love has provided a beacon of light and wisdom for all who are committed to the wellbeing and advancement of young people, in particular all those who will benefit from guided support in surmounting disability.

NOTE TO READER

The stories in this book are drawn from my personal experience as principal of a special school but my hope is that they honour the experience of all families, teachers and schools who have children they care for living with a disability. Names and identifying features have been altered, some characters are composites and some events are conflated. This is a memoir and as such is a very personal view of the events depicted. I have tried to be true to my own perception of things but I acknowledge most freely that others will have seen and experienced the same events differently. I earnestly hope that nothing in these pages will cause distress to anyone. My wish is to make known the exceptional beauty and wealth of spirit I have experienced in these children and in their parents who have been made extraordinary through the gift of their children. As an educator, I hope also to have laid bare my halting and uncertain approach to change guided not by theory but by the bone-deep conviction that all children, however endowed by birth, have the same spirit and the same needs and rights.

FIRST DAY

A sassy blonde girl with arms crossed stood in front of me, a disapproving set to her jaw. Her blue eyes confronted mine. 'Miss Bossy!' she said in a scornful voice, her chin tilted reprovingly at me. My welcoming smile faded awkwardly. I had felt a little nervous coming to the school for this first day but for goodness sake, I had told myself, you have been principal for thirteen years of a school of nearly one thousand boisterous adolescent girls; what can be so hard about sixty-seven primary-aged students, vision impaired and blind? Now looking down at the stern eyes of this youngster with Down syndrome, I wondered. She held her stare for a long moment then, suddenly relenting, flashed me a jaunty smile and without another word, ran off across the playground.

I looked after her. The drab playground was emptying as teachers led their classes away to the surrounding dark brown brick buildings. I stood alone on the dull black asphalt, wondering what had gone wrong. I had been as pleasant and likable as I knew how, yet the children couldn't have been less interested and as for the staff, they were too busy trying to hush their charges and stop them running away to pay much attention to what the new principal said. As the noise level rose with odd high-pitched vocalising and general commotion, I had raised my voice. It was the habit of years of teaching, but not a good move, judging by the feedback from my young critic with the stunning smile.

It was deflating but I was puzzled too. It was supposed to be a primary school for blind children but not many of the children assembled on the playground had been blind. Most were strange to me in ways that I had not expected nor prepared for and I wondered with some concern what I had gotten myself into. All the written material I was sent when I applied for the job was about a school for the blind; the website images and text spoke only of educating vision impaired children. I had been told that if there were unfilled vacancies in the school, children who had other kinds of disability were accepted, but I had assumed they were the exception. It is my way to over prepare when I take something on and in the months between my appointment and when I was due to start, I had swotted up the braille alphabet and the most common contractions, written a research paper for my psychology degree on reading problems in children blind from birth and even learned to play scrabble with a blind friend's brailled scrabble set. My appointment had not been welcomed by everyone and I wanted to get myself up to speed as best I could.

I was as surprised as everyone else when I got this job. I applied more or less on a whim. I had retired at fifty-eight which people told me was young, but I was tired. I had been headmistress for thirteen years at St Catherine's, a very old Anglican girls' school in Sydney's Eastern Suburbs, which I had loved. But Costi, my husband, died suddenly a couple of years after I started at the school and I had not fully dealt with the shock and pain, just buried myself in work. Now I felt it was time to face the shadows that haunted me on nights I couldn't sleep. Besides, I had a goal. There was much that we had achieved at St Cath's in my thirteen years as principal there that I was proud of, but not the way we provided for children with special needs. We had tried all sorts of things, special curriculum, additional support, varying our methods to suit individual learning needs. We had an excellent 'special needs' co-ordinator. It all helped but still, compared to our success with more able students, it felt like we were failing those who needed us most.

We are odd in Australia, the way we judge a school by how well its most able students do and publish league tables based on the academic success of high flyers who would do well no matter which school they went to. It is not how we estimate the worth of doctors. We would be outraged if a hospital closed its doors to the sickest patients and think it odd if doctors boasted of their success with patients in the pink of health. Children who need the most skilled and expert teaching, in my experience, were regularly turned away from private schools and in no school were they given the top quality teaching their needs warranted.

So my goal when I retired was to start a school for children with disabilities as a kind of halfway house that prepared them for successful inclusion in regular schools and then supported the schools that took them through the period of adjustment. It wasn't to be however. Two years of finishing off a psychology degree and taking courses in special education, two years of meeting with principals and winning their support, two years of investigating the statutory and legal requirements, all came to nought when it turned out that the available government funding was not sufficient for the student-to-staff ratio that children with special needs must have. I didn't have private means to make up the shortfall. It was in a dark mood of disappointment and frustration that I came upon the advertisement for a principal at a non-government special school whose name I knew well as it had been quoted to me several times as flourishing despite the negative funding environment. I decided to apply. If nothing else, I could discover how the school managed financially. I wrote a candid letter of application listing all the ways I was unsuitable: not Catholic, no experience of special schools, a history teacher who had never taught in primary schools, retired and at sixty, decidedly old. By return mail came an invitation to interview.

'So you think you'd like to be principal of a special school?' The voice was warm and tinged with laughter. I turned from studying the certificates on the wall of the school foyer to look at the speaker and saw a dark haired woman in her early forties who radiated an empathetic kind of energy. Her brown eyes were alight behind her huge glasses and I felt instantly drawn to her. She held out her hand: 'I'm Gae, I am the Chair of the Board.' I loved that interview. Gae took me around the school and encouraged me to tell her all that I held most dear about teaching and education. She listened with tilted head and when I became hotly passionate, smiled sympathetically instead of recoiling slightly as most people did when I became vehement. I found myself pouring out a stream of words about how schools should be joy-filled places where learning is an offshoot of the adventure of living, not treadmills shaping students to be widgets in the country's economy.

'Look around, see how dark and depressing these buildings are,' I said rashly. Instead of taking offence, Gae laughed and I knew I had met a soulmate. Suddenly I really wanted this job. I realised as I drove away in a state of euphoric excitement that I had found out nothing about how the school managed financially.

My appointment when it was announced a month or so later caused consternation. Catholic schools were expected to have Catholic principals and special schools were supposed to be led by experts in special education. But Gae was breezily confident of my capacity and was supported by Sister Clare, one of the Dominican Sisters on the Board. I wasn't used to religious sisters and Sister Clare was a surprise to me, remarkably urbane in what she knew and talked about and always fashionably dressed with professionally coiffed and tinted hair. At the same time, she was uncompromising in applying spiritual principles to worldly issues. She told the Board that choosing an Anglican as principal for a Dominican school was a truthful application of the Sisters' commitment to ecumenism.

No one asked the staff. In my first few meetings with them they had let me know they were less than impressed at having a new principal who had never been in a special needs classroom. I had vainly believed my extensive experience in administering a large college meant I would be a gift to this little special school. The gaps in my experience could be quickly overcome, I thought with a bland confidence that now faltered as I stood on the bare playground, feeling exposed and uncertain. But I am the 'crash or crash through' type and so, straightening my shoulders, I prepared to get on with it. It was then that I noticed a girl standing about ten metres from me, very still. Had she been there all along? She was dark skinned with brown eyes that stared blankly in my direction. Her body was hunched in a kind of sullen misery and instinctively I moved forward to see what was wrong. Only as I got close did I recognise with a start of annoyance at my slow wits that she was holding a white cane in her hand. *D'uh!* I thought, She's blind. What did you expect? She seemed frozen to the spot. 'What's your name?' I asked her gently.

'Leyla.'

'I'm the new principal, Leyla. Did you get left behind?' A faint ripple of returning competence: here at least was something I could do. 'Tell me what class you are in and I'll help you find it.'

I was startled to hear a man's voice call out abruptly from somewhere behind me. 'Leyla, you know your way to the classroom. Move along.' I turned to see a senior staff member, Jack Cornford, staring past me at Leyla, his grey eyes fixed steadfastly on her. He moved past me towards Leyla saying in a steady voice, 'You can do it. Use your cane and find your classroom.' Leyla seemed inclined to stand her ground but as Jack drew close she turned and moved off slowly, giving her cane a desultory swing from side to side as she went.

'Leyla plays on everyone's sympathy,' Jack said as he watched Leyla's departing back. 'Wait till you see little Kacey.' He turned to me then and the furrow in his brow softened. 'Kacey's only four and has no more vision than Leyla but she flies around the place like a hornet. The trouble with

Leyla is her parents. They spoil her, do everything for her. They are her worst enemy if they only knew it.'

Watching the lone little figure as she slowly made her way to the concrete stairs, I felt a rush of sympathy for Leyla's parents. I would want to make her life easier too. Jack was looking sideways at me. 'You think I'm hard,' he said his eyes narrowing. 'Let me tell you something. Leyla is cute now and you want to make allowances for her. But when she gets older, she won't seem cute any more, nor will any of the children. If we haven't taught them to be independent and well-behaved, no one will want anything to do with them.'

His lips were clenched in a tight line, as though shut firmly on any unwanted emotion. *Not as hard as you like to make out,* I thought to myself. I knew him to be highly regarded as a leader in vision education in Australia and in the few encounters we had had during my induction, had found him to be intelligent and efficient, but there was something about him that kept me at a distance. I understood what he was saying. Tough love. But it was not my way – I had always sought to draw the best from children by encouraging and supporting them. Noticing my silence, Jack turned back to me and acknowledged my unspoken discomfiture with a quizzical smile. 'You'll get used to us in time,' he said, crossing his arms. I nodded silently, not wanting him to know how dismayed I felt. I muttered something and headed off after Leyla. I'd see if she did find her room, I thought, and then I'd visit some of the classes. I wanted to find out what I had unwittingly taken on.

Leyla had moved surprisingly quickly and was already at the door of her upstairs classroom. As I caught up with her, she disappeared inside and shut the door in my face. I looked along the brick-walled corridor. It was studded with scratched and dented classroom doors, each painted a different colour. I knocked on the next one and too late remembered that the principal I had replaced said she never went into classrooms. 'It disturbs the children and the teachers don't like it,' she had told me. I turned the door handle and tentatively poked my head in. I could not see the teacher at first and as I stood looking around for her, a short barrel-shaped boy scooted under my raised arm and out through the door. An adult aide pushed past me then in hasty pursuit. I paused on the threshold, dumbly blinking.

'Shut the door!' said a loud and authoritative voice. 'We don't want to lose any more.' I sensed the words – *thanks to a stupid principal who knows nothing about special schools* – hanging unvoiced in the air and I looked for the speaker. She stood at a nearby desk, a tall, striking-looking woman standing with one hand on a desk looking impatiently at me, the annoying intruder. I began to apologise and her dark face slowly lightened until she grinned and shrugged her shoulders. 'It's all right. It happens all the time,' she said. I must have been looking mortified because she added,

'Don't worry, you'll get used to us after a while.' Softening further, she held out her hand. 'I'm Sybil'. The amused look in her dark eyes was disarming and it was only later I realised that this was the teacher I had been warned about as a powerful personality who had made herself a centre of discord in the school.

At that moment there was a noise at the door and the small, cheeky face of the escapee peeped in, his shoulder in the firm grip of the aide. With a deft twist, he shrugged her hand off and threw himself at my legs, wrapping his plump arms around my knees. 'Halyo,' he said with adenoidal breathiness, 'I'm Shpiro' looking up at my face with mischievous eyes. I couldn't help but respond to this first warm gesture of the day. I bent down to give him an answering hug when Sybil's voice came warningly, 'Ignore him! Spiro, where should you be?' Spiro straight away stood erect and marched with every sign of obedience towards the seat to which Sybil stood sternly pointing. But halfway across the room he stopped, leant over and waggled his plump little bottom at me, squinting over his shoulder to check my reaction. I was about to giggle but Sybil's face was steely and her eyes fixed unmovingly on Spiro as her long arm continued to point imperiously to the chair. I gave a feeble wave.

'Thanks, Sybil,' I said and left quickly.

Outside in the corridor I hesitated, not game to go into another classroom. I was considering a quick retreat to my office when at the end of the corridor a door opened and a woman with a head of red, frizzy hair called out in a cheerful voice, 'Do you want to come to our class?' Gratefully I hurried down to the door she was holding open for me. The room I entered was large and I guessed would have been light and airy except the drawn blinds blocked the windows. There was nothing on the walls: no posters, no pictures, no charts or photographs. Sybil's room had been like this too. 'You don't decorate the rooms or put up the children's work?' I said to the friendly aide.

'Oh no,' she replied instantly as though it were obvious. 'They pull everything down. Besides, the autistic ones can't cope with a lot of stimulation.'

'Is that why you keep the blinds drawn?' I asked.

'Partly, but mostly it's for the vision impaired children, to stop the glare.' I nodded, as though understanding, but I felt troubled. Didn't these children's brains need stimulation to grow, like other children? I looked around at the students. They were very settled, almost passive. I counted eight of them, sitting on a mat at the front watching their teacher turn the pages of an ABC book as she echoed with careful articulation the sounds made by a jolly voice from a CD: *Ants in the apple a..a..a.* A little fair haired boy thrust his leg out to touch the boy next to him. The chirpy red-headed aide was at his side in an instant. *Control, control.*

Back along the corridor in the next couple of classes I

visited, it was a similar scene. The loud voices of the adults dominated the room and the children moved at their command. I had to remind myself that it was a special school and my ideas of good teaching didn't apply here. But then I went into the senior classroom they called FHS (Foundations for High School) and almost at once drew a breath of relief. This was more like it. The children were laughing. Their lanky, bespectacled teacher, whose name I remembered was Robyn Thomas, called on them one by one to introduce themselves to the new principal. 'Hi. I'm J-J-Jayden,' said the first boy with a gappy-toothed smile. 'I c-c-come from G-grossmere p-public s-school and I-I-i.'

'Take a breath Jayden.' The teacher, Robyn, spoke in warm Irish tones.

'I'm gonna be a train driver' he got out in a rush.

'Tell Mrs Karaolis why you're here then.'

'I g-g-got bullied. S-s-some b-b-boys punched me when I c-c-couldn't t-talk.'

'Not here,' a tall, good-looking boy interrupted. 'No one calls you stupid here.'

'And we learn heaps,' said a third boy. 'Miss talks nice and slow so we can understand.'

'Yeah, Mith Thomath ith the greateth,' said a pale-eyed ash blonde girl next to him, smiling shyly. I stayed longer than I really should have, relieved to feel at home at last. This was the kind of special needs I was used to: sweet funny kids able to interact with their teacher and grateful for any help. Robyn, their teacher, was impressive. She looked slightly spinsterish in her thin wire glasses and shoulder-length bob, but her hi-octane energy and good humour filled the room and her firm, clear direction had the children relaxed and trusting. I was smiling when eventually I left and stood looking at my watch. Nearly eleven o'clock. Soon it would be recess when I could repair to my office and deal with the chaos in my mind but I had one more class to visit. And that was when I met Freddy.

He was sitting surrounded by wooden desks that formed a physical barrier between him and the other eight children in the room. Ginger haired and freckled, he didn't look up when I came through the door. Nor did he seem to pay attention when the rest of the children gathered around me gesturing and vocalising. Eventually pulling away from them, I moved across the room towards where he sat isolated behind the assemblage of desks. Immediately the teacher and aide hurried over. On the wall behind his head was a large map of the world and on the barricading desks were pasted flags of different countries.

'This is Freddy's office', said the aide brightly. 'Freddy likes it here, don't you Freddy?' For a moment, the boy ignored her but after a long pause he lifted his head and stared balefully at me before once more dropping his eyes. I heard him mutter and caught a couple of words that sounded very like 'fucking woman'.

'Hello, Freddy. I am the new principal,' I said brightly.

Freddy's foot kicked out and the desk next to me rocked on its legs.

'Fuck off!' he shouted, the glass in his round spectacles catching the light as his head jerked. The teacher nodded her head towards the door, alarm in her eyes. I thought it wise to leave quietly. The bell was ringing for recess as I headed down to my office, stopping in the foyer on the way to exchange a word with Bev, the school secretary whose head just showed over the large and imposing receptionist's desk. She was as short as me but more comfortably cushioned and a ball of matter-of-fact commonsense, as I'd already discovered.

'How's it going?' she asked me with an amused lift to her voice. I felt desperate for a sympathetic ear.

'Oh Bev, I'm so out of my depth.'

'Don't worry, you'll get used to us!' she said, and added, 'There's something on your desk that might cheer you up.' The something proved to be a large bouquet of pink and red roses mixed with big creamy carnations and a card that read, *Best wishes for your new school, Jo. We hope they know how lucky they are.* It was signed by some parents from St Catherine's. I could only look at it and shake my head, fondling the ribbon on the bouquet. The world it came from seemed a thousand miles away. Here the staff didn't think themselves lucky to have me – and I myself was filled with foreboding. On the evidence of the last few hours, my appointment was most likely an error. I found a vase for the flowers in the first-aid room and filled it with water, allowing myself a few weak tears in the safe knowledge that Bev couldn't hear me with the tap running.

I set the glowing mass of flowers on my desk and went in search of Freddy's file. I wanted to understand his anger. On his application form, under the heading 'Disability' the word Autism was written. There was a lengthy psychologist's report stating that Freddy had refused to answer any questions, making it impossible to assess his IQ and adding, *His parents report that Freddy reads film magazines and can repeat the entire cast of his favorite movies but no evidence of his being able to read was apparent during assessment.* It went on to say that Freddy demonstrated a high level of echolalia, repeating phrases and sometimes whole scripts, but that no functional language was observed during the assessment. I wondered. Telling the principal to 'fuck off' was functional enough it seemed to me.

I put the file back and shut the drawer with a bang. There was a more pressing puzzle than Freddy. On my classroom visits I had counted only six or seven children with serious vision impairment and only three who were fully blind. There were more than that with Down syndrome and plenty of others who seemed quite intellectually disabled. I went out to the foyer again to ask Bev about it but she headed me off. 'Best you talk to Jack,' she said. 'He's the expert.' I made a face but she only laughed. 'Now's a good time. He's out cleaning the swimming pool,' she said.

I found him changed into a tracksuit and gym shoes, skimming leaves off the top of the water of the small-sized pool. He nodded at me and continued with swift, efficient movements as I told him how baffled I was at the small number of blind children in the school.

'Blindness is a low-incidence disability now,' he said coolly. 'What with the rubella vaccine and improved management of babies in humidicribs, there aren't as many blind children and anyway, they can go into mainstream schools if they don't have anything else wrong with them.'

'So we aren't a school for the blind any more?'

'Yes we are.' He looked at me then and said very deliberately, 'We're a centre of excellence for the blind. Our standing is second to none. Vision impaired children come here every Friday for braille classes and I give itinerant support to all the vision impaired children in Diocesan schools. We hold braille camps for vision impaired children every school holiday. And besides, all of our staff are expert teachers of braille.' His voice had an edge to it.

'But most of the children have other disabilities; shouldn't we be expert in those? Why hasn't the school changed how it brands itself?'

'Would you give money to a school for retarded children?' he challenged. 'Blind children tug at the heart strings. We can't afford to change.' He then told me jokingly how they used to whip sunglasses onto the children who weren't blind when visitors came. 'There are too many to do that to now,' he added, 'but we don't advertise the fact.' He turned his back on me and studied the now clean surface of the water.

I went inside to my office to call Gae, the Board Chair. 'How is your first day going?' Her voice came down the phone, positive and encouraging.

'The children are much more, well, disabled, than I expected,' I blurted out. I heard her laugh.

'I thought that was probably so.'

'But most of them aren't blind.'

'No.'

'But it's a school for the blind ...'

'Well, it changed very gradually,' she said in tones of warm honey. 'I don't think we have quite registered the change. You've come in and you see us with fresh eyes. But you'll get used to us. Go gently.' And with another merry laugh, she hung up. I sat there, staring at the phone, panic rising. Had I made yet another rash life-choice I would come to regret, like retiring at fifty-eight?

Retirement hadn't brought me the peace I had hoped for. I was restless, returning over and over again to the questions that beset me about Costi's death and whether I should have stopped work to care for him when he went on kidney dialysis. Was it ego that had kept me working at St Cath's while he dialysed at home and waited for the transplant that didn't come? Instead there was a phone call put through to my office at five o'clock one night from an ambulance officer who said my husband had had a heart attack and he was taking him to hospital. I should hurry or it would be too late. But it was already too late. You can't know what sudden death is like until it happens. We got through it somehow, but as my nineteen year old son said, life as we knew it was over. He and my daughter left home. I took refuge in workaholism.

That was ten years ago. I had stayed at St Cath's for another eight years and then retired, hoping that in retirement I would learn to live my single life at peace, without self-medicating on work. I took up bushwalking and journalling and bought a block of wild bush land and camped on it for long stretches, but a feeling of vacant emptiness persisted. There were no more life goals to give me direction, only my funeral at some unknown time in the future. The person who stared back at me from the mirror was a stranger with a disturbing likeness to my mother. Now as I sat at my desk uncomforted by Gae's cheerful words, I had a despairing feeling that in taking on the role of principal I had seized blindly at a passing branch and landed in a place where I didn't fit and for which I didn't have the necessary skills.

The phone rang, breaking into my mood of dejection. 'Berenice is here and would like to see you,' Bev's no-nonsense voice came down the line. 'Can you spare a minute?' I tried to remember who Berenice was. 'President of the Parents and Friends,' Bev prompted.

'Of course. Ask her to come in.' Berenice turned out to be a small, round, twinkling sort of woman in her late forties, fair and rosy, with dimples in her soft cheeks and a self-deprecating little laugh. Something about her made me like her instantly.

'How has your first day been?' she asked.

'Challenging,' I said pulling a face. 'And don't tell me I'll get used to it.'

'Well you will,' she responded gently. 'I'm a teacher too. I know how strange it must seem to you. It's another world, disability. I have wept and wept over Selina, you know. She's my youngest. The others are all fine but Selina was a real shock. I grieved so hard for her, and for myself if I'm honest. But I'll tell you something. The day came when I just accepted that that's who she is. She's Selina. Now I'm fine with it. We couldn't love her more. The day I accepted her was the day I learned to be happy again.'

There was a kind of radiance in her as she spoke. I guessed it was that which had instantly drawn me to her. Grief and love had etched deeply into her, carving an interior peace that made her beautiful. My woes suddenly seemed superficial and self-pitying and, irrationally, I felt hot tears well up. Berenice abruptly changed the subject. 'Let me tell you about the P&F,' she said and in a kindly way led our talk onto the familiar and safe ground of parent politics.

MEETING THE PARENTS

I spent the next few weeks in a fog of unremitting work. It was what I knew and I had to build confidence from somewhere. I studied all the children's files, I looked up information about their different diagnoses on the internet and downloaded scholarly articles on autism and the various syndromes I was learning about. I was shaken to discover how many different ones there were. Down syndrome, Fragile X, Bardet-Biedl, Prader-Willi, Williams, San Filipo, Velocardialfacial, Cornelia de Lange. It went on and on, a parallel world of which I was ignorant, a host of different ways of being born and developing. Each day after everyone had gone home, I stayed back reading and when I finally put the files away, turned off the lights and locked up the school, I drove off to the house I had rented nearby wondering at the luck required to have a so-called 'normal' child.

My heart went out to the parents. They had held in their arms the most precious thing life can give, their baby, and learned that a tiny mutation on a single arm of a microscopic chromosome condemned their infant to ten percent or less of what other children could expect from life. I found it hard to reconcile with my belief that creation is benign and that what happens has meaning. What must a mother feel towards God and the universe when the cruel lottery of genetics delivers a life sentence to her baby? And what was my job then – responsible for improving the chances of all of those compromised babies who were now students in my school?

I went to my first P&F meeting uncertain what to expect or how to behave but guessing that the sympathy I felt would not be welcome. The upstairs staffroom where the meeting was held was a large, welcoming room with walls covered with posters and a big table in the centre around which fifteen or more parents were gathered. They were mostly mothers but with a few fathers too, quite a spread of ages I thought, and a warm atmosphere of chatter and laughter. Berenice had told me it was an issues meeting and likely to get quite heated as the topic for discussion was how to talk to your children about their disability. 'People say what they think at these meetings,' Berenice had said. 'We don't have to pretend because we're all in the same boat and we know what it's like.' Everyone seemed very relaxed, passing plates of sandwiches and cake to each other as Berenice got through the preliminaries of the meeting and opened the discussion topic for the night.

'My daughter doesn't have a diagnosis,' said a sweet-faced woman with short dark curls as she started off the discussion. 'I think it'd be easier if she did. If she had a label everyone would know what to expect.' She smiled towards me and I suddenly recognised her as Honor's mother; I had seen her drop her daughter off at the front of the school some mornings. Honor was the first child whose name I had learned. You couldn't miss her. Though she was only ten she looked older, very tall with big bones and long limbs and a deep booming voice that seemed to surprise even her when it erupted out of her. Her file said she was being treated for gigantism although the cause was unknown.

'The other day we were at Toys R Us,' Honor's mother went on. 'I had to buy a gift for my nephew but Honor made a bee-line for the barbie dolls. She loves them to death. I couldn't get her away so I thought I'd leave her there for a bit and make a quick detour to the toy cars. There was a woman standing nearby and while I was trying to decide between a truck and a racing car, I noticed her two kids start giggling and pointing. I looked and it was Honor they were sniggering at. Her large head was sticking out above the shelves and she was cuddling a barbie doll to her cheek, singing to it in her gravelly voice. I was red hot mad at that woman. I wanted to scream, *how would you feel if it was your child?*' but it was none of their fault really. Honor does look unusual. I'm sure people would understand more if she had Down's.'

A woman sitting opposite jerked back sharply. 'I hate my son being called a Down's boy,' she said and her back was suddenly ramrod straight. 'It sounds like that's all he is.' Berenice at the head of the table bent forward.

'I heard the other day about some young people with Down syndrome,' she said, smiling gently around. 'They wanted the name to be changed to Up syndrome because they reckon they're more Up than most people.'

'Well that's true,' said the father sitting on my left. 'Rory's the happiest of my lot. He's our sunshine.'

'Does he know he's got Down's?' asked the mother who hated the label.

'Gosh no, we none of us think of him like that. He's just Rory.'

'Well, I had to talk to Selina recently about having a disability,' said Berenice. 'She wanted to know why she is different.'

'Rory doesn't think he's different. He probably thinks other people are.'

As the discussion went on, I sat there marveling at the openness and frankness of these parents. They were different from the others I'd known in a way that I couldn't at first put my finger on. Then it dawned on me, these parents weren't competitive. They listened to each other with genuine empathy and gave each other time. When at the end of the meeting Berenice asked me to say a few words, I fumblingly tried to convey my sense of their difference, and my admiration and, well, awe.

'We're not different to anyone else!' The words came from a handsome woman at the end of the table. 'We laugh and cry and stuff up like everyone does.' She looked at me hard. 'No offence, mind. I know you mean well but we're not special. None of us is. I got married late and my best friend already had her first child. He was born with cerebral palsy and had lots of problems. I used to say to her, "You're so patient and loving. I could never be like you. That's why you've been chosen to have this child." And then I had Bill. I learned to be all the things I thought I never could be. We just do what we have to.'

I had been hoping to meet Hailey's mother among the parents but she hadn't come to the meeting. Hailey was the girl who had called me Miss Bossy on my first day. I had often noticed her about the school since then and been struck by the unbridled enthusiasm with which she threw herself into life. I'd see her whooping with glee as she careened down a small children's slide or grinning broadly as she walked with her arm around her best friend Gareth. With straight blonde hair, squinty blue eyes and a mischievous grin she was an escapee from the land of joy and I wanted the chance to tell her mother how special she was. In fact though Mrs Harris rarely came up to the school and my first meeting with her was the official one to set goals for Hailey's education plan.

I had expected her to be an extrovert like her daughter but despite having the same fair hair and blue eyes, Mrs Harris seemed subdued when she came into the meeting room, even despondent I thought. Kelly, Hailey's teacher, got quickly down to business, going one-by-one through the goals that she had set for Hailey and reporting verbally on each in her precise way. 'She can identify five letters of the alphabet,' said Kelly. Mrs. Harris sat erect suddenly. 'That's not what last year's report said. It said she knew ten letters.'

'Well, when I tested her last week, she got five right,' said Kelly, biting her lip, a slight frown above her thick-framed glasses.

'How can she go backwards?' Mrs. Harris wanted to know.

I ran my eyes down the report. It was pretty discouraging. Hailey didn't seem to have mastered any of the numeracy goals either. The only outcome that was ticked on the report was Taking Turns and Sharing. Reading this you got no hint of the gutsy little person who scattered joy and sunshine over the day. If Mrs. Harris sat through this kind of experience twice a year, no wonder she was leaning back with that detached look on her face as though she just wanted to get through it with as little pain as possible. After the interview, I repeated Mrs. Harris's question to Kelly. 'How come Hailey's gone backwards?'

'We don't know she has,' said Kelly speaking slowly in deference to my inexperience. 'What we know is that when I tested her, she correctly matched five letters to their sounds.'

'But last year her report said she knew ten letters.'

'Perhaps it was the way she was tested. She could have been prompted in some way, or maybe she was given a couple of letters to choose between, or it could just have been a bad day when I tested her this year, or else...'

'Kelly, is Hailey any closer to being able to read now than she was twelve months ago? Can you tell me that?'

'Oh yes, in class when I do reading groups, Hailey recognises a lot of words. And she often does letter-sound matching. It's just that with these kids, what they know one day, they forget the next. It comes and goes. So you get different results each time you test them. And often they don't like a test situation and get stubborn and won't answer.'

'Then why do we test them? Why don't we video them in reading groups or just write down what we see them do?'

'Well, because that's not objective testing.' I wanted to shout my frustration. We were talking in circles. Hers was the textbook answer but as the days went on I found myself increasingly irked by the gap between the textbook and the reality of the children. Some of my impatience, I had to admit, came from ignorance. When Jack told me that the previous principal had attended every goal-setting interview, my first thought was what a waste of time that would be. Most interviews ran to an hour or more and while the parents obviously appreciated the principal being present, I couldn't see how I could afford the nearly seventy hours it would total. Not when there was still so much to learn and to do in the school. But I found I was wrong. In those seventy hours I got a quick insight into every child in the school, the way they were at home, and in class; and l came to know all the parents and to look at their child through their eyes, understanding their hopes and fears, their pride and their disappointments. Each interview was pure gold. And of them all, the one that stood out most for me was the meeting we had with Vanessa Holgrave to set goals for her son Gareth.

I already knew Gareth by sight from seeing him in the playground. He was a nine year old ball of confidence: organising everyone, friends with everyone, always on the alert for fun. The staff dubbed him 'Chairman of the Board'. He waddled up to any visitor in the playground and introduced himself before making them welcome with a sweep of his arm and a bow. Everything Gareth did was over-sized, mannered and artful. He loved fancy dress and his mother let him come to school in a purple cape or a tight Buzz Lightyear outfit or dressed as Dorothy the

Dinosaur. Some of the staff tut-tutted about it, muttering that his mother was not helping Gareth to fit into society. I could see what they meant; Gareth would be the butt of jokes anywhere else. Here though, among these kids, Gareth was king.

His mother Vanessa floated into the meeting room for her interview, a small wavy haired woman with a purple chiffon scarf trailing from her neck and a bright aura of optimism about her. Her laughter-lined eyes darted between Gareth's teacher and me as she settled herself onto the violet striped couch with a murmur of pleasure. 'What a lovely colour.' She took some papers from her copious pink handbag and waved them in the air. 'Thanks for sending the goals for Gareth. They look fine.' I glanced at Gareth's surprised teacher as we took our lead from the mother and sat down. She was a young teacher, hard working and very keen and I knew she would have sat up late to prepare the goals that Vanessa was offhandedly waving as she proceeded to take the meeting in hand. With someone else I might have objected, but Vanessa had a bubbly manner and an air of amusement at the vagaries of life that I found very engaging.

'Gareth loves coming to school,' she said as she leaned back into the couch, her short legs causing her feet to rise up like a doll's from the floor. 'He's not going to be a brain surgeon, so I don't worry too much about his Maths and he loves books even though he can't read. So I'll just sign off on the goals and we can relax and have a chat.' She fiddled in her large pink bag for a pen and flicked through the six pages of detailed reporting. At the end she signed her name with a flourish and handed the whole lot to the teacher who was sitting on her hands in silent frustration. 'It's all right,' Vanessa said and patted her. 'You're doing a great job. Gareth really likes you. But here's the thing,' and she began to tell us what she had come to say.

Gareth, she explained, had Prader-Willi syndrome. This was one of the syndromes I had read about, the outcome of a defect on chromosome 15. I knew it affected the hypothalamus and led to an insatiable appetite. We had several times found Gareth scavenging in the garbage bins at the end of lunch and Julie, his keen young teacher, was forever reminding staff to keep children's lunch boxes in their classrooms where Gareth couldn't reach them. 'His food obsession is getting worse,' Vanessa said. 'D'you know about Prader-Willi?' she asked turning to me.

'I understand about the craving for food. Will he grow out of it?'

'No, it's with him for life. But a malfunctioning hypothalamus hits a lot of gongs.' She listed the characteristics that may accompany the syndrome: low muscle tone, intellectual disability, little or no language, minimal sexual development, poor emotional control. 'Gareth's copped them all,' she said with an attempt at a laugh. 'The only one he's missed out on is emotional instability. He's a happy boy and that's a blessing. But this food thing is getting to be major. Gareth knows he shouldn't steal food but he can't help himself. And I'm having trouble keeping a handle on his weight.' The smile wobbled on her face and I looked away. 'The doctor says it will kill him if I can't get it under control,' she said. 'Obesity is the number one cause of death in people with Prader-Willi.'

'We do keep an eye on it at school,' his teacher, Julie, said. Despite her youth, she was indomitable in defending her students. I'd heard a couple of senior staff get the rough edge of her tongue when they'd let their classes throw food scraps in the bin instead of taking them back inside out of Gareth's way.

'I'm sure you do, but it's like Gareth's got an enemy inside he has to fight all the time. There's no let up. He was in tears yesterday. He took a lock from one of the cupboards – all my kitchen cupboards have locks so he won't be tempted – and he held it up in the air, pointing at it and gesticulating at the fridge. He wanted me to put a lock on that too. It broke my heart.'

No wonder she lets him dress up and give full flight to his creative dramatic side, I thought, shaken. As young Julie took the conversation firmly back to discussing Gareth's academic progress, I sat wondering about the teachers' fixation on making children with disabilities as much like other children as possible. Vanessa seemed to be on a different path, embracing the colourful and ambivalent personality that genetics had given Gareth and encouraging his humour and love of life. I guessed she wasn't unaware of society's norms but that she chose to be blind to them for Gareth's sake. And lucky Gareth, I thought. That was how he'd come to be such a confident, outgoing, gregarious nine year old, mature for his years and supremely comfortable in his skin, despite the limitations of his disability and his perpetual craving for food.

After the meeting finished and Vanessa had left with a laugh and a wave, her ebullient persona fixed back in place, I went in search of Sister Gertrude. It was recess and I found her where I expected, out under the lilly pilly tree with her guide dog, Hoover, and a bunch of children for whom the dog was a magnet. Sister Gertrude was the only Dominican Sister still teaching on staff and served as our chaplain. You wouldn't have picked her as part of a congregation of Irish Catholic women; Gertrude had the dark frizzy hair and strong, long nose of her Jewish grandmother and a sharp incisive intellect. She wasn't born blind and in fact had taught music at the blind school when she was sighted and her pupils were not. The irony of it now being the other way round was not lost on her – Sister Gertrude was a deeply ironic woman – but she embraced the unique insight that her blindness gave her into the children's struggles with their disabilities and at times waged war on the lack of vision she saw in us. I had already learned to count on her to give honest and original and often uncomfortable advice.

'Sister Gertrude, can I have a word?' I called out as soon as I was in earshot.

'I take it that it's the principal speaking?'

'Oh sorry, I forgot again.'

'I actually know your voice, but it's polite to say your name before you speak.'

'I'm sorry Gertie.'

'Move along Spiro and let the principal sit down. In fact, it's time you all went off to class.' She pulled the dog back under her seat and shooed the children away. I came straight to the point. You didn't muck around with Sister Gertrude.

'Gertie, I've just been in a meeting with Gareth's mum and it looks to me as though she encourages his outlandishness. I know our goal is to make the children behave as appropriately as possible, but is that right, I wonder? Maybe they have a right to be themselves even if others find it odd? What do you think? Is it our job to make them as normal as possible?' Sister Gertrude's eyes were resting on my face with such attention I thought for a moment she must somehow be seeing me, but then realised this was what, as a professional teacher of the blind, she would have taught her students. *It's polite to look a person in the face when you speak to them, even though you can't see them,* she would have said. And that's what she was doing now, being appropriate, giving me the illusion of eye contact.

'I suppose you know what normal is, do you Jo?' she

asked. For a moment, I thought she was playing semantics to make fun of me. 'Because I don't know,' she went on. 'I don't suppose it's very normal to shut yourself away with a lot of other women to live a life of poverty, chastity and obedience. But it was my choice.' She chuckled as she rose to her feet. 'I'm not sure I'd choose obedience again. Still, choice is important I think. It's about freedom.' The word *choice* was used a lot at this school, I thought as I handed Hoover's lead to Gertie, but it wasn't about freedom; it was about compliance. Make the right choice and get a reward. Walk to the toilet yourself or be taken by force.

It started me thinking about Freddy. Freddy didn't buy into the system; he scorned to play the game of choose this or suffer that. Sybil had told me that Freddy started calling her The Witch after she put him through a week-long programme of classic conditioning to modify his behaviour. It seemed the positive reinforcement method hadn't worked with him, given that Freddy was still being caged behind a barricade of desks in the classroom to stop him attacking other students. Teachers said Freddy was happier in the security of his little kingdom, safe from triggers to his anxiety. But would we do that to him if he weren't labelled with autism? No one seemed to know what drove him. 'He's used to getting his own way. Father's away a lot on business and his mother gives in to him,' Jack said when I asked what he thought caused Freddy to be so aggressive and difficult to manage.

'The parents say he's much brighter than we realise. I read that on his psychologist's report.'

'Splinter skills.' Jack grunted, scratching his head impatiently. 'It's not unusual for a kid with autism to have some freak skills but still not be able to do basic things like reading. His father blames all the schools Freddy has been to including us; we don't extend him, he says. He reckons Freddy's bored with being treated like a baby and made to repeat letters.' He paused. 'And he hates being with deformed kids, his father says.'

'What about all the films he knows; he has found out somewhere the cast of all the well-known films and can quote half their scripts. That was on his file too.'

'Echolalia,' said Jack. 'That's all. It's an autistic trait to repeat film scripts instead of generating your own words. It doesn't mean Freddy is smart.' He shrugged dismissively as though I ought to know all this.

The next day I was in the foyer when Freddy's grandfather brought him to school. A tall, spare man, he had Freddy by the hand as they walked through the gate. I was surprised at how relaxed and comfortable Freddy was with him, almost like a regular kid. I decided to risk another put down and ask at the staff meeting that afternoon whether anyone else found Freddy puzzling. I was surprised by the sudden silence that fell among the teachers who had been sitting murmuring around the table. Kelly giggled and I looked at her. 'You should see him with Jane,' she said pointing and Jane blushed. She was one of our youngest teachers, not long since graduated. 'Freddy has a crush on her,' Kelly said. 'He calls her Sandy.'

'Sandy?' I queried, looking at Jane.

'From Grease,' she said in obvious embarrassment as the other staff laughed. I stayed silent waiting for her to explain and she hurriedly said, 'I was rostered to supervise him in the library on Monday. When I got there and opened the door, Freddy was waiting just inside. He'd wet his hair and slicked it back to look like John Travolta. I didn't know what to say. I just stood there. And then he did this kind of smooth dance move and wriggled his pelvis and sang a line from the movie.'

'Tell her, tell her,' the others urged but Jane had gone bright red and would say no more. She did have a look of Olivia Newton John, I thought, tanned and fresh-faced and very pretty.

'Was he playing around or was it real for him?' I asked.

'I don't know,' Jane said. 'He was smiling but he was pretty intense. I just laughed and told him to get back to work. But I felt too uncomfortable to stay. That's when I went and got Kelly.'

'If his hair was slicked down and he was waiting for you, he must have known you were on duty.'

'Yes, I thought of that,' Jane said. 'The supervision roster was up on the library wall. It's as though he read it.'

I rang Freddy's mother the next day and told her I'd like

to get in a psychologist to assess Freddy. 'Why?' she asked, 'What's wrong?'

'Nothing's wrong. It's just that we don't have a completed IQ assessment for him and I'm not sure why he isn't making more progress academically when in some ways he seems to be so clued up. And also I'm worried about how aggressive he is especially with the more disabled students but I don't know whether he is angry or if there is something else going on.'

'Well all right, if you think it's important but I'll have to tell my husband and I'm not sure what he'll say. He doesn't like psychologists.'

'I'll call you after the psychologist has been,' I said, hanging up before she could change her mind. The psychologist I brought in was a highly regarded specialist in autism and she spent half a day observing Freddy both in class and in the playground. She also gave him an IQ assessment. 'He's doing as well as you can expect,' she told me at the end. 'He's got a very low IQ and his autism is in the moderate range.'

'Are you sure? He seems to be quite sophisticated for an eight year old and we think he can read when he wants to.'

'He couldn't read a word when I tested him and his teacher says he doesn't recognise a lot of letters. What you're talking about is splinter skills. It's not functional learning.'

'Isn't it possible that he has something specifically wrong

with his brain, not a low intelligence? Could he be trapped by his own hostility?' The psychologist was dismissive.

'He is an autistic boy with serious behavioral dysfunction,' she said. 'I advise you to stop worrying about his academics and focus on his behaviour. That boy is a menace.'

I did not want to ring Freddy's mother now that I had such a discouraging report to pass on, but I had promised. She sounded resigned rather than disappointed. 'I know you wanted to help,' she said, 'but we've been down this track before. The psychologists all say the same thing, they have nothing to offer. We keep coming up against brick walls. We were hoping your school would be different.'

'We aren't giving up on Freddy,' I said. 'I just didn't want us to miss something important that might have made a difference.' But Freddy's father gave up on us: he took Freddy out of the school at the end of the term.

'I can't believe you got in another bloody psychologist,' he told me over the phone. 'A lot of mumbo jumbo and big words and each one of them crap. Freddy acts out because he's bored silly at your school and he has a phobia about abnormals. And as I've just found out, he has a biomedical imbalance, lots of heavy metal deposits in the brain. I'm taking him to a specialist in Queensland, he's going to put him on an elimination diet, do away with all his medication and get his system back to normal.' I wished him well and asked him to let us know how it went but I never heard from the family again.

It was seeing the children through the eyes of their parents and catching their love for them that made me feel more heavily the weight of responsibility for getting what we did right. I wanted so much to fix their children for them. Yet the lesson that each day taught me was how little in the scheme of things we were able to achieve, how small were the steps that the teachers celebrated: a child asking for the toilet or recognising the letter 'b' three days in a row. And then there were children like Finn for whom we could do nothing but simply be there. The photo we had of Finn, placed on the front of his file when he enrolled, showed a happy, handsome little boy with an eager intelligent expression. Four years later, we needed a full-time aide to support him. He could still walk but it was in a kind of shuffle and his fine dark features had grown rigid. He had a degenerative neurological disorder from which his younger brother also suffered although the latter had declined earlier and was wheelchair bound and in a different special school.

Often I would look out through my office window and see Finn going by with his dedicated aide, a beautiful woman aptly named Hope. Hope would be leading him by the hand, leaning in close and singing with open throat, her voice sweet and lilting. It was like glimpsing a madonna and child in real life. Hope's dark eyes would be on Finn's face and the smile that radiated from her was all for him. Other staff had told me what Hope's job was like. She fed

Finn, she played and sang with him, she took him to the toilet and she cleaned him up, and she changed his nappy, heavily soiled as you would expect of an eight year old boy. She counted objects with him and she helped him play the marble run, which he loved. And she walked with him, many times a day, whenever he became upset or unsettled.

'I worry for you, Hope,' I said to her one day. 'Finn is a heavy boy now and not easy to care for. Does it get you down?'

'Oh no!' Hope smiled at me, knowing I did not understand. 'I love what I do. It makes him feel better. When I see him smile and relax, I know he is feeling good again and it means the world to me. It's all I want. I love my job.'

One day I saw Hope in the foyer with Finn. 'I don't think he's feeling very well,' she said. 'He's just not his usual cheery self. And he doesn't want to eat. I'm worried about him. I think I'll ring his Mum.' That was the first time I met Rae, Finn's mother. She had the loping, springy walk of a tennis player and a freckled complexion to match. I had expected her to be weighed down with the tragedy of Finn and his brother but it was as though this was what every mother dealt with, two boys with degenerative illnesses that would take them before they reached adulthood. She chatted away about Finn and also about prizes she was soliciting as donations to our fundraising auction.

'How do you manage?' I exclaimed. 'I'm feeling

overwhelmed and I get to go home every night. How do you hold the pain?' It came out more bluntly than I meant and Rae seemed taken aback. She dropped her eyes and smoothed her skirt; for a moment I thought she wasn't going to answer but she was taking time to think. She looked up at me and smiled slowly.

'I was about to say, what pain?' she said giving a small shrug. 'I do know what you mean, you know, it's just that this is my life. It's what I know. To me it's full of love, not pain.' She glanced out into the playground where Hope had come into view slowly leading Finn. 'When I look at Finn and David sometimes, my heart seems to expand until it could hold the whole world.' She turned from the window and smiled. 'It's a gift, really. The boys are a gift.'

FEELING MY WAY

'What do you like about your new school?' friends would ask.

'The parents,' I'd say 'and the children of course,' and I'd feel my face light up. Then I'd tell them a story about one of the children who had grabbed my heart, or say what a relief it was to have parents who didn't ask about the school's public examination results but only wanted their children to have friends and be happy. There was so much that I loved about my new job, and so many ways that it had already changed my perspective on life, and yet the sense of isolation and displacement remained. I told myself it would pass, that it was just I was used to a very different kind of school and I was missing the crowded streets and inner city terrace that I had given up to be close to this far-out school. I felt like a stranger and all the more so for not being Catholic.

I had not expected it to matter. I was used to going to the Greek Orthodox church with Costi where there were more incense and bells than in most Catholic churches and icons everywhere. And the Dominican Sisters had been a revelation. They introduced me to the social justice side of Catholicism that preached activism for the poor and disadvantaged and downtrodden. It was like coming home for the child in me that cried out against injustice. I began to feel that perhaps I had been called to work in this school, that I was to find meaning and purpose here. But what I hadn't allowed for was the way I'd react to the statues and crucifixes.

In the front garden of the school stood a larger than life statue of Mary in white marble, erected in memory of a young nun who had died. I cringed when I first saw it. I wasn't proud of my reaction. I knew it sprang from the religious prejudice of my 1950's upbringing in northern Tasmania, a sectarianism I thought I had disowned. The statue had a broken finger and I tried to feel sorry for her; sometimes I said hello when I passed and that helped. But my reaction against all the crucifixes in the school was not so easily fixed. The school had, to my unaccustomed eye, a particularly gruesome collection of crucifixes with figures of poor Jesus hanging in agony. I wondered what the children thought of them. My two year old grandson, Alex, my daughter Christina's boy, had halted, rooted to the spot, when he first encountered the graphic wooden Jesus stretched out in anguish above the stairwell. At two, he didn't yet have a lot of words in his English vocabulary. 'Stuck!' he said, pointing. I didn't know what to say, especially as his parents were Buddhist. I swept him away to help me with one of the weekend jobs I was combining with child-minding and found an ice block in the staffroom freezer to clear his mind of the naked man tied and nailed to a cross.

Christina, my daughter, who in a fit of adolescent temper had once said she would never inflict a Greek father on *her* children, had married a Frenchman instead. Guillaume was an actor and for three years Christina lived with him in Paris and it was there that Alex was born. Recently though they had moved to Sydney. I had thought Christina was gone from Australia forever so it was a special joy now to have a grandson within visiting distance and babysitting responsibilities. When I returned him to her care that afternoon, I warned that he might have nightmares.

The next week I saw Stanley Brooks standing staring at the same crucifix. Stanley was seven, a caring, serious boy whose autism made him very literal and very persistent. 'Are they nails in Jesus' hands?' he asked me.

'Yes,' I replied, not knowing how to avoid it.

'Why?'

'He was crucified,' I said weakly.

'Why don't you take the nails out?' asked Stanley. The next day he was back again, staring at the crucifix. 'The nails are still in his hands,' he said.

'I know.'

'Will you take them out?'

I sought out Sister Gertrude for advice again. This time I found her in the staffroom fixing herself a cup of tea while her guide dog, Hoover, with covert skill inhaled crumbs from the floor. I told her about Stanley. 'Poor boy,' she said. 'What a thing to fixate on.' She filled her cup from the zip heater using her finger to check when it was full. 'That's hot!' she said, wincing. 'I don't know why we have the crucifixes around, to be honest. Jesus said that he came so that we can have life. And yet we hang up pictures of him dying.'

'Can I take that one down, do you think? The one that is upsetting Stanley?'

'You can take them all down as far as I'm concerned.' Her face twisted in a wry grin. 'After all, I won't know.'

I took the troubling crucifix up to a dusty room on the top floor of the convent. The head of the Dominicans, Sister Agnes, had suggested the nuns swap the convent with us for the cottage which the school now used only once or twice a year in holidays for braille camp. The

Board had said yes. We all knew it was a mixed blessing: the old and drafty convent needed rewiring, re-flooring and was under a heritage order but it was on a good sized block of land. Much better the school acquire it than some developer with high rise ambitions. I had no idea what we'd use it for but hiding crucifixes there seemed like a good start.

The crucifixes weren't of course the only problem for someone who had been immersed in Anglican beliefs and theology but I knew I had to uphold the major points of Catholic doctrine as the school's principal even if I couldn't sign up to them myself. One of them was the belief in Christ's physical presence in the host, the bread that is broken in memory of Jesus' death and resurrection each time the Mass is celebrated. 'If it's the Lord's Table that we're all kneeling at, why do we create dogma to keep each other away?' I asked Sister Gertrude after I had been denied permission to take the bread at a Mass I attended on behalf of the school. 'I don't get why it has to be such a mystery, the Catholic thing about the Eucharist.'

'Don't worry about it,' she said. But one wild and windy morning when grit and leaves were whipping around the playground, I ran into eight year old Seamus coming out of the gym with his two hands clasped tightly together. He stopped me, holding up his hands and vigorously mouthing something I could not hear. I bent closer. 'I have Jesus in my hands,' he said in an awed voice and he opened his hands just enough for me to see a white wafer of communion bread lying inside.

'It's all right, it's unconsecrated,' said Sister Gertrude coming up from behind. 'I'm preparing the children for their sacraments and I've given them some wafers to practise with at home.'

'But Seamus thinks it's Jesus.'

'Yes, I know. Seamus is very literal. But God doesn't mind'. Sister Gertrude patted Seamus somewhere near his head and hurried off pulling Hoover along behind her. Seamus was still peeking at the bread inside his clasped hands and the look of veneration on his face seemed to me at that moment more important, more to be treasured, than the most fought-over dogma.

When the first term ended, I was glad to escape for the holidays with a friend to Norfolk Island, a place I had not been before. Others had told me about the island's beauty and the solace they had found there. Not for me though, not that year. I felt haunted by its grim history as I restlessly wandered its pine-topped hills and convict ruins. It put me too much in mind of the school I had taken responsibility for. In its own way the school was as cut off from the mainstream as this small and brutal settlement had been and I wondered whether the darkness I had sometimes felt at its heart was a consequence of isolation too. Being principal there was certainly not the comfortable job I had expected. I said this to Ruth, the friend who had come to

Norfolk Island with me. She had been head of the Junior School when I was at St Catherine's and knew me well and now she dismissed my haunting sense of something psychically wrong. 'You're just tired,' she said. 'As usual you've worked too hard and got yourself into a state.'

'No, it's more than that. There's a negativity. Some of the teachers who've been there a long time love to tell bizarre stories about the kids even those from years before. They regale the other staff with some of the grossest things.'

'Black humour,' said Ruth. 'Like nurses in an emergency ward. Laughing at what would otherwise be unbearable.'

'Yes, I think it is that some of the time. But often it's just heartless joking at the kids' expense. The parents love their children totally but some of them the staff don't seem to love at all.'

'Love isn't always expressed in words, you know. The fact that they turn up each day says a lot. It must be wearing.'

'Well, yes, I know it is. And I know the staff do in general love the children. Even Sybil, who is so tough on discipline, visibly melted the other day when I asked her how Spiro is going. "I could eat that boy," she said, "I love him so much." I could feel the emotion in her and there were tears in her eyes. Even so, there is something not right about the school. We all know how it is with teachers, we tend to blame the students when things don't go well, rather than looking at what we could do differently. Well, it's endemic at that school. Any student whose behaviour is difficult becomes the problem and honestly at times all we seem to talk about at staff meetings is behaviour, not education.' I sighed.

'We're here for a holiday', Ruth said. 'You don't want to be dwelling on work.' So I didn't tell her about the day I'd seen a teacher and an aide dragging Leon Masters to the toilets, each holding an arm. When I asked what they thought they were doing, I was shocked by their anger. Leon wet himself deliberately, they said. They jokingly called it 'taking-the-piss-piss'. And on our last day which was a staff training day, when Jack had been giving us a refresher on how to avoid injury from an out-of-control student, he'd laughingly said he had a secret weapon he used that worked without leaving a mark. Others had clamoured to know what it was and Jack had coolly demonstrated how to give a child a 'wedgie' while escorting them from the scene.

I felt very uncomfortable but I let it go. Now I was at Norfolk Island that brief incident chafed my memory. The brutality perpetrated by the gaolers against their troublesome convicts happened because there was no one to see and those in authority condoned it. And they would happen at the school too if I as principal continued to be intimidated by the teachers' expertise. I might be a novice in special education and feel like an interloper, but the children were in my care. I took a long walk along the windy headland of the island, with the lonely call of sea birds and the shuddering of the pine trees. I could not continue as I was, I realised. I had either to give up, conceding that special education was not my field, or if I stayed, I had to back my judgement and my instinct for what was right. 'I've decided,' I told Ruth that night. 'When we get back, I'm going to look for a house to buy, somewhere near to the school.' She smiled.

'Nice to see the fight in your eyes again,' she said.

The house I found several months later could not have been more different from the little urban terrace I had moved into after Costi died. This house was built on the side of a gully and I couldn't even see it when I peered down from the road. I counted seventy-six steps on the way down and half-way I met another house hunter who said, 'Who'd want to buy this place? You'd need a helicopter to get in.' Puffed, I could only agree but when I stood in the lounge room and looked out at the wide treescape of turpentines and ironbarks with a path wandering through ferns and a creek murmuring below a ledge of grass trees, it was as though I had come home. Luckily I was the only person who felt like that and the sale went through easily. There was the usual havoc of moving house, the confusion of boxes half unpacked, the hunt for missing utensils, the panic when the house sprang a leak in the first rain – and then calm, deep calm, as the rhythm of the trees and creek and occasional garden-marauding wallaby took over. My whole mood and outlook were more hopeful, as though I was drawing from the generative energy around me.

I thought about the dreary buildings and playground at the school and wished I could give the children the well-being that sprang from beauty like this. Other schools were re-casting themselves for the new century, creating light-filled, clever, artistic environments to invite and stimulate students' thinking and experimentation. Our school had been built in the 1960's, a period of ugly, brutalist brick and concrete school architecture exacerbated by the Sisters' commitment to doing everything on the cheap if not the wing of prayer. As Dominicans they valued aesthetic beauty as a way to God but not for children who couldn't see, who needed protection from bright light and to whom precious little funding was given for their schooling.

This was a change I could make, a first step towards ending the charity concept on which the blind school was built and make it more like a regular school. I would give the children an environment that said they were valued and precious, a place of beauty to go to each day.

And after that, I thought with a rush of vehemence, I would stop them looking like sad sack charity kids in the frumpy maroon and blue uniform available from a discount clothing chain in Sydney. I was still galled by my memory of the first family picnic after I started when I had barely recognised the children in the trendy, flattering clothes their parents had dressed them in. They were almost indistinguishable from their brothers and sisters. Yet at school they looked so misshapen and plain. I wanted to give them a uniform that showed them at their best: confident and breezy and equal to any mainstream child.

I had an ally ready to help in any ambitious plan for change. The year before I started, the Board had appointed a Development Officer named Zandra who was larger than life in figure and personality, a tall blonde dynamo of unremitting energy hungry for projects befitting her extraordinary talents. We began with the library because the Board had been considering demolishing it. It was a low, round mushroom-shaped building of rugged purple-brown brick that stuck out into the dull playground and provided secret niches for children wanting cover for unhealthy deeds. Inside it was dark with few windows and floor to ceiling wood partitions that divided the space up into small work rooms for making braille books and tactile materials, the main business of the library. The few shelves of books for sighted readers were squeezed into one gloomy segment.

I asked Alec Tzannes, one of Sydney's award-winning architects who I had worked with at St Cath's, as a favour to make the long journey from the eastern suburbs to give us advice on how to transform the library to the needs of sighted children without it costing us anything. 'Strip it,' he said when he arrived. 'Paint it out in white, everything white. If you're prepared to spend some money on a feature carpet it can shape the way the children use the space. We'll design it for you as a gift.' Zandra put her fundraising skills to work and before long had all the paint we needed given free by Dunlop, donations of money for the joinery and carpet and best of all, a volunteer labourer to pull out all the partitions and do the painting. Kevin was the volunteer, a businessman who had changed career direction to train as a deacon of the church. He offered to do the library to meet the service requirements of his course. He didn't know what he was signing up for and neither did we because the ceilings were covered with vermiculite that needed countless coats and soaked up gallons of paint. I thanked God we weren't having to pay for it else I think I'd have settled for keeping the sepulchral grey vermiculite. It took Kevin weeks to do the painting and that was after he had spent a month pulling out partitions. He earned a couple of places in heaven during those many weeks of hard labour, but the completed library was worth a few lifetimes. The vivid multi-patterned carpet glowed against the white walls and white shelving that lined the huge open circular space.

I was standing basking in the transformation when young Kacey, the blind tearabout Jack so admired, came in. She stood looking around, her eyes swivelling behind their thick white corneas seeking the light and colour that provided their only sensation. As she caught the brilliant blues, greens and yellows of the carpet, with spangles of white stars and circles, she began to whirl, slowly at first and then faster and faster, her eyes drinking in the spin-past of kaleidoscoping colours. She lifted her arms up high and sang out in a loud voice, 'My library! My library!' and then slowly wound down to a stop, holding the beauty of it to her as she closed her arms around herself.

Jack was less impressed. 'You want to turn us into the Abbotsleigh of special schools, don't you?' he mocked, referring to the very large and prestigious private girls' school a kilometre up the road. I laughed but his barb shot home. I knew how grand buildings could drive an unpalatable socio-economic wedge between schools. But these children had sub-standard facilities only because no one had considered them worthy of better. They had already drawn the short straw. Surely, I told myself, they have a right to the best we can give them? Kacey was a case in point. She could see nothing only colour and light but despite her blindness she was a feisty, independent, whirling dervish of a child who counted knocks and bruises as nothing in her determination to consume every experience she could squeeze from life.

She had an older and calmer sister Flora whose cataracts had been corrected but was at the school because of her intellectual disability. The girls' father Bruce had recently been awarded sole custody of the girls and overnight had had to give up work and learn to keep house for them. He often rang the ever-patient Bev for advice on what soap powder to buy and what to cook when his money had run out and he didn't have petrol to drive to the shops.

Bruce turned up at school one day more than an hour late with Kacey in tow. Flora had arrived much earlier on government special transport. Bev brought Bruce to my door and pushed him into the visitor's chair, saying firmly that he was to speak to me. I hadn't met Bruce before though I'd often heard him on the phone to Bev. I saw a squarish man in his early forties with muscle running a bit to fat and some confidence leached out of him by life, but an earnest face with bashful blue eyes and raw-looking skin and when he smiled, as now, a miscreant's grin.

'Kacey's not in school uniform. Sorry.' He looked sheepish. 'I've got behind y'know, with the washin' and that.'

'We've got spare uniforms in the uniform pool Kacey can have,' I said, thinking this might be what the eye signals Bev had thrown me were about.

'Nah, we'll be right. Just got to get meself better sorted.'

'They're just sitting there, Bruce. You might as well have them.' Bruce said nothing and I wondered if I had sounded patronising. Could be better for Bev to broach it with him, perhaps. I tried another tack.

'Can you tell me why you have to bring Kacey yourself, Bruce?'

'Jeez, I'm sorry 'bout that. Bein' so late. Car broke down goin' home yesterday. Had to come by bus and train this morning and we missed the second bus. It put us right out.' He rubbed his forehead with the back of his hand. 'Sorry 'bout that. We were real late. We can't leave earlier, but. We have to wait for the taxi to come for Flora.'

'You mean the taxi picks up Flora and leaves Kacey behind?'

'Yeah. See Flora got transport a few years ago but when I did the form for Kacey, I ticked the box sayin' I have a car, so now they reckon I can drive 'er. But the old car's carked it.'

'I'm sure if you call Special Transport they'll...'

'Don't got time right now. Got to go back to court in a week. Their mother wants 'em back.' He slumped in his seat and rubbed the thighs of his trousers. There were shiny patches where he had worried them before.

'Do you have legal help?'

'Yeah, DOCS got me a lawyer, y'know,' he said, referring to the Department of Community Service. He shifted on the seat and looked out the window for a moment. His shoulders were kind of sagging and it hit me how hard it must be for him taking on caring for his girls single-handed at his time of life.

'Do you get a break at all?' I asked.

'Yeah, sometimes. Had a drink with the neighbour last night. Out on his verandah. Great night, stars everywhere. Knocked back a few beers and watched for shootin' stars. Neighbour reckons they were dying stars but there were so many of 'em.'

'Were the girls at home?'

'Yeah, asleep in their beds. They're good kids. I have to

get out sometimes, y'know. All that washing and stuff. Does me head in.' So that was why Kacey did not have a uniform to wear to school that day. I had to hope that Bruce did not escape to his neighbour's too often. Still, with the custody case coming up, I did not feel like rushing to report it. All things considered, the girls seemed among the lucky ones to me. I gathered that Bruce had a battler's canniness and was a terrier for what mattered to him. And obviously what mattered to him was his girls. Both intellectually disabled and Kacey blind as well. Bev had told me they did everything together and the girls adored their Dad.

'I'll contact the transport people for you and see if I can't get Kacey on the taxi with Flora.'

'Okay, thanks.' Bruce nodded and got up to go. 'I'll be off then. Bev's givin' me a hand with Flora's uniform.' He paused awkwardly at the door for a minute. 'There's somethin' else, but. Don't reckon I can pay the fees for a while yet.'

'That's OK, Bruce. We're not worried about the fees.'

'Don't wanna take money from the school, y'know. Yer need it.' I couldn't help but recall a similar conversation I'd had with a highly articulate parent when I was principal at St Cath's. She had become first reproachful and then angry when I said we had to see some financial records before we could forego her daughter's school fees on hardship grounds. I felt bad about it until I saw her drive out of the school gates in her Mercedes with a pile of elegant shopping bags stacked in the rear window. It was for people like Bruce that our school existed. I didn't want to drive them away by making the school too classy. Still I did want to change the uniform.

This time it was the fashion designer Robert Burton I turned to for a favour. It was years since I'd spoken to him but he received my call with warmth and suggested I meet him at a local cafe where I could tell him 'my problem' as he called it. In the time since he had designed St Cath's uniform for me, Robert had moved out of fashion and now had an elegant homewares gallery in chic Queen Street, Woollahra. The clatter and chatter of the busy coffee shop distracted me as I tried over a cappuccino to make the modish and ironical Robert understand what the children were like at this school and why I needed his help. Robert's long hair had silvered since I saw him last but the amused twist to his lips and the mockery in his eyes were the same as I remembered and I stumbled over my increasingly halting explanation. After hearing me out, he told me that what I wanted was impossible.

'You're too small, darling. It's absurd. Sixty students. Even if they buy three sets, that's only 180 items, max. Everything's made in China these days and the factories there need orders in the hundred thousand just to set up their machines. You're only a flea of a school. You have to think like one. Leave it with me.'

A month later, when I was thinking he had dismissed us from his mind, he called back and there was a note of excitement in his drawl. He had found a relatively new children's wear company, he said, in Queensland and had persuaded the young couple to produce a version of their current casual line as a uniform for our school. I knew their brand because I had bought some of it as birthday presents for Alex. 'I told them your weepy story darling and they are not going to charge you any mark up.'

He organised everything, was a stickler for the right sizing and right design, even coming out to measure the children himself in case they didn't fit the normal range. Never charged us a cent. It took three years all up from that first meeting with Robert to delivery from the manufacturers in China but it was worth it. The children looked so different in the new uniform with every item made from pure cotton, as jaunty and up-market as I had hoped, but practical and without pretension. Trousers and shorts in navy denim with stripy t-shirts in cherry and grey and matching jersey track suits. The wonderful young couple who let us piggy-back on their designs, manufacture and transport, swore us to secrecy about their brand name and although we still had to order in the thousands, a five year supply, and the school had to become the point of sale, the Board accepted it as an investment in the children.

Now no one would look disparagingly at our kids when they went out in public in their peppy new threads. And our local Rotary Club came to the party by donating uniform bursaries to those who couldn't afford the upgrade, such as Bruce's girls.

That was all in the future though and back in my first year, I was still trying to sort Bruce's taxi problem. None of my letters brought results so eventually I dedicated a morning to waiting on the phone and finally got put through to the head of special transport. I poured out the absurd story of the taxi picking Flora up for school and leaving her sister on the curbside, to be brought by her father and her having to be late because of it. There was a silence and a rustle of papers and I imagined the man perusing the file.

'Mr Mabbitt has been denied transport for not meeting requirements,' he eventually said.

'What requirement hasn't he met?'

'His letter says he has a vehicle.'

'Yes but it's a clapped out bomb, not fit to drive all the way from where he lives.'

'If the vehicle in question is not roadworthy, then he should not be driving it. I will have to report it to the RTA.'

'You can't do that. He needs to drive to the supermarket to buy food for the kids. He's their sole carer. He just can't risk driving it all the way here.'

'If it's not roadworthy, he should not be driving it,' he intoned again.

I spluttered in frustration at this classic Catch 22

and went on trying to plead Bruce's case. The man was implacable and unexpectedly, whether out of temper or distress, I found myself crying. 'He's doing the best he can,' I said, sniffing. 'He's trying his hardest. Can't you help him?' There was a long silence while I surreptitiously wiped my face on my sleeve.

'All right. I'll give her transport,' the officer said in an aggrieved voice. 'But just for the rest of this year. Mr Mabbitt had better get his situation sorted.' I managed to thank him, after all he couldn't help being a rule-bound tunnel-visioned bureaucrat and in his eyes he was making a big concession. But I'd have liked to smash the phone receiver down. Big deal! It cost the government not a dollar more and I had to cry to get it. No wonder our parents got tired and disheartened trying to negotiate for services that were their child's right.

Bruce did get his situation sorted. Some months later he came to see me. 'I've sold my house,' he said. I was horrified. 'Nah, it's better I reckon. We're movin' in with me Dad. We don't get on much but it's better for the kids and Dad sez it's OK. I'm lettin' the car go. Dad'll do the shoppin' he sez. 'N I can pay off me debts. Been worryin' me. I'll pay off the fees too.'

'No!' I blurted.

'Yep, I want to. Youse all look after everyone. Feels like I'm robbin' yer.'

Bev was angry that I accepted Bruce's back-payment.

She reckoned he needed the money for the girls and she was right. But in a way he needed to pay his debts even more. A matter of honour for that more than honorable man. And in fact it turned out well, moving in with his dad. The two of them seemed to sort out their differences and the girls had a stable life at last. Kacey even got a bicycle and used to terrify the neighbours by riding it blindly along the nature strips of the suburb where they now lived. She often came to school with scratches and bruises from running into trees and low-lying branches but was unconcerned.

I appealed to the Catholic Women's League and they provided a scholarship so there would be no more fees. Bruce was proud that his daughters had won scholarships. A couple of years later we nominated him for Father of the Year and he brought the plaque in to school and a cutting about himself from the local newspaper. 'Here, I'll read it to you,' he said, and he did.

AT A CROSSROAD

The first year ended and the summer holidays came. A chance for Zandra and me to get to work on the bathrooms. Actually she did all the work, sub-contracting the tiling, painting and plumbing and going after donations of basins and toilet pans. There seemed no limit to what her charm and drive could achieve. The young architect from Alec Tzannes' office who designed the carpet for the library also chose the glowing opalescent tiles in green and blue for the girls and boys and the vivid kaleidoscope of colour for the infants' bathroom which she hoped would make up for its undersized space.

The bathrooms had become an obsession with me after a confrontation with a young mother over her son's toilet training. She had come to me angry that his teacher had put him back into nappies because he was having so many accidents at school. 'He asks to go to the toilet at home,' she said indignantly. 'Your staff are just not watching for the signs he gives.' The teacher when I spoke to her rolled her eyes.

'He knows all right,' she said. 'But he doesn't give a sign. He hides. Sometimes we take him to the toilet and he sits doing nothing and then when we get him back in the classroom, that's when he goes!' The mother wanted to come in and oversee her son's toileting, certain that she could have the same success with him at school as she did at home. His teacher was riled but I didn't see what we had to lose. The mother came and hung around at recess and lunch for a few days, trailing anxiously after her son, who responded by becoming badly constipated. When I told her I didn't think it was working, she burst into tears. 'I wouldn't want to go to the toilet here either!' she sobbed. 'They're disgusting. Old and smelly and disgusting.' I thanked her for her advice and promised to look into the condition of the bathrooms. I thought I was just being diplomatic but when I checked with the staff, they were scathing.

'They always smell,' they said. 'They're not cleaned properly.' So I went to Jorge the cleaner who I often saw working in the bathrooms at night, but he said it wasn't the cleaning, that he scrubbed and disinfected them daily. 'It's the mortar,' he said. 'You can't get it clean. Years of boys missing aim, if y'know what I mean. And years of changing dirty nappies.' Okay, I thought, I have to revise my priorities. Obviously in a special school, bathrooms are a core activity. Which was why Zandra spent her summer holidays happily commanding an army of men in white overalls, joking, flirting and cajoling as she drove them on to get everything finished by the start of the new year.

I was in love with those bathrooms when they were finished. No auditorium or sports field ever pumped a headmaster's pride the way those bathrooms did mine. I waited eagerly for the teachers' delight and gratitude when the new school year began but it didn't come. 'Shows how little she knows about special needs', was their judgement. No cupboard for spare clothes; the laminated partitions weren't strong enough, not like the old cement stalls; the cubicle doors were hung too high and the kids could crawl under them; the shower in the disabled cubicle would be a magnet for the kids. They were right about the last; we had to remove the taps on it after children kept emerging from it drenched to the skin. And on the second day, young Seamus went missing and after a whole school search, was found sitting on the floor behind the locked doors of the disabled cubicle. He had a napkin spread out with the contents of his lunch box carefully unpacked onto it and was enjoying a solitary picnic in the tranquil chrome and tile surrounds.

Despite this mild fiasco, I felt ready for a fresh start going into my second year, with a group of new parents and a few teachers who, being new, were not wedded to the way things were done in the past. But fresh eyes brought their own issues. At the first Parents and Friends meeting for the year, one of the new fathers asked why the sign at the front door branded us as a school for children 'who are blind, vision impaired or with other special needs'. 'I rarely see a blind kid when I come here,' he said, 'so what's the deal?' There was a murmur of agreement around the table; he had clearly touched a nerve with other parents.

'I know,' I said, embarrassed. 'It's historic really.'

'It makes out our children are an add on.'

'I know,' I said again, helplessly. I had several times spoken to the Board about the reality gap between the children we now enrolled and the way we labelled ourselves publicly. But Board members knew the Dominican Sisters were invested in the blind school they started and also they shared Jack's view that the school would miss out on valuable legacies if they abandoned its historic identity as a 'blind school'.

I made a point of getting to know the new parents quickly by waiting to speak to them at the gate when they dropped off or picked up their children. It was harder with those parents whose children travelled by taxi, I had to wait for an opportunity, and I jumped at the chance when Bev called through to me one morning to say that a new father I had not yet met was on the phone and wanted to speak to me. 'Hello Mr Vincent,' I said warmly down the phone.

'I'm so glad you called. I've been wanting ...' but I tailed off because the voice on the other end was already in full flow. I gathered that he was upset about something but I couldn't make out his words.

'I'm sorry, I didn't quite catch what you were saying?'

'I said, we won't be picking Will up this afternoon.'

'Oh,' I said, not comprehending. 'What's happening?'

'He won't be coming home to us. Not ever.' His voice trembled and I could hear the effort as he steadied it. 'I've contacted the Department of Community Service. They're arranging temporary care for him.'

'It's only temporary then?' I asked carefully.

'I told you, he doesn't have a home here. We've given him up.' With a harsh intake of breath he hurried on. 'I'm about to drive my wife to a psychiatric clinic. She can't take any more.' I heard what sounded like a sob and the phone went dead in my hand. I put it down wondering what kind of stress could have caused parents to give up their child. I didn't even know their son was a problem. Shaken, I hurried to Kelly's classroom to ask her about Will. He was playing quietly in a corner with a red, wooden train. Sitting back on his heels with his blond hair and china blue eyes he looked the picture of boyhood you'd see on a greeting card. I took Kelly aside to tell her about the father's phone call.

'Is he so difficult?' I asked. 'I had no idea.'

'Well, he can be naughty,' Kelly said consideringly. 'He throws things a lot still and he can turn on a killer tantrum.

But he's already getting better. In a term or two, we'll turn him round I think.' She may have been right but we never found out. The Department arranged a foster home for him in a suburb a long way away and we did not see him again. I felt wretched to think of a little boy losing his place in his family and worried that I was part way to blame for not realizing sooner that his parents were at breaking point. I should have taken more seriously the priority the teachers gave here to behaviour. Had my instinctive resistance to the school's use of classic conditioning to control the children's behaviour somehow played a part in Will's tragic displacement?

In a way, the positive behaviour management practised at the school had impressed me. I admired the emphasis that it placed on acknowledging the good things children did and the fact that it abjured punishment. I heard teachers praising children a lot more at this school than in any I had ever been in and I really liked that. But I was uncomfortable with the singular focus on controlling the children and making them compliant with no allowance for what they were thinking or feeling. Because of this, I had given leeway to those teachers who wanted to use more mainstream methods of dealing with their charges. Now I felt guilty about my ambivalent stance. Certainly those staff who had the most effective control over difficult behaviour in the school were Jack and Sybil and they were the ones who applied positive behaviour methods most consistently. I decided I would have to change. I'd have to let go my natural preference for building up a rapport with children and instead model strict behaviorist methods in the way I dealt with children who were sent to me.

My resolve was put to the test soon afterwards when on a hot afternoon, Kelly appeared at my door with one of her six year old pupils. 'I am sorry, Mrs Karaolis,' Kelly said, 'but Lizzie needs time out. Can she stay with you until the bell goes?' It was twenty minutes to the end of the school day and looking at her pinched lips, I guessed it was Kelly rather than Lizzie who needed time out. She disappeared back to her class without waiting for an answer, leaving me with a small, round, indignant Lizzie who, I learned later, had just trashed her classroom. I shut the door to stop her running off and looked at her. She was a tubby little thing with a determined chin and her face was bright red with anger. My instinct was to get out a toy for her to play with while she calmed down but no more of that. I would not give her the benefit of any attention until I caught her doing something good that I could reinforce.

I told her to sit in the chair and I went on with my work. She swept the contents of my in-tray onto the floor. Papers, letters, notes spread everywhere but I ignored this, waiting for her to do something I could reward. She then got to work on my bookshelves. One by one she threw books onto the floor, looking at me each time to check my reaction. I was still ignoring her when the door flew open and Lizzie's mother stood there, her face contorted. 'Elizabeth', she shouted in a fury, 'WHAT are you doing? You come out here with me at once.' Lizzie stopped throwing and after a long, shuddering intake of breath, went meekly out with her mother, who walked off without a word to me. I sat in a pool of embarrassment. What was I doing, over sixty years of age, putting myself in this position? I started to pick up the books and put them back on the shelves.

'How did you go?' Kelly was standing at the door, grinning.

'I failed,' I said, 'and her mother caught me.' Kelly's grin grew broader.

'It happens to us all,' she said and laughed. I nodded but my mind was in revolt. Lizzie had obeyed her mother because she was scared of being in trouble with her, but there was so much more. There was trust, love, a history between them: relationship. Relationship was what I knew and what made sense to me and I was too old to change. Once again I wondered if I had the kind of personality you needed for being principal of a special school.

At this point I had a visit from an old friend. I had known Margot Canning since I first came to Sydney hunting for a job, straight out of university. Her family had put me up for over a month and I shared a room with Margot, who had been fifteen then. Over the years we'd stayed connected by the ties of that long-ago summer and by fond memories of Margot's father whom she had adored and whom we both missed. Margot had married and now moved in a very different, elite social circle. Her daughter went to one of the expensive girls schools in Sydney where Margot and her husband had connections with the Board. She called me at work out of the blue and said she would like to come up and see the special school where I worked now and I felt a rush of hope that she wanted to make a donation; she and her husband were well known for their philanthropy. But when she came, it turned out that she had something very different on her mind.

Resting her finely shaped hands on her expensive handbag, she told me of her worries for her daughter's school. There had been difficulties with the principal, a recent appointment whose contract had been terminated and the school community was divided and confused. 'We need someone with an established reputation who has the experience to settle the school down. I've come to invite you to apply for the position.' My first reaction was disappointment that this wasn't about a donation after all. Then I felt embarrassed. She didn't seem to realise how inappropriate she was, trying to heist a principal from a little special school for the sake of a school that could buy whomever it wanted as principal from anywhere in the world. I tried to let her down lightly, explaining that the parents counted on me and that I was only in my second year. Margot nodded understandingly.

'Believe me, I have the greatest respect for what you are doing here and I really admire you for throwing yourself into it the way you have,' she said. 'But no matter how hard you work in this little school with these children, it's not going to make any difference in the scheme of things.' She leaned forward and her voice dropped a tone or two as she said with studied emphasis. 'I'm talking about one of the top girls school in Australia. More than a thousand young women who will be the leaders of the next generation or else married to the leaders. That's real influence.' She looked at me and paused before adding, 'It's an opportunity for you, Jo. You can instill all the things that you think are important.' Then after another pause, she smiled and rose swiftly to her feet. 'I don't want an answer now. I'll put the prospectus in the mail to you and let you have a couple of days to think about it. I'll ring you at the end of the week.' Sliding the magnificent handbag onto her arm, she gave me a quick, warm hug and went on her way, leaving me in confusion.

I was flattered, no doubt about it, but her suggestion was impossible. Leave these children who had so little, to go to a place where the students had all been born not with a silver spoon but a whole set of silver cutlery in their mouths? It was unthinkable. But I couldn't stop thinking about it. Silly things came into my mind, like the big deal the staff made when I forgot it was my turn to empty the dishwasher and the worrying clank my car had developed that I didn't have time to get fixed. It would have been noticed and repaired at St Cath's without me even being aware. Why there I used to have lunch brought on a silver tray with a lace cloth and fine bone china. Well, that had been over the top, but still, it was a nice contrast to not having time to open my mail and being afraid my electricity would be cut off like last quarter because I'd missed the bill.

The prospectus arrived two days after Margot's visit. It was glossy and brightly coloured with a photograph of the school on the front and another of the elegant headmistress's residence on the first page. My eyes were drawn to the laughing girls pictured at the school gate. Their hair was glossy, they were bright eyed and confident, intelligence beamed from the page. Nostalgically I remembered what fun it had been, engaging with girls like this, their chatter and their idealism. I glanced through the role description and list of expectations of the principal, all very familiar. No mention of wiping noses or dealing with broken toilets. The emoluments page was an eye-opener: car, meals, ridiculously high salary. I began to waver. With the appealing prospectus in front of me, I rang Gae and hesitantly told her of Margot's visit. 'You're not considering it, are you?' she asked. I was silent. 'Well, are you?'

'Well, yes; or at least I am not sure.' It was her turn to go quiet. After a long pause she said only that she needed time to think.

'Don't do anything until I come back to you on it.'

I couldn't get it out of my mind. I began to wonder if it would be such a bad thing for the school if I took this other position. I could persuade wealthy families there to sponsor the special school I had left behind and assist with fundraising and other things. Zandra would like that. And really I wasn't such a good match here; I didn't fit with the expectations and I didn't have the skills; the staff and I were on a different page, and anyway, it wasn't the blind school I thought I had applied for. I had probably given the best of my capacity in getting the library and bathrooms refurbished. It might well be better for someone more experienced in special education to take over now and for me to go back to what I knew best.

On the Thursday, Gae and I were both booked for the Open Day at our satellite class at Narrabeen. I had felt very touched when Gae had agreed to speak at the Open Day. She was an education consultant and giving her time meant losing income, yet she had not hesitated when I told her how much it would mean to the teachers to have her there. As Chair of the Board, she spent herself unstintingly on the school. She was her usual warm, vivacious self when she arrived at the classroom and neither of us mentioned the phone call. For a couple of hours we met with prospective parents and talked about the school and the satellite class as though nothing was amiss. The satellite teacher, Chris Donaldson, was thrilled to have Gae's charismatic presence and seemed completely unaware of the turbulence in my mind and I suspected in Gae's though she gave no sign.

At the end of the morning Gae helped me to carry the boxes of flyers and enrolment folders back to my car and after they were stashed away in my boot, she took out an envelope and a CD from her handbag. 'I don't feel able to talk to you about it so I've written you a letter,' she said. 'And I'd like you to listen to a track on this CD when you've read the letter.' She placed them both in my hands and turned and walked away to her car that was parked nearby.

I watched her go, thinking how much I would miss her warm, generous friendship and that I'd never have a Board Chair to match her. It would be a wrench to say goodbye, but who knew, perhaps there would be an opportunity for her to work as a consultant at the new school? I got about half-way home before I had to stop and see what was in her letter. I pulled over onto gravel at the top of a hill that overlooked the ocean and stayed sitting immobile in the sun, not wanting to be persuaded by whatever she had written. Finally I ripped the envelope apart and skimmed the pages. Then I sat with the letter lying on my lap a while before I took it up and read again more carefully. Finally I sat staring out to where the sea and sun blended on the horizon. I stayed there a long time, letting the decision I was making seep through my being, silently absorbing all that it meant.

Gae had written at length, for more than a couple of

pages, listing all the advantages of the other school, all those I had thought and dreamt about and some that I hadn't. My first feeling was relief that she understood. It was good to have it all set out in writing, every aspect that lured me.

'We can offer you none of these things,' she wrote at the top of the page. 'All we can offer is life lived at its rawest and most truthful; love given without hope of gain; joy that comes from the deepest springs; work whose only reward is the lift in the shoulders for which you have lightened the burden. We cannot offer what the other school does, but here every day love is on offer, love without ego, love without demand, love that comes from sharing burdens and finding gladness together.'

An odd thing had happened when I read the words, *We can offer you none of those things.* A shaft of understanding and I knew with a funny sense of loss that I would not apply. If I had been younger, perhaps. But at this point of my life I was not looking for what I could be offered, I was looking for meaning. Since Costi's death I had been lost, unsure who I was even. Now in a flash I saw that my search for identity, for personhood, was not a question of Who at all but a question of Where, where did I find meaning? I couldn't leave these children, these families, for a wealthy, privileged school.

Our parents had no choice. I thought of Bruce Mabbitt. He would have liked to be off with his mates having a beer, but he was at home trying to get the girls' uniforms dry. The parents had been handed a task they never asked for, and were stretching nerve and sinew to do it well. My school years had been spent in the 1950's, in the shadow still cast by WWII, when we were taught not to let those millions of deaths be in vain, that we must work to make the world a better place. No one talked like that now but it was what the parents of these kids did, every day of their lives. 'To give and not to count the cost ... to work and ask for no reward save that of knowing that we do Thy will.'

'Thy will'. Since being with the Dominican Sisters, I had found God less easy to ignore. I still disliked the crucifixes and thought it was superstitious to believe a white wafer of plastic bread could be commuted to Jesus' flesh and blood. But I was at one with their call to serve the poor and the suffering, the weak and the lonely. I was at home in a religion that said every human being matters equally to God.

Go as principal to a secular school, where parents dreamed of brilliant careers and even more brilliant marriages for their daughters? Where they berated teachers for not getting their child the marks they wanted? It wasn't for me, not now. That night in my bedroom I played the CD track that Gae had pressed on me. It was one of John Coleman's songs called *The Road Less Travelled* and I listened with a strange calm to the words I thought were probably Gae's message to me:

My friend turned her back on power
She chose another mobility
She finds peace in smaller places
For weakness is the source of grace.
© John Coleman

My daughter Christina came in as I was listening. She and Guillaume were living with me, with Alex, while they searched for a house to buy. They had been all in favour of my enjoying the perks of the other job. I told her about Gae's letter and played her the song. 'Sounds like you,' she said when it finished, smiling in commiseration. 'Bit of a masochist really.'

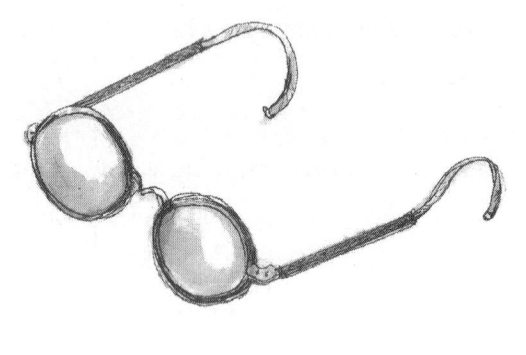

VISION

'Well, don't keep us in suspense. Are you leaving or not?' It was Marta, Italian, ebullient, impatient, who couldn't wait while I took the staff through my labyrinthine thought processes. I wanted them to feel with me the momentousness of the decision I had made and to recognise that I was committing not just myself but them too, to work together and forge a shared vision that did justice to their expertise and my experience. I was conscious of the disconcerting quiet around the staff room table, and uncomfortably aware that not all welcomed my news.

'Yes, I'm staying, Marta,' I finally got out.

'Good because you're down to empty the dishwasher.' A laugh ran around the table, ending the tension, and the meeting quickly broke up. And that was the end of the matter, though Sybil did mutter quietly as she left, 'Good move, Jo', and Marta stayed behind to help me put the dishes away.

Still emotional, I worked late that night. I thought I had the school to myself and the sudden sound of loud footsteps across the foyer floor made me jump. 'Do you have time for a word?' It was Jack. I had come to dread his drop-in visits, always late at night; they portended some matter of great seriousness to him, often something that in his view I'd got wrong. I always felt at a disadvantage because Jack could pin what I was thinking in an instant whereas he remained a mystery to me. I knew him to be intelligent, confident and dedicated and I respected his honesty but we could never find common ground. I was a bit scared of him too and tonight I wished he hadn't come. 'You said this afternoon that now you've had your epiphany, you'll be more proactive in pursuing your vision for the school. I'm hoping you'll tell me what you meant.' He pulled out a chair and I studied his face a moment for clues to his feelings, but Jack, sitting with his arms across his chest, looked blandly back.

'I meant that I don't think we can go on pretending we are a school for the blind.' There was a tell-tale tremor in my voice. I didn't want this confrontation but it was here anyway.

'It's what we do best,' Jack said firmly. 'We're experts in it.'

'Yes, and that's a problem when ninety percent of our children don't have vision impairment. What we have is children whose brain wiring is abnormal,' I said and added rather lamely, 'It's time we were experts in that.' Jack stared at me across the desk and I shifted uncomfortably, wishing there were someone to interrupt us.

'You're in the wrong place,' he said. 'You are principal of a school for the blind but you don't care a toss about vision education.' He looked hard at me. 'You've not been in one of my braille classes for months and I haven't seen you in Disability Awareness all this year.'

'Well, it's true I've not been for a while. I'll come this week.' To my relief, I saw Jack push himself out of the chair.

'People much better than you have given their lives to making this school great,' he said, leaning across my desk. 'Don't destroy their work.' He straightened and without a backward look strode from the room.

Disability Awareness classes were an institution at the school. I didn't know how long they had been going but they were certainly popular with the Catholic primary schools that sent their children along to learn first hand what it's like to have a disability. There was a school booked each Friday for most weeks of the year. I used to see them out in the playground at recess, some of them talking to our students. It looked on the surface like an enlightened kind of programme but I had misgivings about it, mostly because the students who came were taught about blindness. Jack passed out blindfolds and canes and they took it in turns to find their way round the library. He showed them how to be a sighted guide for a blind person and taught them to write their names in braille. It was interesting and in itself worthwhile, but the children they met in the playground were mostly not blind.

On the Friday after Jack challenged me, I sat in on his disability class in the morning and at recess stood watching the playground unseen from inside the office. Gareth the 'Chairman of the Board' was in top form. As the mainstream children emerged from the library, he was there to greet them, smiling and nodding, uttering wordless sounds of welcome and waving his arms about in emphatic fashion. Most of the children gave him a wide berth but a couple of girls stopped to say hello and I could see even from a distance that Gareth's day was made. Then I noticed the slim form of one of our older boys, Sam, slowly approaching from behind the lilly pilly tree where he had been hovering, probably waiting for the visitors to come out of the library.

Sam was a conundrum to us. He couldn't speak and his diagnosis was dyspraxia, meaning that his brain had difficulties in motor planning. It showed up in his awkward ungainly movements and incomprehensible vocalisations. His deep-set eyes always had an alert and interested shine to them and I was inclined to agree with his mother who believed a bright, eager mind existed in frustration inside his jerky body, unable to express itself through words, unable to write and blocked from life by cruel handicaps that a range of therapists had been unable to correct. Now I saw with an ache that Sam was approaching the visitors in hope of making contact and I guessed that he saw in them possibilities that he couldn't find in anyone at our school. Stopping in front of a group of boys, he waved his arms and made yelping sounds. They laughed and nudged each other. 'He's a psycho,' one said loudly and they giggled. As I hurried out to intervene, they scattered.

'Are you okay?' I asked Sam. He was a beautiful looking boy with long eyelashes that now dropped over his dark eyes as he bent his head and turned and walked awkwardly away – embarrassed I supposed that I had seen his humiliation. Back in the library after recess, Jack was standing waiting to debrief the class on the students they had met. I recognised a couple of the boys who had been in the group teasing Sam. They were rumbling each other on the floor. Jack called on them at once. 'Who did you two meet?' he asked.

'We don't know his name cos he couldn't speak,' blustered one of them.

'What can you tell us about him?' Jack asked encouragingly.

'He's psycho,' the other boy said under his breath. Jack frowned.

'Speak up!'

'He's all jerky and makes funny sounds!' The two broke into giggles.

'You probably met Sam,' Jack said with a quelling look. 'Sam has dyspraxia. He has trouble talking but he is probably more intelligent than you or me.'

'We talked to Gareth,' a girl volunteered.

'Who was that?' asked Jack, not quite catching it.

'The fat boy,' a boy called out. A look of disgust crossed Jack's face but he ignored the jibe, instead explaining patiently to the class some of the disabilities they had encountered. But the children were tired and not very interested and soon it was time for them to go. I stayed back helping to put the chairs away.

'How did you think that went?' I asked.

'They were a bit restless but they came round,' Jack said.

''They were making fun of the children.'

'Well, it's their first contact with people with disabilities,' he said reasonably. 'It's natural for them to react. It's part of the desensitisation process.'

'Desensitisation!' I exclaimed. 'Sam was looking for a friend. Bringing children in to gawk doesn't help. Our kids can't be fodder for non-disabled children to learn empathy. They need friendship, buddies who can get to know and like them.' I made an attempt to speak calmly. 'P'raps this was a good program when the children here were only blind and could hold their own with the visitors but now, frankly it's exploitation. I don't want us to continue with it.' Jack put down the chair he was carrying.

'The schools are already booked,' he said flatly. 'I have

bookings right through the next two terms.'

'Then I'll call them and cancel.'

His voice was cold. 'I don't think you understand what this programme means to them', he said. 'It is part of their personal development and religious studies curriculum. I get emails every year from teachers saying how great it is for their students to come on excursion here.'

'Yes, like a visit to the zoo.'

'You just don't get it. Buildings are what you care about and fancy uniforms. We are a leader in vision education, renowned in Australia and internationally. You want to tear all that down.'

'There are five vision impaired children here,' I said loudly. 'You keep fighting for something that's over; it's past. Face facts. This is now a school of children with intellectual impairment.' Jack and I stood glaring at each other. Annoyed at losing my cool, I turned and headed off to my office to start ringing schools. I quickly found Jack was right. They were disappointed and aggrieved, unable to understand why I would discontinue a programme that worked so well.

'It's good for our children,' one of them said. 'It makes them more empathetic.'

'Then let's build on that. Let's have a relationship between our schools; your classes can buddy ours. They can get to really know each other.' But it was too complicated. Our disability awareness programme had been neat and self-contained and fitted tidily into their busy school life; why did I want to fix something that was not broken?

I felt a bit tentative about breaking the news to the Board members of what I had done. Only one of them was the parent of a child at the school; the rest were there to do a favour to the Dominicans and had little or no experience with disability. They were kind and supportive but apart from Gae, not very close to things at the school. Sister Clare was particularly concerned at my high handedness. A psychologist and counsellor, she liked to find the path of conciliation. 'If you explain properly to the schools about the kind of children here and don't focus so much on braille in their classes, they'll still get an awareness of what it's like to be disabled without any of this upset.'

It sounded eminently reasonable and I could see other Board members nodding. But they hadn't seen Sam's face as he turned away from me in shame. They would be horrified if their own children were made the exhibit for other schools' excursions, but that was different because their children were normal. Perhaps I would have thought as they did had I not come to know and care for the children here. I was at a loss how to make them understand. I was huffing incoherently when Gae calmly intervened. She leaned forward, smiling equably as she let her warm, intelligent eyes behind their large glasses move from one Board member to another. 'A lot has changed since we drew up our vision for the school back in 1996,' she told them. 'I think it's time that we had another look. I propose appointing an external facilitator to review the performance of the principal and the school and advise on the way forward. We'll use that report to review the school's vision and mission at our annual retreat.' You could feel the sense of relief around the table as Board members murmured that it was a good idea, a chance to look at the thing in context.

The review process took a couple of months and included interviews with staff, parents and Board members. I was hugely relieved at the end of it to read in the facilitator's report a generally warm commendation of our work of the past two years and my own leadership. But there was a rocket in the tail of the report. 'The school is developing along two divergent paths. No school can flourish with a divided mission. It is the responsibility of the school Board to define the future direction so there can be unanimity of principles, practices and priorities.'

'You're the principal,' Gae said to me when we met to discuss the report. 'It's the Board's job to discern the signs of the times and adjust its vision accordingly but we need to hear from you. After all, you're running the school. I'll give you time at the retreat.' I jumped at the opportunity. I had come to believe we were selling children short because of unspoken prejudice against intellectual impairment. It seemed deeply ingrained in us as a species and a society that the more marked a person's cognitive impairment, the less they were valued as human beings. We were a special school but even we liked the smarter kids best. And we thought learning to read and write were more important than being a life-giving, love-giving human being.

Gae was giving me a chance to persuade the Board to see things differently and there seemed only one way to do it. They didn't know the children and they knew little about education. They were on the Board out of friendship to the Dominican Sisters but that meant that they believed in Jesus who had taught that all of us are made in the image of God. My job then was to help them see these children not as a mistake or error of nature, but as an expression of God.

I had several times said to a parent sitting in front of me, brimming with love for her child and lacerated by judgmental comments – from her family or her friends or strangers in the park – 'Your child is whole as she is; she is made in the image of God.' Those words made sense in the moment and the parents' gratitude at my understanding gave me a warm glow. But sometimes I wondered if I was kidding myself or them. One grey bleak day when I was feeling a bit low, I chose to stand outside in the playground and gaze unblinkingly around me, asking myself to consider honestly without sentimental pretence, in what way did these children present an image of God? God of infinite knowledge and wisdom, God of infinite grace? Little Jillian for example, standing twisting a leaf in her hand, mesmerised by it, her hair falling over her face as she twirled it backwards and forwards, enjoying the sensation that ran along her nerves. I noticed her nose was running and yes, the staff were right, there was a greeny discharge. Why won't parents keep their children home when they're sick, they moaned. We all knew why. They needed to get them out of the house to give themselves a break; they needed it so badly it was worth a sharp rebuke from the teacher.

I took a clean tissue from my pocket – these days I knew to be equipped – and went to deal with Jillian's nose. I almost gagged as I tried to capture the mass of green mucous. Her eyes stared blankly ahead, she was squat and unmoving, standing stock still. And in that moment, like a deep pulse of recognition rising from below, I felt the is-ness of her, the essence of her. It was as though my own self expanded, embraced by the absolute trust with which she stood there, letting me do whatever I felt I must do. The mucous was just body product, nothing important. In that moment I was touched by the shared humanity that connects us all, the one true thing we have to give each other. Jillian lifted up her eyes to me and gave a slow smile. This is what we were about. Standing for all children no matter how great their disabilities in the faith that their very humanity was what we must serve, with all our imagination and capacity. It was this I had to convey to the Board.

I couldn't take the children to them so I decided to look for pictures. I found a photo of Seamus during his Confirmation and inserted it into a PowerPoint. He was standing staring with total absorption at the lighted candle in his hand. I actually knew that the devotion on Seamus's face was for fire. I had to hide the matches from him at school, along with any cash, given his predilection for taking both. But when the Confirmation ceremony was over Seamus's mother said in pride mixed with apology, 'He's a lot of trouble but he has a beautiful soul'. I hoped the Board could understand this.

Children who believe easily and love unconditionally, who don't remember disappointments and failures, whose lives are not stained like ours with worry and fear, who don't call themselves names and run a tape of self-doubt, who trust all who are kind to them – they have pure souls. They project the image of God in a way we cannot.

I added to it a photo of Hailey shooting down a small slide with her legs splayed wide and her face beaming. The abandonment of her movement was heart-catching, there was such trust in her relaxed limbs and shining face. You could see how she lives each day as though it is all there is. She remembers little of yesterday and tomorrow is just a word. When she climbs onto the slide, she has no thought about the possibility of falling; she just gives herself up to the experience.

Then I found a photo of Whitney. When Whitney was born, her parents were told that her disabilities were so severe she would not live long enough for them to take her home. But she had pulled through. Then they were told that she would never talk, but the other day when I brought a visitor to the class, Whitney had looked at my tense body and folded arms (I was hoping to impress the visitor). 'Why are you cross with the children?' she asked with a look at me as true as a die. Despite her calipers, she was now as fast on her feet as the next child. The doctors had expended their best skills and uncountable thousands of dollars to get Whitney to survive. It was our task to make sure the life they had given her was one worth living.

At the Retreat when I projected these and many other photos onto the screen and spoke about the children, I could see the Board members were moved but it was Gae who made the clinching argument. 'As Dominicans, we are committed to truth,' she said. 'Is our current label as a school for the blind truthful? If you think it is not, given that ninety percent of our children are not vision impaired, then we have to put all the school's resources, energies and time into achieving excellence for children of all disabilities. That means shutting down our braille classes, our outreach to blind children in mainstream schools, our braille camps and the compulsory training of teachers in braille.' She then pulled out a small travel Bible and turned to a passage from the gospel of St Matthew that she had bookmarked. 'No one can serve two masters,' she read out. 'Either you will hate the one and love the other, or you will be devoted to the one and despise the other. You cannot serve both.' She raised her head and looked around again.

'It is time for us to choose,' she said.

It was an historic decision and having accepted Gae's ultimatum that it must be one or the other, the Board members made it easily. There could be no question of deciding against the children who made up the majority of the school, the children whose images they had just seen on the screen. I felt great relief. We had clung to the past too long. But there was one glaring consequence that troubled and scared me. Because we would not continue the outreach program to blind children in regular schools, we no longer needed Jack's expertise in vision education. The Board offered him a very generous separation arrangement and he was quickly snapped up by a university. But he was angry and lost no time in letting the world know how I was destroying the work of generations of Dominican Sisters and teachers of the blind. Jack was popular and had a wide network. Feeling ran high against me inside the school and out and it came to a head at the staff Christmas party.

I had been negotiating for some months with the Diocese for us to establish a second satellite class to be set up in a mainstream Catholic primary school. We already had the one on the coast for school beginners, where Chris Donaldson taught. I wanted another one for Year 5 and 6 students with disabilities so we could strengthen their skills and act as a springboard to get them into mainstream high school classes. The Diocese's Disability Co-ordinator recommended that we consider setting the second satellite up at a school in the adjacent suburb because, he said, the principal there was 'a kind of angel'. When I met her, I knew instantly that he was right. Elsa McPhee was immediately enthusiastic and through painstaking consultation won her whole staff and parent body to the venture. I invited Mrs McPhee to our Christmas staff party so I could thank her and she could meet everyone and we could share prayers of hope for the new class.

But that was Jack's last day and I hadn't allowed for the hostility of the staff. I handed out their Christmas gifts in an atmosphere of whispered venom. My words of congratulations on a year of hard work and achievement were received with stony silence. 'Please don't invite me again,' Mrs McPhee said as she left, patting me comfortingly on the arm.

TASHA WINS THROUGH

'Change is painful,' Gae said, looking smilingly around the table at the staff gathered for the first day of the new school year. 'Even when it is necessary, it hurts. Some of you will be uncomfortable, some resentful and some of you will leave. That's the pattern of change in any organisation.' There was a sudden silence as Gae's words sank in and then a buzz of whispered conversation but in the end only one of the staff left. The children were the same children after all: only the label on the facade of the school had altered. We had changed the catchline which defined us to: *excellence in education for children with disabilities*. I had wanted to use a softer term, like 'children with different abilities' but Ernesto, the only school parent on the Board, was impatient with what he saw as evasion. 'The kids have disabilities. Nothing wrong with that,' he said. 'They're fine. In fact they're remarkable.'

The change was not resisted so much in the school as in the wider community which still believed we were populated by blind children and assumed they were now being ejected. I received angry calls from professionals, disappointed letters from past parents and criticism from organisations dedicated to educating the vision impaired. Worst was the hostility apparent in the congregation of Dominican Sisters who owned the school. Most of the Sisters were barely aware that the school had changed from the talented blind children for whom they had introduced a world-class standard of education for the vision impaired. They couldn't help but mourn the past when their students had won piano competitions in the Sydney eisteddfod and defied all expectations by their success in public examinations and in paralympic sports such as skiing.

'It's a classic marketing situation,' Zandra said over the rim of her pink vodka cocktail when I finished telling her about the angry letters I was getting and the septic gossip the grapevine filtered back to me. I was prepared to be unpopular for a time but the reaction by the Sisters worried me and I was hurt by the implication that I had betrayed the Dominican legacy. Zandra's perspective on it as a mere business problem was a relief. I was enjoying the escape from school at the end of a week and the chance to have a laugh with someone who didn't shy from me as the enemy. The surroundings were cheerless, an old-style ladies' lounge at the Northern pub, but Zandra was lending a bit of style in her exotic pink and bling outfit, sipping her summer cocktail while I thirstily downed a beer. 'We've changed our branding and we need to manage the process,' she went on with an airy wave of her shell pink nails. 'The Sisters don't really know the children we have now. We must bring them up to the school. They'll fall in love with them.'

She spun a scenario that sounded too easy. We would hold a special religious observance to belatedly commemorate the school's seventy-five years and the Sisters' work in building it into a place of excellence. We would use the children at every point, to welcome the Sisters, to lead the prayers and to sing to them. Afterwards Zandra would turn on a gracious old-style afternoon tea on the lawn with marquees and cucumber sandwiches and commemorative lace handkerchiefs as a take-home memento. That afternoon I was warmed by the alcohol and cheered by Zandra's sparkling confidence and felt excited and relaxed about it all as we sat in the late-afternoon glow from the amber windows of the ladies' lounge.

I felt less confident when I sat down some weeks later to plan the religious ceremony. The Sisters had no experience with the kind of disabilities our pupils had now. Would they look at our debonair, creative Gareth and just see an overweight, slow boy? Would they feel disturbed by the shouted vocalisations of some of the children with autism? I feared the visit could make them more critical and disparaging of the change. I had heard that some were suggesting the Dominicans should withdraw altogether from the school. Since they owned the land, that could spell the end. With so much at stake, I was tempted to expose our visitors to only our most capable and well-behaved students. We had plenty of cute little children who would win their hearts and some very courteous, relatively articulate seniors who could meet and greet them. It would be much safer to keep our really challenging children hidden.

But I resisted the temptation. We had just gone through fire to restore truth to how we presented the school. We could not hide or pretend again. We had to embrace all the children in all their diversity and I had to trust that the Sisters would respond. But my disquiet persisted especially when we had yet another incident with Tasha. Tasha! I sometimes thought I should never have enrolled her. I had felt ambushed by her mother at the time but I could have refused.

Tasha was nine when I first met her. Her mother had brought a large entourage of family to check out the school, including her ex-husband and his new wife. 'Oh darling,' she had said as she burst unannounced through my door with a pack of beautiful blonde beach people behind her. 'What a special place you have. We love it. We all agree it will be perfect for Tasha. Just perfect.' She pulled up a chair and waved the others into place around her. She introduced everyone but I didn't catch their names because I was too busy trying to work out what they were all doing in my office.

'Bev has taken us into all the classes and your teachers are fabulous. I know Tasha will be very happy here.'

'Um, who is Tasha?'

'Oh darling, we just came in on spec. We live down south at Cronulla and a client told me about your school. Let's just go and have a look, I said. If we don't like it we won't have to bother anyone. But you know, we *do*. We think it's marvellous. Bev said we had to make an appointment to see you but I thought I'd just pop my head in and say hello since we're here.' She rose from her chair and waved the flock of beautiful people out of the door. 'I'll bring Tasha with me next time I come, Jo. I can call you Jo can't I? You'll love her.' She blew a kiss from the tips of her long red nails before sailing out of the room leaving a cloud of scent behind her.

I was still recovering when the phone rang. 'Sorry about that,' came Bev's voice. 'They got away from me.'

'I can see how that would happen! Did they really come all the way from Cronulla?'

'Seems so. The mother, Belle, says that the school Tasha

is in now isn't right for her and that she's tried all the other options where they live.'

'Do you know anything about the girl?'

'I'm not sure. I think she'd be about the right age for Kelly's class. There'll be a vacancy when Sean moves to England.'

'Well, if they do ring back, make a time when Kelly is able to try the girl out in her class and I'll get the story from the mother while she's here.'

I had learned to be wary of families who moved their child from school to school. Often it meant the parents hadn't accepted the reality of their child's difficulties. Still, I wasn't going to jump to conclusions ahead of meeting the girl. And when I first saw her, I felt a sense of relief. Tasha was long-limbed and tanned, unusually tall with a mass of honey gold curls that sprang from her head in a thick cascade. Her blue eyes had a vacant look as she stared vaguely around, otherwise she was a vision of loveliness. When Kelly came down to lead her off to class, Tasha hesitated and drew back until her mother said, 'This is your new teacher, Tasha. You'll be all right with her.' Tasha quietly followed Kelly's pink jumper out of the foyer. I thought it an excellent sign though I was a little taken aback at the mother's assumption that we would accept her.

'Oh Jo, I can't thank you enough,' she gushed as she sat herself comfortably in the chair in my office.

'I'm afraid you've not understood, Mrs Hartfield. We

haven't said we can take your daughter, you know. This is just a preliminary meeting so that I can get an idea of her needs and whether we might be able to meet them.'

'Oh call me Belle. Mrs Hartfield sounds so formal. I'm a podiatrist you know. I get a feeling for my clients just as soon as they take off their shoes. It's made me a great judge of people. I get a good energy from you. I just know that this is the right place for Tasha and you'll be able to see that, I know you will. I feel very positive about it.'

'Personally, I need the facts, Mrs Har..uh, Belle. Would you mind telling me all the details you can about Tasha, beginning with her birth and early years?' I didn't have to ask another question for the next half hour. Once started, Belle poured out Tasha's whole life story and I had difficulty keeping up as I scribbled notes onto the file that Bev had opportunely made up for her. Tasha's diagnosis of autism had come late in the day after she had been through pre-school and started at a normal public school. She was then moved by the Department of Education to an autism school that for some reason had not worked out and from there they had shifted her to a school for children with a high level of disability.

'And that is the school she's at now?' I asked at the end of the saga. 'Why would you take her out of a special school that is near to you and bring her all the way up here?'

'Because,' Belle said, leaning across the desk and looking intensely into my face, 'Tasha is the only one there who can move around by herself. The rest are all in wheelchairs.' She took my hand and held it in both hers. 'Tasha is such a free spirit, you know, Jo. She needs to run, to skip and dance. How can she grow and develop when she has no one to play with, no one who can run around like she can?' She dropped my hand and said sadly, 'They do their best, really they do, but it's not the right place for Tasha. If she comes here, she'll have lots of other children like her.' She reached for a tissue from the box on my desk. 'To tell you the truth, Jo, that's not a nice place she's at. When I go in the afternoon to pick her up, the children are all lined up in the hall in their wheelchairs and there's an awful smell of urine. I know the staff don't have time to change everyone and make them nice but it's terrible. I hate having to leave Tasha there every day, knowing that it's not a school, just a place they put children who can't care for themselves.'

Then she brightened up. 'Tell me, Jo. Do you do the sacraments here? Tasha's Catholic you know. I dream of having her confirmed. I still remember my own confirmation day, how special it was. I wear the cross my godmother gave me all the time,' and she pulled down the collar of her jumper to show me a small gold cross hanging around her neck. The gesture grabbed me, reminding me of someone else. Belle, thinking it was the cross that had made me start so visibly, held it up for me to see better. But it wasn't the cross.

My mind had gone to another interview, another

woman sitting in the chair where Belle was sitting now, a quiet woman. She too had pulled at her collar, but it was to show me that the cross she had worn since her baptism no longer hung around her neck. It had been some weeks before. She had a son with Down syndrome due to start school the following year. She'd been given the diagnosis of Down syndrome during her pregnancy, after her amniocentesis test, she said, and the doctor had asked if she wanted to abort the baby. She was terribly upset and had gone to her priest for advice.

Her eyes were dark with remembered pain as she told me the story. 'He said my child was a gift from God and it would be a sin not to give birth. And in a way he was right. He's a beautiful boy and I wouldn't be without him. Now he's ready for school I took him along to the parish school to book him in for next year but the principal said he was sorry, they didn't have the resources to care for him. He'd be better off in the government school as they have more money for children like mine. I was livid and I went to the priest, the one who'd said I had to give birth. Oh I can't interfere, he said. He said it wouldn't be fair to the other children because he'd take too much of the teacher's time.' I offered her son a place with us but in the end she decided not to take it. 'I've no stomach for it,' she said. 'Not now I've seen what a sham the Church is.'

Now I looked at Belle sitting opposite me, her fingers playing with her cross and her eyes watching me hopefully.

A mother determined that her child would not miss out on life just because chance had dealt her a difficult hand; wanting the same for Tasha as any normal child would be given. Our school had an open enrolment policy, we did not consider religious affiliation when offering places, only the children's needs. But it seemed to me that for a person whose faith was important to her, who got through the challenges of having a child with disabilities by putting her worries in God's hands and living each day in trust, that for such a person to be rejected by a Catholic school was much more than disappointment. It was a slap in the face from God. It made a mockery, turned her faith upside down – as had happened to the other mother.

'Let's go up and collect Tasha now,' I said to Belle. 'She's been there long enough.'

'D'you mean you'll take her? Will you take her?'

'Well, I have to see how she's been today, what the teacher says about her,' I said, but seeing Belle's face fall and her eyes fill suddenly, I thought, why am I stalling when I know my mind is made up?

'It's all right,' I told her. 'I'm going to take Tasha.' She grabbed me in an enveloping hug for a moment until I coughed from her perfume. 'Let's go,' I said, leading the way upstairs, hoping we would find that Tasha had settled in like an angel.

At first it seemed it might be so. Tasha was sitting by herself playing quietly with a mechanical toy bird, making it bob back and forth on its branch. The aide was sitting with her and Kelly was on the other side of the room, busy with the rest of the class. Belle called to Tasha who looked up and smiled, rising slowly to come over to her. I smiled too. But then I caught Kelly's eye and she shook her head at me. Tasha followed her mother quietly as we made our way downstairs. As soon as I could get away from the two of them, I hurried back upstairs to check with Kelly.

'I'm sorry,' she said. 'It didn't go well. She didn't leave the other children alone. Kept touching them and pulling on them and she pinches too. I'm sorry. I know you wanted to take her.'

'Maybe she's just not used to being in a class like this? At her school they are all in wheelchairs.' Kelly shook her head.

'I don't think so. Frankly, I wouldn't want her in my class. She's pretty well uncontrollable.' I was in a spot. Kelly was very experienced and her judgement was usually sound; and the vacancy was in her class. It was possible Tasha would settle in all right once she got used to us but on the other hand, she might be beyond our skill. We couldn't know and I wouldn't be the one having to handle her day after day if Kelly's prediction was fulfilled. On the other hand, I had already promised Belle and under those layers of ebullient charm, I sensed she was desperate for help.

It was a judgement between the good of the many and the needs of the one and it left me dithering but I was given a reprieve. Belle's application to the Education Department for Tasha to travel by government special school transport was rejected on the grounds that she lived more than the maximum forty kilometres from the school. Belle appealed against the Department's decision, offering to drive Tasha to an agreed pick-up point within the forty kilometre zone and to pick her up from there each day, but to her dismay her appeal was rejected. She couldn't take so much time from work each day to drive Tasha and as the weeks ran on, I selfishly thought I had been saved a difficult decision. But one day Belle burst into my office looking darkly angry, waving a letter at me. 'I wrote to ask him to help with my appeal,' she said, 'and look what he has written. Is it true? Is it true Catholic schools don't take children like Tasha?'

I read the letter. It was from the Bishop in Belle's diocese. It was two pages of formal jargon that basically said the forty kilometre limit applied to everyone and Belle had better suck it up and added that, in any case, Catholic schools did not provide for children with severe disabilities like Tasha and our school had made a mistake in offering her a place.

I had to read the letter a second time, unable to believe that these stony words came from the Bishop, looking for some pastoral concern but it was all bureaucrat-speak. Then the sentence stating that Tasha had a severe disability struck me. The term 'severe' denoted an IQ below forty points. But the psychologist's report I had from Belle said

Tasha had been too unsettled to be tested and so no IQ score could be obtained. Whoever drafted this letter for the Bishop had private information from the Department to use, information I didn't have. The powers of State and Church had aligned against Tasha and the ugliness of it drove me to a decision.

Belle had been sitting silently watching me as I read, a look of misery on her face. 'Is it true?' she repeated, this time in a whisper of anxiety. 'Is it the rule that Catholic schools don't accept children if their disability is severe?' I folded the letter and handed it back to her.

'We've never had a child with a severe disability before,' I heard myself telling her. 'But no, it isn't true. Jesus' heart is open to everyone and so is ours.' And so Tasha started without the benefit of the special government transport provided for children like her. Instead Belle organised her entourage of beautiful people into a roster of drivers and Tasha arrived with her uncle one day, her father another and Belle's brother another. Belle's mother did all the afternoon pick-ups. Belle said Tasha was a changed girl, always happy to go to school instead of crying and resistant as she used to be. Kelly was the one who was crying now. Tasha was even more difficult in her class than she had feared and I felt guilty that I had landed her on Kelly against her wishes and judgement.

The driving roster fell apart a few months later when Belle's mother had a bad fall and broke her ankle. Her doctor said it would be a long time before she could drive again and in his opinion it was too much for a woman of her age anyway. Belle was desperate, struggling to juggle appointments with her clients around the drive up north with Tasha. What made her maddest, she said, was that each day she would sit on the freeway alongside the special government bus. She'd look in and see its empty seats and spit chips, she said. She had even struck up a friendship with the driver who joined her campaign for Tasha to get a seat on his bus. By now she had her local Member of Parliament writing letters for her and the local radio station talkback host focused on her story, but nothing changed and Belle grew increasingly tired and disheartened. Then out of the blue, she received a standard pro forma letter from the Department stating that Tasha had been allocated transport commencing the following Monday. When she rang to check if it could really be true, an official let slip that our local MP, leader of the Opposition in State Parliament, was behind the change of heart.

Our local Member was a good friend to our school. He had hosted a couple of parent seminars for us on how to advocate successfully for children. I knew one of Belle's many letters had been to him but I'd not expected the result to be any different. When not long afterwards he came out to the school to do a book launch for us (a collection of healthy lunch box recipes Zandra had compiled with a few parents) I couldn't resist asking how he had managed to swing transport for Tasha when all else had failed.

'Ways and means,' he replied briskly, moving towards the exit. I thought I was to be left none the wiser but at the door he relented and, turning back, told me how he had seized his chance in Question Time when the Minister for Education was getting a lot of heat from Opposition members. 'I walked up to The Table and put Tasha's file under her nose and said if she'd have a look at it, I'd call off our fellows. So she did.'

'It's all about who you know then,' I said feeling a bit miffed.

'It's about getting heard, not special favours,' the Opposition leader corrected. 'As soon as the Minister read in the file how Tasha's mother drives each day alongside the half empty bus coming from the southern suburbs and even waves to the driver as she passes, she said, "How ridiculous!" and agreed to intervene with the department. Bureaucrats have to apply the rules, you know,' he added. 'It's our privilege as Members of Parliament to get sensible exceptions made.' Nice if you can get it, I thought, remembering Bruce Mabbitt's struggle with Kacey's transport. Still I was relieved for Belle.

By the time of the anniversary celebration for the Sisters, Tasha had been with us for nearly nine months. From the first day she was hitting and kicking children in her vicinity and descending into violent tantrums we could not manage. Kelly was in despair and in the new year

I had thankfully accepted Sybil's request to be her teacher. 'It will get worse before it gets better,' she warned me as she set herself to teach Tasha that rules have to be followed and that doing the right thing is the only way to get what you want. For weeks she kept Tasha in the classroom with her for both recess and lunch. Sybil emerged with bruises and scratches but after some weeks, she could bring Tasha down to the playground for longer and longer periods without an incident, provided she herself stayed close by. It was poignant to watch Tasha's eyes search frenziedly about and then calm the moment she caught sight of Sybil's tall, dominant figure striding towards her.

There were still violent episodes. Just the week before the anniversary celebration, Tasha, having watched in alarm as Sybil disappeared through the big glass doors that led inside from the playground, threw herself in fury against them. The safety glass shattered into a thousand diamond pieces that scattered around Tasha's feet; she stood transfixed staring uncomprehendingly at the glittering carpet. Sybil was unruffled. 'It's only a door. I expect you have insurance. Tasha will learn in time.'

As I stood waiting at the door of the gym for the Dominican Sisters to arrive for the anniversary liturgy, I wished fearfully for it all to be over. I knew they would be punctual – it had been drilled into them as novices Sister Gertrude told me – and now here they were crowding into the playground, not dressed in the religious habits of pre-Vatican II days but still discreet in black and white with their Dominican crosses speaking of a life of prayer and good works. I smiled as warm a welcome as I could, praying that these controlled and proper looking women would be able to embrace the idiosyncrasies and singularities of the children they were about to meet.

At first all went well. I had planned a very simple liturgy. One of the Sisters was at the keyboard and the children were all gathered quietly in the gym, awed by the mass of black and white Dominicans filling up their hall and the seriousness of sitting in chairs instead of on mats as they usually did. Tasha was seated quietly at the end of a row, Sybil next to her with a safe two metres separating them from anyone else. We had put together a small and much practised choir for the event and these children now moved with some show of poise to the front of the gym where they launched into a loud and clamorous version of *Clap Your Hands and Sing to the Lord*. The Sisters smiled at their unbridled enthusiasm and a few started clapping along. 'That's good,' I thought to myself. 'They're warming to the children.'

At that moment Tasha rose from her seat and pushed impatiently out of the row. Sybil made a quick lunge for her jumper and missed. She started to get up but I caught her eye and shook my head. If she stopped Tasha now there would be a scene. The best we could do was pick up the pieces afterwards. Tasha made her way to the front and stood staring around glassy-eyed, surprised by the mass of people. For a moment she stood frozen and then began gently to sway as the music pounded around her. When the chorus of alleluias began, she raised her arms high above her head and started to turn. Slowly at first and then faster and faster she spun, her beautiful thick gold curls swinging out behind her. Her face was lifted to the heavens and a slow smile was forming on it. As her movements became more abandoned, so her exultation grew. She seemed no longer attached to the ground but to have risen upward into a sphere of bliss. Totally lost in movement, she went round and round. Then the music and singing stopped: the song was over. The look of joy faded and Tasha's face puckered as she realised the music had vanished. She came to a halt and looked around vaguely. The nuns broke into loud applause, shocking Tasha. She turned and sped across the floor and out the door, Sybil onto her feet and dashing after her.

The rest of the liturgy went without incident. I lingered behind making an excuse of packing up chairs, unwilling to face the Sisters and hear their condemnation of Tasha. Would they be alarmed that we had so little control of one of our students? Would they feel she belonged in some other kind of institution? Finally I went outside to join them on the lawn where Zandra and her helpers in dainty lace aprons were already serving the high tea.

'Who is the girl who danced? Wasn't she wonderful!' said the Prioress, Sister Agnes, grabbing me as I slid past.

'I thought that girl was just beautiful,' said Sister June, turning warmly towards me.

'Tell us about the girl who danced,' said others. Tasha was on everyone's lips. I was hugely relieved but puzzled too that the women whose judgement I had feared were better able to see beyond Tasha's impairments than I. It was a lesson to me. Deeply immersed as they were in a spiritual life, the Sisters had seen Tasha's moment as an epiphany. They responded to the soul of her, so apparent in the radiant joy with which she danced. In those few moments, they understood the call to provide for such very different children. I realised then that truth is its own best advocate. Everyone has the capacity to see the beauty in the children. They only need to be introduced. Thank goodness Tasha was a free spirit and had introduced herself.

THINKING CREATIVELY

It should have felt like success. We had re-cast ourselves as a radically different school. We now embraced publicly our commitment to children with all kinds of disability and, after only a few months, most of the opposition had faded. It had happened surprisingly smoothly – too smoothly in fact. There had been no revolution: in the classrooms everyone was doing what they had done before. I still heard the monotonous chant of Ants in the Apple from every room. I still saw children tracing letters over and over. Hailey, who was smart enough to pick me as Miss Bossy on my first day, still muddled her letters. I wondered at her patience with us, the way we asked her to fail at this arcane set of hieroglyphs each morning.

Every day was the same. Time on the mat saying what day

of the week it was and whether it was rainy or sunny; time at desks matching letters and sounds; time doing Maths – if Maths means counting by rote. 'These children thrive on routine,' Robyn Thomas said, kindly setting me straight. She took over this role when she replaced Jack as senior teacher. But our public slogan was 'excellence in education for children with disabilities'. Was this excellence? I asked myself. What we did was textbook best practice for special needs children. We identified the learning task, analysed it into steps and drilled the children, praising and rewarding any sign of success and being careful not to move them on to the next step until they had mastered the one before it. But what about children like Hailey who after three years were still stuck on the first step? What about the senior students who had been learning to tell the time for six years and were still baffled by the big hand when it moved past the half hour?

When I spoke to the staff about the children for whom our methods were not working, some teachers argued that they needed more help in the classroom and others wanted us to devote even more time to 'academics'. Sybil on the other hand argued for throwing out the academic programme and focusing on basic life skills like self-care and road rules.

One day I called in on the class that included the dapper Gareth and irrepressible Hayley. Mrs Mack, the aide in that class, had stopped me on the stairs the day before. 'Come along to our class if you want a surprise,' she said, smiling archly.' As soon as I appeared, she and the teacher, Yolanda, marshalled the children into a group ready to perform. I assumed I was to hear a new song they had learned but instead the children started a chorus of sing-song rote counting. I knew this class was still struggling with counting, unable to keep the 7s and 8s in place despite years of repetitive teaching. Today though they sailed through to the end with barely a pause, giggling and triumphant as they went, laughing at my surprise that they were counting in French. I applauded and exclaimed and made a big fuss of them but I couldn't wait to get the teacher Yolanda by herself afterwards. 'How come they can count in French and not in English?' I demanded. She shrugged.

'I don't know. It was Mrs Mack's idea to teach them because she was bored with the usual counting. They were very excited to be learning French. And of course their parents are terribly proud and make a big fuss of their cleverness.'

I remembered how Freddy's father had said it was boredom that stopped Freddy learning at school. I was pretty sure I could see other bored children. The sullen and recalcitrant Leon Masters was one. 'He's not smart enough to be bored,' Mrs Mack retorted when I suggested it. 'He's very delayed you know'. Leon dragged his feet, kept his head down and urinated when he was upset. The staff were sure he did it deliberately. When an invitation came from a mainstream school for one of our classes to visit their school, Leon's teachers immediately said that they'd go but they couldn't take Leon. 'You know what he'll do,' they said warningly.

But I insisted. 'It's okay with this school. I'll explain in advance,' I said. 'They want to give our kids a good time and I think Leon should have his chance.' Yolanda, his teacher, didn't say no; she just crossed her arms and stared at the floor, her cheeks flushed but Mrs Mack regaled me with dire details of what we could expect. I held my ground but I was apprehensive and on the day of their visit, I was on tenterhooks all day until in the afternoon I saw their bus pull up. I shot out into the foyer to greet them. My eyes scoured the bunch of children as they poured off the bus, looking for Leon; but there was no sign of him and I started to be nervous.

'Where is Leon?' I asked Yolanda as soon as she appeared at the door of the bus.

'He got off with the others,' she said, looking around. 'Didn't you see him? Oh there he is, over there. See him?' I hadn't recognised the shiny-eyed lad with his head high and a smile on his face. 'He had a wonderful time. You must have said something because the children there paid him a lot of attention. He loved it. There were one or two girls he really connected with and he joined in everything, even art which he won't touch usually.' We smiled at each other and I walked away feeling rather pleased with myself for insisting. Only later did I wonder what we were doing wrong at our school if going to another environment could transform Leon like that.

But it was Martine who finally impelled me into action. Martine had a vivacious, dark-eyed mother who was often up at the school talking to us about different interventions she was trying with Martine to help with her autism. Martine was not at all like her mother, lank-haired and morosely hostile to other children, she spent her time out on the playground picking up leaves and sticks and even dirt that she surreptitiously snuck into her mouth. I knew it was a recognised symptom called 'pica', the liking for eating non-food items, but I wondered which came first in Martine's case, her isolation from the other children or her pica.

Her mother tried some less traditional interventions for autism like sound therapy and behavioral optometry and then found a new speech therapist who taught her to use social stories with Martine. We started to see a change at school, even an occasional smile, and her mother excitedly reported how well she was doing at home, starting to dress herself and get her own breakfast. And then one day her mother came up to the school to see me and she was in obvious distress.

'What is it?' I said. 'I thought things were going well?'

'I'm embarrassed to tell you,' she said, her pretty face flushed beneath her dark cap of hair. 'It happened last

Sunday morning; John and I slept in. I heard Martine moving round in the kitchen and I got up to check and she was cooking something in the frying pan. I went over to take a look. She was frying the goldfish.'

My shocked laugh died away quickly when I saw that Martine's mother was near to tears. I guessed she was wondering what kind of an unfeeling, monster-child she was raising. We talked through possible explanations and I suggested she get help from the speech therapist who worked with Martine.

The speech therapist, a small, round woman, came to see me a few days later. 'I don't think that Martine will cook any more goldfish,' she said with a grin as she flopped into the chair in my office. 'It sounded bizarre to you I know, but it is not so strange if you allow for how literal children are who have autism.' She explained how Martine's parents had cooked fish for dinner the night before and that when Martine got up feeling hungry in the morning, she saw the goldfish in the bowl and did what she had seen her parents do. 'But she gets it now,' she said. 'I used Venn diagrams with her, you know, with the overlapping circles that they teach in Maths and logic? Martine likes Venn diagrams a lot. I drew a big circle that I labelled *fish*, and then a small circle inside it and wrote *fish for eating* in it, and another circle and wrote *fish as pets* in that and I made Martine see that those two circles do NOT overlap. And she understands it now.'

Venn diagrams? I had used those in history classes sometimes and often found even senior students unable to grasp them and yet to ten year old intellectually delayed Martine they made the mystifying world comprehensible. I was relieved to know it wasn't sociopathic tendencies that had made her cook the family goldfish but instead I had to face the fact that we were blind and deaf to her intelligence at school.

When I reflected on it, I saw other signs of intelligence in the children that didn't translate into classroom learning. There were the funny stories the staff enjoyed telling about the cute mistakes the children made, such as when the Bishop processed grandly out of the confirmation ceremony, all togged up in his white vestments and pectoral cross with his shiny gold mitre on his head, and Anjelica cried out, 'Don't go, God. Don't go!' And in Mrs Mack's account of being stopped by a girl in the corridor who had said to her very seriously, 'Mrs Mack, you are small. But you have breasts.'

'I told her, I am short, but I am grown up. I have two children and breasts.' The girl had stood solemnly, visibly trying to re-compute. When you paid attention, you could see that the children were thinking all the time, analysing, synthesising and inventing.

The new boy Logan insisted that his best friend was an invisible dragon who went everywhere with him. In a regular school, we might have commented on his lively imagination but not here. In the special school context it was a fixation that needed to be remedied.

We got it wrong, I thought, whenever we looked at the children as impaired, focusing on what we labelled as abnormal. We would do better to see them as children first and treat their differences as a mask obscuring their abilities and gifts. After the goldfish incident with Martine, I began to visit other special schools not just in Sydney but also in Melbourne and Adelaide to see how they managed. Then at Easter time a couple of principals in Adelaide invited me to join an overseas tour they had organised to check out some well-known special schools in Singapore, Scotland and England. I jumped at the chance. For two hectic weeks we visited different special schools in the daytime and at night discussed what we had seen and learned. Those two weeks made a huge difference to my confidence. I bounced back into school at the start of the new term eager to try new ways to reach the abilities of our students.

We were constrained though. One of the strongest trends I had found was for schools to specialise. Autism schools were mushrooming with low-stimulus environments adapted to the calm, the structure and the predictable routine that children with autism seemed to need. Other special schools were focusing on physical disabilities, or communication deficits or cognitive impairment within a certain range and even children with disordered behaviour were being channelled into specialist schools. But our school existed to provide for children who couldn't get an education elsewhere, those who fell through the cracks, especially those who wanted a Catholic education.

We had to be eclectic. And we had to keep our fees low so that parents like Mr Mabbit could afford them. Many of the innovations I saw in my travels required very small classes with a lot of one-to-one teaching and therapy. These schools were necessarily extremely expensive. Parents had to pay or donate up to $40,000 per year. Our classes had twelve or so children with volunteers to help out so that we could keep our fees below $3000. I would have to come up with an approach that didn't rely on professionals guiding and prompting each child at every point. Our children would have to do some of the learning themselves, as they do in regular schools.

I mulled over what I knew from my own years of teaching. These children were not so different, that was my starting point. Over years of teaching I had formed some principles I held firmly. Children who are happy are much more open to learning than children who are unhappy. When children know they are loved and respected, an innate curiosity and desire to learn drives their development. Children aren't stupid. They know whether they are succeeding or not, and a taste of success will keep them trying, providing they respect the task. It is demeaning to expect children to learn things just because the teacher says they must and will reward them for it. At least some of the time, students need to be partners in the learning task, freely participating and contributing, otherwise how can they stay motivated? What we remember best from school are exciting things we did ourselves, attention-grabbing stories and learning that aroused our emotions. And while direct instruction with drill and rewards works for teaching mechanical skills like reading and simple arithmetic, anything that requires the student to understand needs multiple learning pathways and many modes of reinforcement.

When I said all of this to staff at the day-long workshop we held after the Easter holidays, not many bought it. They stared at the ceiling or glanced surreptitiously at each other. Some sighed and others whispered. I understood how they felt. They were comfortable in their structured paradigm of systematic instruction, drilling, testing and reporting; it was reassuring to operate within a conceptualisation of learning as right and wrong answers, correct and incorrect. They had been doing it for years, their colleagues did it and it kept them in control of children who in other ways were unpredictable and confusing.

What I needed, I realised, were disruptors, people who operated in a different paradigm, who valued the journey more than the outcome. I needed artists. The arts are about expressing and communicating, not about reproducing right answers. Chris Donaldson, the teacher at the satellite class on the coast, soon afterwards gave me a chance to put my hunch to the test.

Her much loved teacher's aide had just decided to move interstate and Chris decided to turn her loss into gain by requesting someone creative as her next aide. 'I know it's my weakness,' she told me. 'I'm excellent at literacy and numeracy but I'd like an aide who can do art and drama with the class. Do you know anyone?' I thought of my daughter-in-law who was an actor by night and beauty consultant by day. Olivia was an uncanny observer, she could discern things about people just from their body language and even their body smell. I found it unnerving at times. And she was wonderful with children. She had had her own TV show for children for a while. She and Chris Donaldson, when I introduced them, took to each other straight away. I was apologetic, though, when I told the staff about her appointment. 'I wouldn't worry,' one of the older aides said. 'You're her mother-in-law. She won't mind what we say about you.'

My nepotism embarrassed me at the time but looking back it was the most unequivocally good act of my life. It was not just the great partnership that developed between Chris and Olivia and the way the children's language blossomed as they interacted with the puppets that peopled her lessons. It was not only her later work when she began drama lessons with all the classes. Olivia went on to get a double Masters in Special Education and Drama and later in the USA she was invited to lecture on drama and autism; her work was unique. And then she and my son

Michael adopted twins with special needs and afterwards Olivia transferred what she had learnt from the twins into working professionally with babies born with disabilities.

At the school, to begin with, Olivia just worked her magic with Chris's class, using puppets to teach them everything from safety rules to sharing and how to handle a bully. But once I saw how well the children were communicating in her lessons, I brought her up to the main campus as well. There she teamed up with a new art teacher I had recently added to the staff. Zandra had found Mab for me after I told her in frustration how I'd watched one of our teachers take a class in the art room. 'No, no, Francis,' I had overheard her say, 'You can't use that crayon. It's red. Trees are green.' How could we expect children to communicate with us through their paintings if we wouldn't let them draw red trees? Mab, when I met her in her studio, was darkly beautiful and dressed in layers of black muslin relieved by shining, jangling bangles and bracelets with deep circles under her eyes from a life sustained by coffee and cigarettes and long, late nights of painting. She gave little of herself away at that meeting and I played safe by giving her a temporary role as artist-in-residence.

But Mab dropped her protective walls when she was with the children. Using music, stories, precious objects and imagination, she magicked original drawings and paintings from them and over weeks that turned into years they produced art that was so fresh, unselfconscious and eloquent that our exhibitions in galleries drew sales from people who didn't know they were the work of children with disabilities. At first though it was the impact on the children's language that I noticed, especially when Mab and Olivia began to build on each other's lessons. One day when I passed Mab's room, I looked in and was captured by the sight of young George with his head bent over a large sheet of paper. He said something in a guttural voice. 'What was that?' I asked. I hadn't heard him speak before.

'He said, *snow*,' Mab told me. 'It's what he's drawing, see? Their pencils do the talking for them and then after a while, sometimes after a long while, some spoken words come along with their drawing. George has taken a long while but look at how Stanley's mind has run along here.' She held up a drawing that looked like a sausage with five L-shaped legs and spots, scribbled over in blue and brown crayon. Above it she had written Stanley's words: *This was my dog but it is now my caterpillar with chicken pox in a sea of lava.* All those concepts and yet in the classroom Stanley was mostly silent.

I was excited by what I saw happening but not many of the staff felt the same enthusiasm. The aides said the lessons were often too noisy and questioned whether there was enough control. Of the teachers, only red-haired Yolanda seemed to like it. Yolanda was a closet drummer who after finishing her lessons and preparing for the next day, used to beat her troubles away in the old convent. After observing Mab and Olivia at work, she was inspired to try out percussion with her class. The weeks of deafening lunchtime practices drew complaints from staff but when the first performance came, we were stunned. Gareth was the star drummer with Francis playing the xylophone and others clashing cymbals and tambourines. Mrs Mack had dressed them up as punk rockers in black leather jackets and dyed their hair black and gelled it into spikes. They looked so cool, everyone said, not like 'special kids' at all.

It gave me a jolt, seeing the boys in their tough gear and recognising that they were on the threshold of puberty. We were like most primary schools, rather feminised and now I wondered how we could provide for them. There were a few older, tougher boys who were drifting into using their size to intimidate the smaller kids, not having anything else to feed their self-esteem.

I was particularly worried about a new boy, Tyler Brandt whose language was mostly limited to F-words. When he couldn't make himself understood, he kicked. Or spat. His mother told me how he arrived home from school in an angry mood each day, marched straight through the house and out the back door and pushed a mower around the perimeter of their garden until dinner time.

These boys were on the brink of adolescence: they needed someone they could bond with, who would stimulate and excite them. This time I conscripted my son-in-law, Christina's husband. Guillaume was an actor who had studied commedia dell'arte and physical theatre under France's legendary Jacques Lecoq and I knew how crazy and funny he could be with the right audience to egg him on.

'What d'you want me to do?' he asked.

'Whatever you think will work.' Very unhelpful, I knew, even for a mother-in-law. I didn't tell anyone he was coming. I wanted the children's raw reaction unhampered by the teachers telling them to be polite to a visitor. I was also too embarrassed to tell the staff I was bringing in another member of my family. Easier just to do it. I felt a bit disappointed when he arrived in the foyer. He looked the same as always, a tall, impeccably dressed Frenchman, reserved and courteous. 'I thought you'd be wearing a clown suit,' I said.

'No, I just brought this,' and he pulled a round red rubber nose from his pocket. It didn't seem much. I was filled with sudden doubt. What was I thinking, putting him out in the playground with no preparation for him or the children or the teachers? Nothing for it now though, but to go ahead. I showed him through the foyer to the red wooden door that gave on to the playground and, feeling dreadful, I left him to go through it alone. Then I hovered by the photocopier where a small window gave a view out. There was not a sign of Guillaume. In his place was a loose-limbed, shoulder drooping, rather sad looking figure with an uncertain smile and a large red nose, tripping over his feet as he wandered over to a group of children. He juggled two small balls as he went, dropping one and retrieving it awkwardly – bashful stumbling Valentino, the voiceless clown. Very soon a crowd of children gathered around him. Valentino didn't speak at all. He was a stranger without words, like the children. But he mimed. A centuries-old European tradition of expressive movements, exquisite in their precision, took life: more powerful than the spoken word, they conveyed nuances of emotion and meaning in single fluid gestures.

It was the non-verbal children who caught on. As if they instinctively recognised the potential of this language, one by one they began to respond. After some minutes the younger children drifted away to new interests, but the older boys moved in closer. Excitedly, they began to pull on his arm, copy his actions, laugh up into his face. Relief surged through me. It was going to be all right. Better than all right: it looked like the magic I hoped for.

And then I noticed Tyler Brandt. He was standing at the back of the circle of children, his eyes fixed hypnotically on Valentino. As Valentino scratched his head, Tyler scratched his. When Valentino dropped the ball, Tyler dropped an imaginary ball with scrupulous mimicry. And when Valentino tripped over his left foot, Tyler awkwardly stumbled. His class teacher had bluntly let me know, soon after Tyler started, that *this one was probably a mistake*. She was doubtful we could do much with him. He was 'ineducable'. And here Tyler was, his eyes on Valentino, with a light shining in them I had not seen before.

When Tyler went to class after recess, his teacher, who had heard about Valentino's visit along the speedy staff grapevine, asked him who the strange man was in the playground. Tyler usually just looked at the ground if questioned but this morning he precisely re-enacted how the visitor had scratched his head, bounced an imaginary ball, stumbled over his feet, and laughed out loud. She told me afterwards she had never heard him laugh like that. 'And he remembered it all. I've not known him learn a thing.'

I established a visiting drama class for the group of boys I was worried about. They met with Valentino once a week in a small cupboard-like room we had to spare. The shouts of laughter that leaked through the door were a delight to my ears. They grew louder the worse the social taboo Valentino taught them to breach. They learned things that never appeared in our school curriculum: how to make farting noises when shaking someone by the hand; how to seem to pick your nose and admire the pickings, and how to trip over your feet without falling. Silly stuff, silly enough and glorious enough to overcome the hurts inflicted by a self-important, self-regarding 'normal' world. The boys loved it and Valentino became a regular visitor to the school.

That was it though. Exciting learning was happening but in regular classes there was precious little creativity or teaching that increased communication. And then one Monday morning Sybil strode into my office, her usually impassive face alight with excitement. 'I brought this in to show you. How good is that? Have a look, read it.' She thrust a newspaper cutting in front of me from the Sunday paper. I skimmed it quickly. A journalist had visited the municipality of Reggio Emilia in central Italy and reported on its unique approach to pre-school education. I knew the Reggio Emilia philosophy and had introduced its principles into the junior classes at St Cath's but I had never thought about it for this school for one simple reason. In Australia it was viewed as a way to teach gifted and talented children.

'Look what it says.' Sybil was impatient at my slowness. Her long index finger jabbed at a paragraph about children with special needs. 'See, they call them children with special rights. Rights! How cool is that? We should ask the Board for scholarships to send us to Italy to have a look.' I wasn't sure she was joking. There was an electricity about her: her usually ironic, dismissive expression had given way to an unguarded excitement. Gosh, if she could keep that, what a leader she would become. And as I thought about it, I saw that the Reggio Emilia philosophy was exactly what we needed: a learning framework to encompass the whole of teaching in the school, not just the visiting artists. Reggio Emilia was ideal because it was founded on a belief in the innate abilities of even very young children, the curriculum was directed by a creative artist who worked alongside the class teachers, it didn't rely on the spoken word but on the '100 languages' of children, it started with each individual child's current understanding and measured the progress of each through photographs, videos and documentation, not through tests and assessments.

It was easy to get Sibyl and Robin Thomas on board with Reggio Emilia principles as the new framework but I wasn't surprised to find that other teachers felt uncomfortable with an approach so different from what they were used to, even though we would only use it for the afternoon programme and wouldn't replace the direct instruction we used in the mornings for literacy and numeracy. The strongest opposition came from one of our most successful 'academic' teachers, Talieh. 'This Reggio Emilia pedagogy is a mistake,' she said. 'It requires conceptual thinking and the students we have lack capacity for thinking conceptually. Their frontal lobes are not developed, they use their adrenal system and respond from emotion. All your evidence of benefit is anecdotal. Where are the quantitative studies?'

Talieh was from Iran where she had gained her Masters in Special Education and held the position of school principal. At our school I generally gave her the Year 2 children we were preparing for mainstream. Talieh excelled at bringing their reading and basic arithmetic up to the mainstream level by intensive hours of direct instruction. But when they went into mainstream, they weren't prepared for the self-direction and creative thinking that the rest of the curriculum required. The Reggio Emilia framework would help them think for themselves. But how to convince Talieh? I wasn't subtle.

'Just do it, Talieh. If after your best effort at provoking inductive thinking you don't see any gains, then you may go back to direct instruction. But right now you are to come up with a project for your class that fits the Reggio Emilia model. I'll be up in your class on Thursday to see the project you've got going.' I wouldn't have spoken like that to any other teacher but Talieh was from Iran and she was comfortable with a direct order.

On the whiteboard in her classroom when I went to check the following Thursday, alongside words like *sun* and *fun,* appeared in Talieh's well-formed hand, the topic title: Living and Non-Living Things. *Oh no, I thought, you couldn't try something simple first, could you? You had to choose something like Living Things.* But this was Talieh. If she had to use a Reggio method, she would give it a rigorous test. She showed me on her computer the table she had drawn up ready for the electronic whiteboard with two columns. In one was a list of living things and in the other were non-living. There were half a dozen items in each. I was disappointed. 'Are you teaching them by rote?'

'No, I get a child to suggest a thing and then I ask the class to decide which column it belongs in, living or non-living.'

'But I want the children to have direct experience

that they can make their own deductions from. Maybe tomorrow you can take them out onto the oval and search for things that are living and not living?'

'If you insist,' she said with a doubtful shrug. I supposed she wasn't accustomed to crawling around in the grass.

'I'll come with you,' I promised and she looked more doubtful still.

We all lay on the grass and looked around us. 'Now remember,' Talieh said to the children, 'If it moves, or breathes, or grows, or reproduces, it is alive, a living thing.' Oh dear, she was asking too much – she needed to start with small steps – but Talieh knew that. Did she want them to fail?

'The cloud is alive,' James said thoughtfully, lying on his back and gazing upwards. 'It's getting bigger and bigger.'

'Getting bigger isn't the same as growing, James,' Talieh told him.

'My Mum's getting bigger and that's the baby growing,' James responded.

John had his ear to the ground. 'I can hear something,' he said. 'I think it's the earth breathing. Is the earth alive?'

'Well, not really,' said Talieh uncertainly. At that point Martine held up a worm in the air and watched it squirm pinkly between her outstretched fingers.

'That's it. Well done, Martine. Look everyone, Martine has a living thing,' said Talieh. 'Now how can you tell it is alive?' And then to forestall a mistake, 'Because it's moving'.

'Not moving now,' said Gideon as Martine put the worm in her mouth. Talieh threw me a look of disgust though there was a hint of something more in her eyes.

'It is time to go in now, class,' she said firmly. 'We'll all wash our hands in the bathroom and then you can have a nice play inside.' After the school day ended she came in and sat perched on a chair in my office.

'You are right and you are wrong,' she said. 'It is true that they can think but what they think is not correct.'

'Get on with you, Talieh,' I said, 'I saw how proud you were of them.'

'Yes, but without direction, they make errors and that is not learning.'

She wanted more control over the children's experience of living things, she said, so I suggested she take the class down to the village. 'Prepare them carefully, Talieh. Have them help you plan the trip and identify what living things they can expect to find.'

'A dragon,' Logan said eagerly.

'A lion,' said Gideon.

'No, no,' Talieh told them very firmly. 'Dragons don't exist and there are no lions in Australia. Only things you can touch or see or hear are real.'

On the chosen day Talieh led the class on a slow walk down to the village. It was the first time she had taken them out of the school. She had them run their hands along the fences, feel the leaves that hung from low-lying branches, smell the rose bushes in the park along the way until finally they reached the shops. Both Talieh and the children were exhausted by the time she got them safely back to school but she was not going to miss the moment. 'What real things did you see?' she asked. 'What did you find that you could touch, or smell or see or hear?'

'Lion', said Gideon.

Talieh gave up at that point. She was back in my office at the end of the day annoyed that she'd allowed herself to be led along such a fruitless path. 'It's slow and it's harmful,' she said. 'I am the teacher and I am letting them learn things that aren't true.'

'It takes longer but they are really learning,' I urged. 'Don't give up now. Why don't you let the children work it out. Ask them if they saw a lion. Take them down to the village again and say Gideon has to tell you when he sees a lion. The other children will set him right, if you give them time.' I hoped they would anyway.

Talieh put her head in my office door a couple of days later. 'There is a lion,' she said. 'It's on the base of the Anzac memorial. Gideon showed me.'

INCLUSION

'Catholic special schools are an historical anomaly. They have no place in this day and age.' I looked at the speaker, standing there in his nice grey suit with his well-manicured hands. He was safely tucked away from reality in the Catholic Schools Board on the tenth floor high up above Madison Street. The clock above his head showed eleven am. Recess time back at school where the teachers would be scrambling to get the children into the playground, changing nappies, jumping in the way of trouble, probably getting a kick or two. And here the man responsible for the seven Catholic special schools was saying they were an anomaly. I glanced around the long conference table at the other principals and the couple of provincial leaders at this quarterly meeting. They looked as flabbergasted as me. The redoubtable Sister Agnes was there for the Dominicans. 'An anomaly?' she clanged in quelling tones. 'I thought they were the outworking of the Holy Spirit.'

'I am sure that was the case when they started, Sister,' he said smoothly, 'but now that mainstream schools enroll children with disabilities, there's no reason for special schools. That's my opinion. However I expect we're stuck with them for the present,' and he sighed. It was not until we were in the lift descending the nine floors to the ground that the shock cleared enough for us to speak. 'Pompous ass,' exploded Doug, principal of Boys' Town, his face red with anger. 'As though our kids are like the special needs kids they've got in their schools. They shoot their boys off to us because they can't handle them. He's a bloody idiot pronouncing on things without bothering to find the facts.'

'Then we need to give him the facts.' The calm and reasonable voice of the consultant for the Christian Brothers schools brought a moment's silence. 'We need a research paper that gives the statistics and details of children in the special schools compared to those in regular schools.'

'I'll write it,' I heard myself offering and straight away wondered what on earth I was thinking. I needed it like a hole in the head given that I couldn't get through the work on my desk as it was. But I had been challenged before by officers of the Catholic Schools Board who said that many of our students should be in regular schools. It bemused me, knowing how much their parents would have liked to get them into mainstream schools but hadn't found a school to give them a place. This was a chance for me to get to the bottom of the contradictions and assure myself that there was still a justification for special schools – or not.

The Christian Brothers offered to pay for a research assistant to share the task with me so I contacted a friend who had once worked as an academic in the field of special needs and asked him to recommend a research assistant. 'I can give you a couple of people to contact but I don't like your chances,' he said. 'There's not an academic who will touch special schools. They see them as bastions of discrimination and believe children with disabilities should be normalised.' It turned out he was right. One of them emailed me back saying, *I could not in all conscience take on this project. I believe that special schools are an invitation to mainstream schools to contend that some children are not worthy of inclusion.* So I was left to do it by myself.

I began with official reports and documents and found that ten years earlier Australia had officially committed itself as part of a UNESCO agreement to accommodate all children in ordinary schools regardless of their physical, intellectual, emotional, social, linguistic or other conditions. Despite this, the most recent figures available showed there were 106 government special schools in Australia and over 545 special units within mainstream schools and the numbers were growing. I discovered a very different picture in the USA where integration of kids with disabilities was the norm and only a few special schools existed. There was a difference too between Australian states, with NSW having the most special schools and Queensland for example having almost none. So Mr Grey Suit was right. We were an anomaly.

Why then, I wondered, did so many parents say fervently, as they regularly did, that getting a letter of acceptance from us was like winning the lottery? I read up all the research I could into the quality of special education in mainstream and segregated settings but there was little in the way of rigorous comparisons. There were a lot of government reviews especially in the UK and a few in Australia but they relied mostly on anecdotal experiences and personal opinion of teachers and parents and I couldn't find a consistent pattern.

The experience of one mother in England was enlightening. She had two children with disabilities both of whom were placed in mainstream schools by the local education authority. 'What worked for one was terrible for the other,' she was reported as saying and added, 'Thank God there was a special school she could go to'. Another mother complained of the pressure she felt to mainstream her child. 'I have no quarrel with the inclusionists if they are content to insist upon inclusion for **their** children. But when they try to force me and other unwilling parents to dance to their tune, I find it highly objectionable.'

Unable to find quantitative objective studies, I went to talk to colleagues in charge of Government Schools for a Special Purpose to ask them about their experience. After all, they were operated by a government that had signed up to include all children in regular schools. One principal told me she used to get a lot of pressure from a Director of Education whose goal was to close down all the special schools, 'It's eased off in recent years,' she said. 'I think someone worked out how much it would cost. I'm glad because honestly they don't have a clue what our students are like or the mayhem that would happen in a mainstream school if they were integrated.' Yes, I thought, but if all the special schools were closed, the government would have to put the money and specialists into regular schools to make inclusion of every child possible. The schools would work it out eventually, just as we had with Tasha. But how many children would be hurt in the process?

While I kept on with research for the report, I vowed to be very careful whom I accepted in the future and to do all I could to support the inclusion of students in mainstream schools. So when I had a call from the principal of a nearby Anglican college about a student with Down syndrome who had been with them since kindergarten but had recently started waving his penis about in the playground, I resisted her suggestion that he should be in a special school. 'It's just a stage, I'm sure,' I said, and offered to send one of our staff around to help with strategies to deal with it. I sent Kelly because she used to work at the college and knew it well. She came back laughing. 'He's getting a real kick out of it,' she said. 'Loving the attention. Best fun he's had for a long time, all the fuss the teachers there are making.' I rang the principal to put it in perspective for her but she was not in the mood to listen. The father of another student had lodged a formal complaint with the NSW Ombudsman saying that his daughter had been sexually abused by the boy, Drew.

'She says he touched her with his penis. I have no choice in the matter. He'll have to leave.' Soon afterwards Drew's parents rang Bev and said the college had recommended he come to us. 'We shouldn't be a party to it,' I told Bev. 'Schools need to deal with puberty in kids with disabilities. They'll never learn if they send these kids off to a special school the minute they have a problem with them.'

'But what do I say to the parents?' Bev's arms were crossed and there was a glint of reproach in her eye. 'They can't make the school change. And they can't send their son there if nobody wants him. At least you can have a chat with them and suggest some options.'

I saw them standing under the lilly pilly tree. It was recess and some of the children had gathered around the visitors who looked uncomfortable. They were a tall, dignified couple and as I watched them awkwardly interact with Gareth and Sam, I felt at first offended by their stand-offishness but then just as suddenly I was sorry for them. They must have been so pleased and proud to have their son in a normal school with normal kids and now he had been expelled and told to come to a school like ours where all the children looked to their unaccustomed and fearful eyes, I guessed, abnormal and confronting. I wanted to reassure them and I hurried out to introduce myself. 'The principal told me about what happened,' I said so as to cut through their embarrassment quickly. 'It probably seems worse than it is. It's pretty common in boys who don't have a lot of inhibition. It doesn't mean there's anything wrong with Drew or that he has to be in a special school.'

The two of them turned slowly and stood without speaking. The mother's smile was grateful but the father seemed shrouded in a kind of helpless anger. I turned to the boy, Drew, who lounged at a small distance from his parents. He was already as tall as me and solidly built with a freckled face and a sticking plaster on his forehead. He gave me a cheerful, thin-lipped grin. His father sharply snapped at him to straighten his shoulders and Drew in answer turned and wandered off towards the sand pit. The father shouted after him to come and say hello to the Principal and then shouted again but Drew was already at the sandpit and had spied the shovel. His father started towards him whereupon Drew, sizing up the situation, dropped the shovel, climbed back up out of the pit and lumbered towards us.

'Drew,' the father said loudly, taking the boy by the elbow. 'You are to shake hands with the Principal. Lift your head and look her in the eye. That's right. Now shake her hand. You know how to shake hands, Drew.' Drew stared directly into my eyes as he had been told but in a seeming trance left his hands hanging and I wondered if he was deliberately defying his father. The three of us stood there, me not sure how to break the impasse, when Drew emerged from his reverie and with a saucy grin reached up and planted his two hands firmly on my breasts.

'Nice boobies,' he said with warm approval, still staring me in the eye. I blushed bright red and wrestled his hands off, cursing inwardly at the too low-cut blouse I had bought on impulse at the weekend. Drew's father turned his back; I didn't know if he was embarrassed or hiding his laughter.

'Well now, let's have a look at the school,' I said in as cool a voice as I could manage and with rapid stride led them off to the library. After they had left, with warm handshakes all round, I found I no longer felt qualms about accepting Drew. The other principal had had a point. Without expert management, a boy like that was at risk with his overt sexuality and sense of mischief. Still, I couldn't help a fleeting tinge of amusement that at my advanced age I had scored such uninhibited commendation.

I continued spending most of my evenings reading academic studies and seeking out whatever data was available on the relative benefits of integration or segregated schooling. Some of the advocates for disability were very strident in their hostility to special schools and their criticisms made me squirm. At times their passion for 'normalising' children with disabilities sounded like a form of discrimination itself. I didn't find in their writings any recognition of the children's originality or humour or the unconditional love they showered on others, just their right to be included with the normal population.

One day I took an early morning call from a mother whose daughter Abbey had been in our 'preparation for inclusion' program a while back, before I came to the school. She did very well, so much so that her measured IQ rose by sufficient points to bring it within the normal range. The psychologist advised her mother to transition her to a mainstream school. 'She'll start to identify herself as disabled if you leave her in a school where all the kids have a disability,' the psychologist warned.

I had met Faye a couple of times when she attended our public events with Abbey and found her easy going and relaxed with a ready laugh and given to humorous realism about her daughter. She was not laughing when she rang me though. 'I am sorry to do this to you,' she said after apologising for the earliness of the hour, 'but I want to find out if Abbey can have a place back with you.' I was surprised. The school she now attended was one of the few that made a point of accepting children with disabilities and I expected Abbey would have flourished there. She had a mild form of a fairly rare syndrome typically causing a range of physical, sensory and emotional problems but she was a good little learner.

'Why, what's happened?' I asked doubtfully. Faye gave a heavy sigh down the phone.

'Things aren't going well,' she said. 'They've suspended her.'

'Suspended? She's only ten!'

'Yes, well they have. They had to do something. Some parents came up to the school and threatened to take their children out, on account of Abbey.'

'Why, what had she done?'

'She kicked a girl in the head. Oh, she didn't mean to. She got upset, you know. The teacher had the class sit on the floor all together and Abbey gets anxious like that. She panicked and tried to get to the door. This girl was in her way and Abbey just walked over her.' Faye, strong woman that she was, sounded near to tears. 'They've asked me to come for a meeting at the school. I expect they'll ask me to find another school for her and I wanted to know if you'll have her back.'

'Of course we will but I don't think it's necessary. It sounds like an easy situation to fix. Why don't I come to the meeting with you?'

'Would you? I don't know I can face them by myself. I get upset just thinking about it.'

Abbey was then in Year 4, very small for her age. She had impaired eyesight and a deep, husky voice that tended to boom out suddenly from her small body, and sometimes shot up to a squeak. She was quirky and funny, and a deeply loving and compassionate child but you had to look past her thick glasses, bushy eyebrows and repaired cleft palate to appreciate her. It was typical of her syndrome that Abbey's oesophagus was ulcerated and scarred its whole length and she was often in pain from acid reflux. She also suffered from obsessive anxieties. I could well understand her getting into a panic and blindly trying to fight her way out of the crowd of children to safety. In her distress and with her poor eyesight, she probably did not even see the child whose head she kicked.

I thought it would be easy enough to explain to the school and the parents and help them put structures in place to stop Abbey getting so anxious – and give her a clear line of escape from the room in case she did. We arranged to meet in the car park of the school about ten minutes before the meeting was scheduled. Faye was dressed in a cheerful red coat that contrasted with the grey dampness of the day. 'It's for courage,' she said, and made a face. I felt a bit nervous myself. We spent a few moments discussing how she could approach the meeting and what we might expect to come out of it.

'Let's be positive,' I said. 'After all, they took Abbey on, and most regular schools wouldn't have done that. I am sure they'll want to find a solution.'

We were met at the door by the principal herself, a small plump woman with a comfortable, managing way about her. She reached up to give Faye an encouraging hug that Faye rather rigidly returned and then led us down the corridor to the meeting. It was in a confined meeting room and there was quite a crowd there: the school counsellor, the classroom teacher and the learning support teacher as well as the principal and the two of us. The principal began by thanking me effusively for coming along. 'We are all here because we want the best for Abbey,' she began, smiling brightly around at us all. There were no answering smiles from her staff and I noticed a grim set to Faye's jaw too. She wasn't buying it. Both she and her husband were teachers. She knew that if the stakes are high enough, principals are likely to put the good of the school above the welfare of any individual student.

Now the principal was inviting the class teacher to explain about *The Incident*, as she called it. The teacher began calmly enough. She stared straight ahead as she talked without looking at Faye. As her story unfolded, her voice rose in pitch and became almost shrill as she described how Abbey 'just walked over Lisa, she walked straight over her and kicked her in the head. Poor Lisa started crying. She was terribly upset. All the children were. Abbey just didn't care.

She was grunting and waving her arms and then she ran outside. It was horrible.' Folding her hands in her lap, she added, 'Afterwards Abbey showed no remorse. She wouldn't even say sorry.' Her lips were pressed tight, two bright red spots in her cheeks. The learning support teacher turned confidingly to me, one professional to another.

'We have a lot of students with special needs here,' she said in an undertone. 'Lovely children. We are proud of how well they do. But we can't have children who won't do the right thing. Abbey has been in a lot of trouble. She kicked someone in the shins for no reason last week.'

'There would have been a reason,' I objected, a little shrill myself. 'Perhaps Abbey wasn't feeling well and was in pain.'

'Well, I must say that's not a reason for kicking someone.'

'I am afraid that if you have Abbey's many difficulties, it is quite enough reason.' The learning support teacher looked affronted. She pulled herself up on her hard-backed chair and eyed me severely.

'It's school policy to distinguish between disability and behaviour. The parents all know that. A child may have disabilities but it's not an excuse. If they can't behave, they can't stay.'

'But their behaviour is part of their disability,' I protested. And then more calmly, reasoningly, 'Look, there are simple things you can do. Let Abbey sit near the door so she doesn't get so anxious. Use visuals with her so she knows what is happening. Keep the noise level in the classroom down.' The classroom teacher looked pained.

'I do have twenty-seven other children to think of,' she said. I was about to retort when Faye stumbled clumsily to her feet.

'I have to go,' she said, pushing her way to the door.

'Poor dear, she is upset,' said the principal. 'I was hoping we could find a way forward today.' I stood up to follow Faye out and the principal walked me back down the long corridor, tucking her arm into mine, repeatedly thanking me for my advice and saying she would love to talk some more, 'at a better time'. Outside in the car park, Faye in her red coat was leaning over the car bonnet. She straightened up as I approached and turning, said bitterly, 'They don't even like her. They haven't tried to get to know her. They only care about the other children.'

'I think they are at a loss,' I said, 'but it's early days.'

'No, no! I want Abbey to come back where she is loved. You all know her. You know what she needs.'

I would have tried harder to persuade her but I was not feeling hopeful myself. The rigid face of the learning support teacher and her chilling belief that 'bad behaviour' is not to be tolerated augured ill for Abbey. And the class teacher seemed overwhelmed and frustrated. It was a conscientiously Christian school and the principal seemed genuinely anxious to help but the love they practised had conditions attached. Special needs children had to be *nice* children to be accepted here.

It was good to have Abbey back with us. She was a bag of laughs. A real drama queen. Even her problems were newsworthy. One of her obsessions was picking at her fingers. She would pick and pick until she broke the skin. If blood appeared, she went into alarm mode. She would rush to the office, crying loudly in her little foghorn voice, demanding a band-aid and escalating into full-scale panic. At first I tried urging her to be a brave girl, but it only made her worse. I realised that *being a brave girl* to her signalled an injection or worse from her hospital stays. I began to see that she was seriously worried by the blood and we took to rushing the band-aid into place. She would go off happily but before long would begin picking relentlessly at the band-aid. Despite the dramas, she was delighted to be back and life settled down again for Faye.

Meanwhile the second satellite class we'd established a couple of years before in the Catholic primary school along the Coast was thriving, thanks to the brilliant Mrs McPhee, the principal there. Despite the misleading impression of her diminutive stature and sweet blonde curls, Mrs McPhee had proved to be a dynamic force field who regarded our special needs satellite as the most positive thing that could happen to any school. She treated our students in the unit as her own, visiting the classroom every single day, joining in their lessons or their prayer time and standing by our teachers through any crisis or conflict that sprang up. It's the Mrs McPhees of the world who do much of the heavy lifting for the Church. They don't hesitate to put their beliefs into practice and they face the challenges and risks with a cheerful confidence that comes from a deep and trusting faith. And they win through. Thanks to Elsa McPhee, our satellite class there was the best of both worlds: the children were friends with their peers in the regular classes but had the protection and guidance of specialist teachers in a small class of children with needs like their own. I wanted Abbey to take a vacancy we had there knowing that Mrs McPhee would manage lovingly any challenge that she threw up, but Faye did not want to move her again. 'Let her stay here till high school,' she pleaded. I sent young Brett instead. It was the perfect answer for him.

Brett's mother had walked in from the street more than a year before driven by a dark desperation. 'I know you're a special school,' she blurted out as soon as Bev showed her into my office with a look that said this one needs help. 'My son is pretty bright, I think, but he doesn't do well at school.' She twisted her fingers as they lay in her lap and smiled a little. 'He is funny, he says lots of really deep things and his drawing is fantastic, but he can barely read and he is often in trouble. He hates himself, he really does. And then this morning when I went to get him up, he said he was going to kill himself. He's only ten. I don't know where to turn. I drive past your school every day and this morning I had to come in.' She bent to fumble in her bag and I felt a rush of sympathy for this poor woman who was so desperate she would throw herself on the mercy of strangers.

I also felt frustrated. I believed I recognised the kind of student her son was; a kind I used to try to help at my previous school. Kids who were gifted but 'right brained' as we used to say, clumsy, disorganised and apparently unfocused because their brain processed everything at once, not sequentially and logically the way school learning requires. We had special programs at St Cath's for creative, original, failing children like this and with the right kind of teaching and a ton of encouragement, they had done well. It annoyed me that all these years later, other schools still missed kids like this because they taught to the old 'one size fits all' model.

I tried to explain to the frightened woman tugging at her handkerchief the kind of teaching I believed her son needed. 'Can't you take him here?' she said. 'Since you know what he needs.' But that isn't enough, I tried to tell her. It's important he gets the right help but it has to be in a regular school with boys as bright as himself; our children were intellectually disabled, I explained, but she cried. She didn't want to walk away from the one person who seemed to have an answer for her son when she was terrified for his life. The only way to make her understand, I thought, was to take her to meet our students and see the kind of learning they were doing. I led her up the stairs to Robyn's senior class and after an apologetic word to Robyn, I showed her some of the children's work books so she could see for herself the one-syllable words they were reading and the very basic sums they still struggled with. She opened a couple of the books and I seized my chance to spend a few minutes with the children.

As Sybil always said, I didn't get into classrooms enough and this class was such fun. Alexander wanted to tell me about the green pooh he had done that morning and Amanda had a new riding ribbon to show off. Robyn and Marta, the aide, were moving quietly from group to group, encouraging this one, praising that and laughing with another. I looked up to see how Brett's mother was going with her inspection of the workbooks but she was no longer there. I swivelled around and saw her standing at the blackboard with her back to the class. Concerned, I went over to her and glimpsed tears running down her cheeks. Oh no, what had I done? Had I made her think that Brett was disabled? I led her out of the room, saying a quick goodbye to the children. 'What's wrong?' I asked as soon as we were outside.

'It's the children!' she said. 'They are so happy! I would give anything for Brett to be happy like that'.

I ended up taking Brett into the satellite class on the coast, within the mainstream school where Mrs McPhee was principal. The inspector at the Catholic Schools Board was understandably outraged. Here was an able student without a diagnosis enrolled in a special school. 'You won't get any funding for him,' she warned. But I already knew that and recognised that I was out of line. Nevertheless, it worked for Brett. The slow pace of the class, the constant repetition of material, the frequent tests and assessment built his confidence. He began to master basic skills that had eluded him all those years in his regular school. And he made friends, never seeming to mind the huge gap between his intelligence and the others', enjoying their jokes and letting down his guard with them in a way he couldn't with peers whose scorn he had feared. He still seemed depressed at times and prone to anger that he turned inward into a black moodiness but these episodes came less and less. I was determined he would go to a mainstream high school but I worried that he might not be robust enough mentally to survive.

I talked to Mrs McPhee and she suggested that she ask the school's parish priest to have a chat with him. 'The priest takes your Special Needs class for religion,' she said, 'and he likes Brett. He's a good counsellor and he'll have an insight into how well he'll manage.' I wasn't sure Brett would like being chatted to by a priest but he proved more than able to hold his own.

'I've been listening to you bang on all year about Jesus and God making the world and that,' he told the priest. 'I can't fathom that a grown up can believe such stuff.'

'It's a question of faith,' the priest began.

'Well, I'm a science man myself, and science tells me it's a bunch of bloody lies,' Brett responded. The priest was laughing when he reported the conversation to Mrs McPhee.

'I think our boy will do just fine in high school,' he said. He did too. He was accepted into the local government high school and never looked back. To me it was evidence that kids can develop in any setting provided they are loved and appreciated, given the time, structure and stimulation that they need and the freedom to learn the way that best suits them. I felt good that we were there when we were needed.

I hoped Faye would try mainstream again when it was time for Abbey to go to high school but she decided not to risk it. Abbey had recently started calling herself Margaret and she obsessively insisted that everyone else call her Margaret too. If you said Abbey, she ignored you. 'I hate Abbey. Abbey is stupid,' she told her mother, who was shattered. 'I want her to love herself but I don't know how to teach her to do that,' Faye said. 'I want others to love her too and I don't know how to teach them.' Abbey had been to a Christmas party with her family and their friends, and a little girl there told her she didn't want to play with her because she looked yucky. Abbey burst into sobs and insisted her mother take her home straight away. After that, Faye's mind was made up. 'I'm going to give her the gentlest life I can,' she said, and enrolled her in a high school for children with special needs. 'I can't spend every day she's at school worrying. I can't put her at the mercy of teachers who may not understand her. Abbey has the same right to expert education as any other child only the expertise she requires is different. Inclusion is all very fine in principle but in practice it can be just too hard.'

I had nearly finished the research for the paper on Catholic special schools and was writing up data the other principals had collected from interviews with their parents. The pattern was similar. There were children who thrived in regular schools and children damaged by their experience there. There were children no regular school would accept and children they expelled. And in each of our schools there were children with extreme needs that we were struggling to manage, let alone provide well for, but to whom we continued to give a place. Frank Pitt, the principal of Mater Dei Special School wrote a postscript for the booklet that captured the experience parents reported in their interviews:

For many families and children we are the face of Christ. We are the hand that is held out in friendship, in love and in compassion. In doing this we also give hope to families and a sense that they are not alone.

The paper was eventually published in booklet form. We sent copies to all the bureaucrats and church leaders and I had courteous acknowledgements in reply. I doubt it made any difference. Within a couple of months it had sunk out of sight like a stone. But at least I no longer had doubts about the importance of the safety net we provided for those children who fell through the cracks of mainstream schooling.

FINDING ENOUGH LOVE

The new uniforms arrived just before Christmas. Boxes of trendily styled jeans and denim shorts with t-shirts in grey and cherry red crossed with horizontal cream stripes, as well as tracksuits in grey and pink for sports day and casual wear. I couldn't wait to see the children in them.

I'd had to warn one mother that we wouldn't have a size to fit her son whose syndrome gave him a girth so great that only custom-made would fit. She was upset and angry. 'You're a special school. You're supposed to cater for difference,' she'd said heatedly. I wanted to shout back, protective of the long and painstaking process we'd followed to get to this point, and frustrated that Robert Burton's herculean labours were unappreciated. Unaccustomed to children of any kind, Robert had spent three days on his elegant knees measuring every shape and size of child in the school in order to accommodate the many ways they fell outside normal dimensions. But even Robert couldn't create a size for everyone and we had arranged for a local tailor to custom make uniforms for the scattering of children we couldn't fit, at no extra charge to their parents. It was unreasonable but I understood her anger. It was about how much she loved her son and wanted to protect his dignity and self-respect.

By now I had come to recognise the power of that love, how it kept the children feeling safe and confident and at ease with themselves, and how the extent to which they thrived was a measure of the love with which they were enveloped. The teachers and I were professionals, not parents and we couldn't expect to match the parents' unconditional love for their children. No one expected us to and in fact, talk about love was fairly inappropriate in a school setting. We were professionals. A new spirit was established now among the teachers, a readiness to try new ways to reach the children, to understand the function of their behaviour and the pathways by which they learned. We did it professionally, keeping data, recording antecedents and consequences, using video evidence. Yet painfully I discovered that our failures, when we failed, were always because we had not loved enough.

Francis was a boy who liked to play at monsters. Being a monster and scaring others to death. He had himself suffered the nameless terrors of hospital treatment, month after month, as a five year old with leukemia, separated from his mother, not understanding and not able to speak and say what frightened him. 'We thought he wasn't going to live, so we gave him whatever he wanted, anything that would distract him or give him moments of happiness,' his mother told me when I asked her to come and discuss the problems we were having with Francis.

His mischief had amused me at first. I found his adventures refreshingly boy-like. He had recruited a young partner in crime, six year old Andrew. It was odd how children were drawn to others with the same syndrome as their own. Andrew like Francis had Downs. One day the pair of them were caught jumping up and down on the roof of my car and another day they locked themselves in a disused bathroom with a bottle of detergent while we searched everywhere for them, until an overflow of soapy water from under the door gave them away.

Later though as Francis grew older and showed the signs of early puberty, his name started cropping up in staff meetings in stories that were no laughing matter: incidents in which he got weaker or smaller children alone to frighten them. He said he was being a monster but it looked like bullying. Francis was now a big boy with a truculent manner and the staff said he seemed to enjoy the power his size gave him. I called a red alert: he was to be watched continually in the playground and no incident of bullying allowed. But Francis was tricky and used to wait for a moment when no one was looking. Came the day a teacher heard screams and found him with a small girl's head jammed between the bars of a locked security gate. Horrified, I rang his mother to request a meeting. His mother was a solicitor, sharp and intelligent and I really liked her. But as she sat in my office in response to my call, I spared no detail in telling her our worries about Francis and described the panic the little girl was in when she was extricated from the security gate. His mother lowered her head and studied her fingers in her lap but I kept on because I felt we couldn't keep Francis at the school unless she got help for him and for us. After long moments of silence, she briskly pushed her handbag onto her shoulder, rose to her feet and told me in a voice of detached professionalism that she would make enquiries and get back to me.

She was as good as her word and a few days later called to say that she had managed to get a behavioral psychologist assigned to Francis's case. Usually there was a six months wait but she had told the Department of Community Services that he was at risk of being excluded from school. The psychologist was going to work with Francis at home and in a few weeks would come to observe him in our environment. I put the phone down feeling satisfied, but it didn't turn out the way I expected. I was busy in an interview a couple of weeks later when a youngish man in jeans with his sun-bleached hair tied back in a rubber band casually put his head around the door. 'I'm young Francis's case worker but I'll not bother you now,' he said, gesturing a half apology at my visitor. 'This morning I'm just observing. I'll come and see you when I'm done,' and he vanished.

He dropped back later in the day when I was having a hurried sandwich and spread his legs under my desk as he told me in a lazy drawl that Francis was doing well at home now. 'We've put a few things in place. He needs to know the rules and have his boundaries enforced but he's a good kid. Funny boy. I like him. But at school he's a monster and I think you're to blame.'

'What do you mean?' I asked indignantly. He grinned at me.

'I think you told your teachers they were not to let another child be hurt, didn't you? Well, that worked. For the whole of recess today, all I heard was "What are you doing Francis? Come back from there Francis. Stop that Francis."'

'But we have to. We have to stop Francis hurting the little ones. I didn't create that.'

'Look, I understand. You reacted to what you saw and flew into emergency mode. It's puberty. Francis's hormones are kicking in and his testosterone levels are high. He is full of repressed fear, confused and angry and he likes the power he gets from scaring children. But what he needs is to feel better about himself, not to be treated like a villain. You're making it so the only fun he gets is from being a monster. In time he'll see himself the way you do. What choice will he have?'

I was mortified. The words that sprang hot and instant to my defence fell into silence before the plain truth of what he said. After he left, I sat uncomfortably reflecting back over how I had reacted with dumb hostility to Francis, letting my distress for his small victims drive out any consideration or affection. I should have asked more questions about what was driving him and not needed a stranger to point out the harm we were doing. I called a special staff meeting the next day to report the psychologist's observations and got a stony reaction at first, especially from the aides. Making excuses for Francis was how they saw it – and what were we going to do then, let the little ones get hurt? I realised how easy it was to demonise a child and how hard it could be to reverse.

'Let's start again,' I said. 'Let's do all we can to make Francis feel loved. I want you to go over the top.' The staff were good. The next morning they started lavishing attention on Francis. They called out cheerful welcomes when he arrived in the taxi, they talked to him at recess and asked him about his dog and what he had for lunch, they praised him for his gentleness and at the end of a fortnight they nominated him for an award as a good friend to the younger children.

Soon he was looking less hunched, more at ease; he started walking taller and making jokes. He still occasionally bailed up a smaller child but such incidents became rare. The lesson wasn't hard to draw. Only those children we loved, thrived. And when they thrived, they were easy to love.

I pondered on the hidden human biases that make us as teachers like some children more than others. And some parents. There was the usual personality stuff of course, but I had to admit that ego defence played a part, defending my own ego that is. Mrs Grale was a case in point. Her daughter Jasmine had had severe uncontrolled seizures since she was a baby which the neurologists thought could be the reason she didn't learn to speak. Mrs Grale was a nurse who worked the day shift while Jasmine and her older sister were at school. She had been to lots of courses to learn how to help Jasmine and in particular had studied sign language using key words such as hungry, thirsty, toilet and a lot more. Our own staff now used key word signing with the children but we all had difficulty understanding the signs that Jasmine used.

Kelly her teacher suspected that Jasmine and her mother had developed their own idiosyncratic sign language to communicate between themselves. 'Jasmine has to learn standardised signs,' she told Mrs Grale. 'Otherwise she won't be able to communicate with anyone other than you.' But Mrs Grale complained to me that Jasmine was making her best approximation of the standardised signs and the teachers should learn to recognise her attempts. When Jasmine's tantrums became an issue for us at school, her mother was sure whom to blame. 'She's frustrated because she can't communicate here. She doesn't act out at home,' was her explanation.

On her good days, Jasmine was a delight. She laughed and played tricks and had no trouble making her needs understood. But there were days when the shutters fell. Nothing satisfied her then. Her screaming spiralled into violent tantrums and the teacher would have to evacuate the other children from the classroom until she could calm Jasmine. I wondered whether the seizure medication was exacerbating her manic moods but when I suggested this to Mrs Grale she said in an agitated way that I was ducking responsibility and that Jasmine got upset only because we didn't handle her correctly.

A couple of times she brought in work that she said Jasmine had done at home, to prove how misunderstood she was at school but the teacher insisted her mother must have been guiding Jasmine's hand. I didn't know who was right. I had an idea that if Mrs Grale videoed Jasmine at home we could see her doing the tasks that seemed beyond her at school but when I asked, she flared up and said I was accusing her of lying. Eventually I gave up and started asking Bev to say I was busy when she called. One morning as I passed her desk, Bev signalled to me that Mrs Grale was on the line again. I steeled myself to take the call but Bev put her hand over the receiver and whispered in an undertone, 'She's saying she's going to kill herself.' I took the phone and heard Mrs Grale's voice high pitched and slurry.

'And then I hit her,' I heard her say. 'I hit her! All she's ever done is try to help me. She's so good and quiet and I never give her any time. It's because of Jasmine.' And then she sobbed, 'I can't take it any more.'

'Mrs Grale, can you tell me where you are?' I hoped she wouldn't react to hearing my voice in place of Bev's but she didn't seem to care.

'I'm in the car. I've got Jasmine with me.'

'You seem upset. D'you want to tell me what's wrong?' I was playing at calm, desperately afraid of bungling and pushing her over the edge.

'What's wrong? What's wrong?' her voice came brokenly down the phone. 'How can you ask that? Everything's wrong. Me, and Jasmine. We're no good to anyone. Her screaming drives me crazy. I hit Caitlin today. She was shouting at me because I'd forgotten to wash her sports uniform and I slapped her across the face. She just walked out of the house. Just went. I'm a terrible mother to her. It's all Jasmine with me. And I can't take it any more. I can't take her. I'm going to drive us into a telegraph pole. Soon as I see one I can get to.'

'You can't do that, Mrs Grale. Think about Caitlin, how she'd feel. She'd blame herself. She loves you.'

'She hates me. She said she wishes Jasmine was dead and me too. I don't blame her. She'd be better off with both of us dead.' Her voice was quieter now and I could hear her breath heaving down the line and then a choked sob.

'Mrs Grale, do you know where you are?' There was a silence.

'No ... yes ... or I'm not sure, actually.'

'Are you in traffic?'

'Yes, there's traffic. There always is out here.'

'Where's here, Mrs Grale. Can you tell me? What can you see?'

'Westmead. I can see Westmead hospital.'

'Westmead?'

'Yes, I'm going to the clinic. I'm going to book myself in.'

'The psychiatric clinic?'

'Yes, I rang them and they said to come straight in.'

After I had hung up, I just sat frozen to Bev's desk and stared numbly at Bev's comfortable, steady face. 'So she was on her way to the hospital all the time?' Bev asked.

'Yes, it seems so.'

'Then why did she ring us?'

'I think she wanted someone to talk to so she could keep going, keep driving.'

'But what's going to happen now? She obviously isn't stable enough to care for Jasmine.'

'You know, I think she's shown how stable she is, deep down. She knew she needed help and she got Jasmine in the car and went for it; and got us to talk her there. I think she's going to be all right.'

Both of them were admitted to Westmead psychiatric ward and stayed for four weeks. Mrs Grale got the rest she needed and the specialists had an opportunity to trial different medications with Jasmine. Mrs Grale came to see me when they were discharged. She had had a new hair cut and looked younger and brighter. She gave me a tentative sort of smile. 'You must think me hopelessly neurotic – after my phone call that day?'

'No, I don't. I was grateful that you turned to us. I hadn't seen how bad it was for you.'

'I didn't want you to know. I didn't want anyone to know. I wanted everyone to see Jasmine as the beautiful, clever girl she really is. At her best. How I like to imagine her. That's what they said at the clinic. But they say they can help with her moods now she's on new medication.'

'Well, that's great.' She frowned.

'It makes me wonder why they didn't get the medication right in the first place. I shouldn't have had to go through all that, just to get her medication right.' I felt a flash of exasperation. Had she learned anything at all? Unexpectedly, she grinned at me. 'You've got your principal's look on,' she said, and I quickly smoothed my features back to pleasant. 'No, it's OK.' She cocked her head and gave a girlish smile as though to placate me. 'I called you that day so you'd scare me into staying alive, me and Jasmine.' Thank God, I thought. It could have ended differently and me left facing the worst kind of failure. I knew I'd shut her out to make it easier on myself. Blocking out responsibility or discomfort. That was another temptation of the role. Pain avoidance. It was Harry Townsend and his father who taught me you had to accept pain.

Four year old Harry came to school for an interview part way through my first year, along with his little brother and his father. 'Hi, I'm Lyell,' the father said, getting up from the long stripy lounge where the three of them were sitting waiting for me. He smiled gravely at me for a moment as though the meeting had a special significance for us both. He gestured to the two boys still sitting on the couch. 'This here is young Jake and this is Harry. We think it's time Harry started school and your place seems to be about right for him.'

The boy was slight for his age, his hair carefully slicked into place except for a few hairs that stuck up stubbornly at the back of his part. I was about to suggest that he and his brother go outside to play while we talked but Lyell was already sitting back down and he now patted on the seat for the boys to join him. 'My wife Jo is at work, she's the breadwinner, otherwise she'd be here too. I gave up work when Harry was diagnosed. My wife's a lawyer. She earns a lot more than I can, so I'm the carer. And I'm pretty good at it, aren't I?' he said to Harry and Jake. Harry gave him a weak punch in the arm.

'You're all right,' he said with a small grin, 'but Mum's a better cook.'

Lyell then took me through a story that I guessed he had repeated many times and still found relief in telling. Of Harry's on-going illnesses and the growing suspicion Lyell and his wife had that something was seriously wrong; of the many different tests in different hospitals, both in Tasmania where they lived and then up here in Sydney where they moved to be nearer specialists. His pleasant face took on an angry almost bitter cast as he spoke of the many frustrations and disappointments they had been through with the medicos unable to arrive at an explanation or a prognosis for Harry, except that it was some form of mitochondrial disorder and that it would be fatal. I must have flinched because Lyell said, 'Oh it's all right. Harry knows he's going to die, don't you mate?'

Involuntarily I looked at Harry. He leaned a little closer to his father and silently reached out to take his hand, smiling a little at me as he did. Harry didn't have a disability as such, just a death sentence. I had past experience of what it does to a school to watch a student die, especially when they are much loved – and they are all much loved. I wasn't sure I could handle it myself, not another death, not another loss. But then Harry took his father's hand and smiled at me and I had no choice. 'Well, if you'd like to come here Harry, we'd love to have you,' I said.

He started with us the following January. I put him

in Chris Donaldson's class. Chris, who I had brought up to the main campus from the satellites to strengthen our leadership, was the only person I could ask to take on Harry. Small things could ruffle her but faced with the big issues of life, no one was as stable or trustworthy as Chris. I invited a grief counsellor to our first staff day to prepare the teachers and aides for what they might soon be facing. The counsellor took a long time telling us that unsettled griefs in our own lives might resurface. I found it difficult to stay seated calmly at the table and had no doubt that others were feeling equally as vulnerable but no one said a word against having Harry join us. It was life, and he needed us.

The first day of the school year is always a special time with all the new little children to get to know and their nervous, tearful parents. But on this first day I couldn't wait for the parents to leave so I could get along to Chris's classroom to see how Harry was settling in. When I peered through the glass, I saw all the new little ones sitting in a circle on a mat watching the Wiggles on the electronic whiteboard and Harry's slight figure on a chair in their midst. Good, Chris had remembered that sitting on the floor was hard for Harry but I wondered if he minded being perched up so prominently like that. As I watched, he reached out a foot and nudged the boy nearest him, grinning mischievously, and then leaned down and pulled the pony tail of the girl in front. Obviously being on a chair wasn't going to hold him back. 'Hi horsey,' Harry crowed, grinning as she turned around. He seemed in no doubt that everyone here would become as much his devoted slave as everyone else in his young life. When he saw they were not to be shaken from their focus on the Wiggles, Harry joined in too, chuckling and clapping as on the screen the purple Wiggle fell into one of his characteristic sudden sleeps. 'Wake up Jeff,' Harry shouted loudest of all. He could have been any child with all his life before him. Sitting on the floor near to him was Seth, one of our few blind students, his blindness and slight cerebral palsy the result of a brain tumour. Seth's face and unseeing eyes were turned away from the screen. Harry leaned his thin body down and rubbed his head. 'It's *funny*, Seth!' he said loudly.

'Funny,' Seth shouted, excited by the invitation in Harry's touch. 'It's funny, Mrs Donaldson.' He giggled loudly. Harry's blue eyes stared thoughtfully at him for a moment and then, smiling, he leaned forward to massage his head again.

A few weeks into the new term, on a day when it was pouring with rain, Lyell drove Harry to school as usual but this time Mick, the maintenance guy, and I were out the front doing 'kiss and drop' so the parents wouldn't have to walk through the rain. I leaned into Lyell's car to help Harry with his seatbelt. 'Lyell says you're the boss', Harry said, deadpan, as I struggled with the clip.

'Mmm, I guess I am,' I replied.

'Not if you can't undo my seatbelt, you're not' he hooted and laughed at his joke. I finally had it undone and helped Harry climb out onto the footpath. Mick had already taken his backpack from the car boot and he went to put it on Harry's bony shoulders. 'You can carry it', Harry said with an airy wave of his arm. He took my hand. I was touched and as I looked down at his small thin face, I felt a catch in my heart. 'If you're the boss,' Harry said giving me the full force of his blue eyes and most persuasive smile, 'Tell my teacher I don't have to go swimming today, will you?'

Then came a day when the emergency button on my phone rang. The small digital screen read Room 4, Chris Donaldson's room. I rushed out my door and down the corridor, joined by Bev carrying the first aid bag. We burst through the classroom door and stopped still. Chris was perched on one of the small kindergarten chairs with Harry's small body straddled motionless across her lap. Chris was rubbing his back and humming quietly. She looked up briefly and waved us back. After a horribly long moment, Harry lifted his head and Chris gently levered him onto his feet. 'Harry had a bit of a choke,' she said. 'You're all right now, are you?' she asked as she looked closely into his face which had a kind of grey pallor. Harry stared vaguely back at her and gave a small nod. 'It's happened before,' she told me afterwards. 'Lyell says the main thing is to keep him calm and let him get control of his breathing himself.'

I waited for Lyell that afternoon, wanting to have a

word with him before he collected Harry. Bev had rung him about the incident and said he hadn't seemed overly concerned which somehow made me feel the responsibility more heavily. I wandered aimlessly about the foyer until eventually his warm, pleasant face appeared in the doorway. I jumped on him. 'Lyell, I want to know what we're supposed to do,' I blurted. 'If it happens again. How will we know if it's bad enough to call an ambulance. What are the signs. What should we have in place?' Lyell gave me his slow grin.

'If it's a bad one, there won't be time for an ambulance.'

'But we can't take the risk, Lyell. What if Harry dies, here at school?'

'Well, he could. He could die anywhere. We just don't know when it's going to happen.'

'But I'd feel terrible. What if we got it wrong somehow? How could I ring you, and say it had happened and we'd let your boy die?'

'The dying is not what's important,' Lyell said, fixing his eyes on me but keeping his soft, wry smile. 'It's the living that matters. Giving Harry as much fun and joy and life as we can, each day that he's alive. That's what it's about.'

I was silent then, standing staring in wonder at the man, seeing him resolute in the midst of flames of grief and certain loss, brushing them aside, making himself a shelter for Harry. Banishing the grim and gloomy with jokes and banter. And my protests, my concern for duty of care and responsibility were all because I couldn't stand the heat, couldn't bear the pain.

'Lyell' came Harry's piping voice at the door. 'I choked again and Mrs Donaldson sang to me.'

'What's her singing like? Is she as good as me?'

'You sing flat!' said Harry scornfully and took his hand. Lyell smiled at me over Harry's head.

'You're right then, are you?' he asked, and I slowly nodded, for what more was there to say?

COMMUNITY

In 2007 Won Bhin came into our lives. He was tiny, so small you could still hold him in one hand, but enough to fill all our hearts, the answer to prayer. He arrived on a Qantas flight from Seoul and came through the arrival gates in Olivia's arms, with Michael behind struggling with the unaccustomed baby gear. It strengthened our bonds as a family, having this tiny baby. Olivia and Michael with Won Bhin, Christina and Guillaume with Alex. We held a naming ceremony at my place, with Gae acting as celebrant, something she fitted into her spare time. With friends and family gathered around to share our gratitude for this precious new addition to our lives, the special day wove another memory into my house in the woods and sealed Won Bhin's place with us. Family, friends, ceremony, shared experiences and shared memories – together they create community and the sense of belonging from which one's identity springs.

Community was missing at the school when I started there. The classroom was home for each child but they had no sense of belonging to a school. There was just the classroom and the playground – and on that dull, bare plot of asphalt they didn't run around playing with each other; they sat passively on the margins or mooched slowly around, except for the times when one of them punched or kicked another. It felt institutional to me and I missed the vibrant life that most schools have, where friendships and community are at least as important as the learning in the classroom.

Early on I tried to start a daily assembly, to create a ritual the children could enjoy and share in. We used the cavernous old gym and put out the old blue gym mats for each class to sit on but it didn't go well. The space was big and impersonal and dark, and sound echoed around its high, bare walls. The children sat inert, or put their hands over their ears, or took flight, escaping up the wooden climbing ladders attached to the walls, with the teachers trying frantically to talk them down. It was obvious to me that, as in any school, we needed singing to engage the children but I am a terrible singer. Even those who love me giggle or throw me quelling looks if I try to join in any community singing. I pleaded with the staff to help me teach songs to the children in assembly the way they did in class but they wouldn't risk it in front of their colleagues and anyway I was then still the new principal with alien ideas and they couldn't see the point. Marta our IT fix-it person, kindly brought in a CD player for me to use in the gym and downloaded some God songs she thought the children might like but when we tried it, those children who didn't run off, sat oblivious on their mats while their teachers looked at their watches.

It was Hailey with her unconquerable Down syndrome spirit who made the breakthrough for me during a song called *Hearts on Fire* by Michael Mangan. Jack and I had heard it at a vision educators' conference on the Gold Coast and we both thought it had the kind of rhythm and energy that might rouse the children. As the song started on the CD player, I seized the microphone in a tight fist and began to sing, my thin, wavering voice, flat and off tune, magnified painfully through the microphone. Nobody joined in. The teachers were too embarrassed to look at each other. Hailey was sitting near the front, her bright slightly squinting eyes fixed on me, seeming to smile encouragement.

When the song finally came to an end, I boisterously urged everyone to join in as we tried it a second time.

The teachers, ignoring my fake cheer, continued to study the floor but Hailey bless her, began to copy my actions, banging on her breast with increasing force every time 'hearts on fire' sang out. Then incredibly, she started to sing. At first it was a kind of quiet hum but by the second chorus she had gained confidence and her voice was ringing out loudly and tunefully her own version of the words.

Everyone stared, galvanised, and soon a couple of teachers sitting near picked up the tune to help her out. On the next play through, more children and teachers joined in and the room was suddenly full of smiles and people banging their chests. Hailey was pumped up, knowing she had started it. As she left the gym with her class, she turned at the door and raised her thumbs at me. *Hearts on Fire* became her song and whenever we played it, she would light up and prepare herself to belt out the chorus, thumping on her chest as though she was giving herself pulmonary resuscitation.

That day marked the beginning. Eventually morning song became the most special part of the school day and our repertoire of God songs became a kind of lingua franca, sung and played in our families' homes and in their cars. I wrote a simplified version of the Lord's Prayer for the children – and later one of the Sisters formulated a Creed that they could understand. But none of this happened quickly or easily. For one thing, Hailey only liked *Hearts on Fire*, her signature tune that had made her a star. As soon as she heard the first bars and knew it wasn't *Hearts on Fire*, her bottom lip would protrude and she'd clam her mouth shut and dart a look of disgust my way. So we sang *Hearts on Fire* a lot and after several months you could sense a change. Children began to gather outside the gym doors in the morning waiting for them to open and then rush in to take their places on the mats and join in the singing they were now convinced was the way to start the day.

Transforming the playground came next. I became conscious of the role of the environment when Sybil, Robin Thomas and I joined an Australian study tour to Reggio Emilia in Italy. We were sitting in a dark, underground conference room being told in Italian and English that the environment impacts children's learning to such an extent that in their Reggio Emilia schools they call it 'the third teacher'. I could believe it. Right now the cramped musty room we were in was making me feel confined and restless. Next to me Sybil was in a grumpy mood, muttering darkly about what would happen in her classroom if she did what they were demonstrating and created an attractive classroom display of leaves and twigs, or seaweed. 'Kids will chuck it or eat it,' she whispered. I shrugged and laughed, worried that she might be right and that the studies and experiences the speakers were citing might not transfer to our school. The children had to have an environment with minimal stimulation, the teachers always said it. And that made me think about the playground, an area the teachers didn't control.

Going by the Reggio studies, our dull, ugly empty asphalt wasteland could be contributing to the children's behaviour as much as their developmental problems. We had no equipment for them to play together on, apart from an aging adventure playground that was only suited to the youngest children. Did those kids, whose names appeared in the incident book day after day, do their provoking and hitting as a way of making contact with other children? Or was it out of boredom, to make something happen? Or was it in fact an inevitable effect of their disabilities that they couldn't learn to initiate or co-operate in play?

As soon as we got back from Italy, I fired up the inimitable Zandra with my vision of a playground so fantastical as to magic our children out of their isolated meanderings and into a new universe of interactive, exploratory play. Zandra went to George's father, Ernesto, who had offered to help raise money for our next project.

The black-eyed, suave Ernesto had introduced himself to me when George started school at the 'tissues and tears' morning tea we held for new parents on the first day. My mind was more than usually distracted at the time as that was the morning Harry started too, and I nodded and thanked him politely, ignorant of his respected position in the financial world and never dreaming that he planned to extract large donations from Sydney's brokers and investment managers who needed his good will. He raised the money so quickly that Zandra was able to sub-contract the transformation over the next Christmas holidays and have everything ready for the start of the new year.

There were the usual construction hiccups of course and the green rubber play surface was only just dry in time for the first morning when children returned for the start of school. I was on tenterhooks waiting to see how they would react, no longer complacent as I had been the previous summer after we finished the bathrooms.

Suddenly Ernesto appeared at my side. He had never been at school at this hour before and I was a bit slow to realise what he was doing there. 'We won't see a change immediately,' I warned him when I finally twigged that he wanted to check on delivery of the transformation I had spruiked. It was a hot morning and I was conscious of perspiring more than usual as we waited together, me twisting my fingers and Ernesto standing beside me with an inscrutable expression.

Then the big glass doors opened and the first taxi load of children sidled through into the playground and stood in small knots looking wordlessly about them. For a moment nothing happened. Then young Andrew broke from the spell and started running across the green rubberised surface towards the huge sandpit backed by a mural of colourful beach huts on the far wall. Another child followed and another. Soon children were running everywhere, climbing onto the large rockers, walking over the wooden decking, sitting at the new lunch tables, digging in the sand, pushing between the multi-coloured squeeze barrels. Ernesto looked at me in wonder.

'It's like someone turned a switch,' he said. 'They usually just sit about like sacks.' I couldn't believe it myself. To this day, Ernesto and I, if we get together, speak of the miracle of that moment of metamorphosis.

I had pushed the boundaries in selecting playground equipment. The climbing spider was four metres high, the flying fox attached to the big eucalyptus was more than twenty metres long and two metres above ground and there were twenty bikes of different sizes and types for the bike track including two-wheelers.

I had been open about the risks with the parents. 'Schools are all about safety these days,' I wrote to them in a letter before the start of school. 'Children aren't allowed to climb trees and equipment is not to go higher than one and a half metres. We forget that taking risks and testing skill is part of how children learn. Your children will develop faster and go further if we give them these challenges. We'll teach them safety rules and supervise them but I can't guarantee there won't be a few broken arms. I'd like your support.' Not a single parent protested, not even when Andrew who'd learned to climb up the huge rope Spider but not down it, solved his problem by letting go and dropping heavily three metres onto the softfall. Luckily he bruised only a shoulder and after that we taught getting down before any one went up. Our children were the envy of the kids at the Catholic school next door who often came over to use our equipment but were not allowed to climb to the top of the Spider and were barred altogether from the flying fox.

Recess became the excitement of the day. Staff reported positively about the emergence of friendships between children who favoured the same zone of the Spider or together frequented the queue for the flying fox, or spent every recess and lunch trundling round the bike track together. Some of the children began to invent their own games. Louisa pulled reeds from the creek to make herself into a unicorn, Logan and his friends played chasings with his imaginary dragon and the older boys started a game of prisoners, with the girls as their captives, which ran for days until the staff had to intervene.

Some of the teachers were uncomfortable with the new wildness in the children and the aides understandably worried about accidents. They made deputations about the jacaranda tree needing to be pruned back to a safe height and for the railway sleepers in the bridge to be sanded. 'The biggest risk is that the children won't know the joy of being a child, and won't develop their potential – not that they suffer a scratch or two,' I kept responding. 'What I need,' I exclaimed to the patient Bev, 'Is a Pied Piper to make these staff remember their own childhoods and what fun it is to play unhindered.'

And then on cue the Pied Piper turned up. It was Olivia who introduced her. She and Michael broke the news to me that they were following their theatre ambitions to Los Angeles and taking precious Won Bhin with them. 'I won't leave you in the lurch, Mumma,' Olivia said and told me of a young actor who she thought would be an excellent drama teacher. I was sceptical that anyone could draw the children out the way Olivia did and I was upset at losing them. So it was with some resentment that I agreed to meet Pia Lombardi. 'I'm Italian,' she said at that first interview. 'I'm loud.' Her laugh was full of humour and her energy filled the room. Despite myself, I felt a rush of hope. Pia had not heard of Reggio Emilia before she came but she embraced it like it was part of her DNA. She was an actor, not a teacher, but she knew instinctively how to create situations that provoked the children to leaps of insight and it was in her nature to make life a celebration.

Within a few weeks of her arrival she was taking a public address system into the playground and turning the children's dress-ups into a fashion parade. She broadcast a race commentary as the children rode their bikes. She played music over the loud speaker and the children standing silent on the playground started dancing. Every day was a party. With Pia in charge, the teachers were able to relax and acknowledge the fun the children were having and the way it expanded their imagination and connected them to others. They stepped back a pace and became observers instead of generals.

But I missed Olivia. I missed the sight of her green tweed coat flicking by, the comforting presence of family. There were signs on all sides of the growing community, all the more so now that Pia was here, but I wasn't part of it, not really. The children didn't know me the way they knew their classroom teacher, I had no relationship with them and I had little chance to create it, preoccupied as I was with all the challenges of building up the school. One father, collecting his boy in the afternoon gave him a poke to say goodbye to me. When the boy hesitated, the father asked, 'Who is this? Do you know?' and his son said shyly, 'She's the microphone woman.' I laughed but it said it all and I felt sad.

Then young Gideon started hanging around my office window. Gideon was about eight at the time and had recently been diagnosed with Fragile X syndrome, a genetic disorder closely linked to autism. I didn't know what prompted his interest in me; perhaps it was because I was drawn to him. There was a humorous gleam in his eye that I loved. I'd look out to the playground from my desk and see him staring in at me. As soon as my eyes met his, he would look away, a secret smile on his lips. If I kept looking or waved, he ran off. After a bit he took to walking past my window, nonchalantly, as though he had no idea it was my window. As soon as he saw me glance up, he'd hurry off. His hyperactivity fascinated me. I'd known plenty of students with ADHD but Gideon's was on a different scale altogether. His hands moved all the time, his eyes flashed about him, he would grin suddenly and go solemn suddenly; his whole nervous system seemed to be tuned at a higher speed. Now whenever he saw me, his hands started to flap like frenzied birds, out of his control.

One day as the children were leaving after morning assembly, I noticed Gideon standing next to the CD player and looking at me. 'Be careful,' I said automatically. In a flash he had bent to the CD player, removed the disc, put it in its jacket, carefully placed it in the CD stack and run off. He did the same the next day and the day after and before long he was hanging round at the start of assembly as well, waiting until Marta or I told him which song we were having that day.

When a year later we replaced the CD player with more sophisticated audio equipment, Marta taught Gideon to operate it and he became my morning 'techie'. I had no idea what he was doing. His hands flew through the controls, switching this, turning that, finding the CD, putting it on, taking it off, turning another control. My eyes could barely keep up so fast was the speed of his hands; my brain had no hope of checking that he had it right. But he mostly did and when the technology failed, as it does, his hands would fly even faster than usual, no other sign of stress, and generally he'd get it going again. I'd see him smile quietly to himself. He was now nine and had a diagnosed intellectual disability and Fragile X and I depended on his skill and self-assurance.

The minute I emerged from the office, he would appear from nowhere and walk wordlessly at my side, his hands flapping and a small half-smile on his long face, his eyes fixed on middle distance. Gideon's attachment gave me an identity the children could grasp. I was Gideon's friend. Now children started to come up to me when Gideon did and just hang. Sometimes they shared news of what had happened in the playground and although I still couldn't often understand their words, I learned to stay quiet and let them try again and again until I got it. They were wonderfully patient with me.

By now the impact of the children's art, drama and music lessons was apparent even to Gae and the Board who urged that I work with the architects to establish a creative arts centre in the old convent. We were stymied though by the heritage status of much of the convent and especially the internal staircase which we were barred from touching but which was not compliant for use in a school because of the low height of the balustrade. 'Face facts, you can't use the convent,' said Sybil at our weekly leadership team meeting. Sybil and Chris Donaldson now shared the role as joint senior leaders, taking over after Robyn Thomas left us to become principal at a neighbouring special school. Sybil, who preferred the role of rebel, only agreed to join the dark side because I promised wine and laughter at our weekly meetings. I wasn't laughing though when she dismissed my plans to convert the convent. My mouth must have dropped open because she continued, 'If you want creative arts to be at the centre of the curriculum, then the creative arts centre shouldn't be way off in the convent. Why don't you pull down the gym and build it there?'

'We can't,' I exclaimed in horror. 'We can't tear down a perfectly good building. We don't have that kind of money to waste. Besides, think of the noise and disruption to the kids if we built it in the very centre of the school.' But Sybil continued to argue. The gym was designed for very different children and should be replaced with a building that would meet the needs of the students we had now.

'It can be a really good space for assembly,' she added persuasively, 'with the acoustics to do justice to your singing, Jo. And you're right, it will be hell but think how the kids will love the bulldozers and tip trucks.' The architects, when I consulted them, much preferred Sybil's suggestion. They proposed using the foundations of the gym and rebuilding in glass to bring in light and make the layout transparent to the children. They were implementing Reggio Emilia principles but my head held images of all the special schools I had ever visited. Solid brick with high walls and even barbed wire.

'Glass can be as indestructible as brick,' Jonathon the

architect in charge assured me. 'It will be like an Italian piazza. The children will feel free as birds.'

'Great,' I said darkly, my mind going instantly to Spiro's latest exploit. Pia and Guillaume were now running after school theatre classes with the help of some senior boys from the college across the road. The week before, Spiro had taken a fit of the sulks at being excluded from an activity because of his behaviour. When the teachers weren't looking, he slipped out through the Library doors. Marta saw him go and raised the alarm. Although Guillaume quickly set off into the playground after him, Spiro was too fast. He sprinted across the asphalt and into Jorge the cleaner's van which Jorge had left unlocked on the playground. As Guillaume ran up, savvy little Spiro shot the door lock down and grinned at Guillaume's helplessness as the latter banged frantically on the rear window. Then he bent forward, turned the key in the ignition and drove the van forward. It bumped along a few metres and then rumbled into the sand pit. We had to call a tow truck to pull the van out; Jorge was indignant at the damage to his vehicle, Spiro's mother was hysterical that he could have been killed and an overwrought Guillaume offered to resign.

But Jonathan responded to my horror story by suggesting we secure the new building electronically, with swipes instead of keys. He had an answer for my every concern except the cost and the noise.

Just before construction began, we had one last event in the old gym. Some of the school's most loved students were going on to high school the next year, including Berenice's daughter, Selina. Berenice came to ask me if the parents could hold a graduation party for them. 'Not a Year 6 graduation!' I exclaimed without thinking. 'Can't we let children be children and not have them ape Year 12 formals and graduations?' Berenice looked at me in dismay.

'All my friends who have children in Year 6 in regular schools, they're all talking about their child's graduation party,' she told me, her face going rather pale and blotchy. 'I just want Selina to have the same as other children have.' I started to explain my dislike of the way children these days are hot-housed into would-be adults before their time. Her mouth was pursed and she looked stubborn and I realised how absurd I was being. These Year 6 students would be young and unsophisticated all their lives. What was wrong in having a party for them to make them feel celebrated and fabulous? I quickly backtracked. When the night came and I looked around at the balloon-festooned tables of parents all dressed in their best, and listened to their proud tales and heard the excited giggling of their children, I was mortified that I could have missed the importance of this. I glanced around for Berenice to tell her how glad I was she had insisted.

I couldn't see her at first and then I glimpsed her almost out of sight in the kitchen doorway. That didn't seem right;

she should be out with the others enjoying the fun. I hurried over and saw she had been crying. I assumed it was just the emotion of the moment and started exclaiming over how beautiful Selina looked in her long white dress. 'She's had her hair done, hasn't she? It looks lovely.' Berenice leaned forward to make herself heard over the party noise.

'You know how much I wanted this night for her,' she said. 'I wanted it so badly. But yesterday we went to the pre-party for my friend's daughter and all the children there were amazing, they were confident and full of life. As I watched and listened to them I got a jolt realising how different Selina is. Somehow I thought that having a graduation party would make her like all the other girls but nothing can do that. She will never have what each of them has.' There seemed nothing to say. I wanted to hug her but Pia's voice came booming over the microphone calling the principal and the president of the P&F to the stage to present the graduation certificates. Berenice quickly fished out a tissue from her pocket. Together we headed for the podium, pasting broad smiles onto our teary faces as we went.

It was everything a graduation ceremony should be. The children were solemn, funny, proud and bashful, by turns, as they came up on stage to receive their certificates. Their parents applauded and shouted as if each child had won an Olympic medal and a citation from the Queen to boot. Berenice's face was beaming. As the last child left the stage and we walked off out of the limelight together,

I asked her was she just putting on a brave show. 'Oh no. The moment Selina came up on the stage and I saw her so excited, so proud of herself, I wondered what I'd been carrying on about. I was silly.' I squeezed her hand.

A few days later she appeared brightly at my office door. 'I came to say sorry for getting upset at the party,' she said, all shadow of sadness gone. 'I lost my bearings for a bit but I'm right again.' Seeing the doubt on my face, she laughed. 'Oh it's true,' she assured me. 'I saw the light and I owe it to Rene Rivkin.' Rene Rivkin was one of Sydney's colourful characters of the time, a financial high flyer famous for his lavish lifestyle and his gold worry beads.

'Rene Rivken?' I repeated, puzzled. 'Did you know him?'

'No,' she said. 'They were replaying an interview with him on the radio. He was talking about his life, his yachts, his mansions, his travel. It made me think how small and sad my life would seem to someone like him.' She gave a deprecating shrug. 'We don't go away on holidays. If we go out to dinner, it's at the local pizza place. But I love my life. It's all I need. I realised it's the same with Selina. The life she can have seems small to me, but it will be all that she knows and all she'll want.'

The day before one of the Year 6 mothers, coming to say goodbye, had commented to me how the chronic grief crept up on her at each milestone in her child's life. I wondered how many parents had shed secret tears at the graduation. 'Did we do the right thing, having the party?' I wondered aloud. Berenice smiled.

'You should ask Selina that, and the other kids. They say it was the best night of their lives.'

It was now nearly Christmas and Pia Lombardi and I decided to end the year with a Carols Night. The gym was already half-demolished, but with the new playground we had the perfect setting for a summer evening picnic. We would hold it by candlelight under the stars, with each class performing one of the carols and all the families joining in. I sent out notices to the parents telling them to bring picnic baskets and rugs, Zandra summoned up a supply of candle-shaped torches, Marta recorded the carols for the teachers and Pia was stage manager.

The day of the carols was bright and sunny but after lunch grey clouds began to gather. Hastily I tuned in to the latest weather forecast and caught a warning of a rain storm on the way. Without the gym we didn't have a big enough covered space for all the families. Feeling badly disappointed, I wrote a note to go in each child's bag saying that in view of the terrible weather, we wouldn't be offended if they decided not to come. Not come? Families had been talking to their children about the carols for weeks. Under lowering black clouds they started to arrive, spreading their rugs under sheltering trees, unpacking their eskies in defiance of the looming skies. When spots of rain started they crowded in a huddle under the cover of the children's lunch tables or in the shelter of the lilly pilly tree. But soon the rain grew heavy and lightning shot across the sky. Surely they would head for their cars now but no, they were looking at me, waiting for me to lead the way somewhere. I offered the library and with great good cheer they packed up and followed me there.

At a squeeze, we could fit sixty children into the library. That's what we thought. But this night more than 160 people were sardined around the walls and between the bookshelves and massed on the carpet, making a crowded tapestry of expectant faces. Their voices reverberated under the domed ceiling as they called across the room to each other and I wondered how the children with autism were coping. I could hardly hear my own voice as I took the microphone and called Chris Donaldson's kindergarten class onto the makeshift stage to sing Away in a Manger. I was sweating. The air conditioning was having no tangible impact on the heat from all those bodies. Outside the rain continued to hammer down.

Chris waved urgently to me across the crowded heads; she couldn't get the children through the press of bodies. A father standing nearby reached down and picked up one of the kids, passing him forward and then another and the crowd bore them aloft and onto the stage where everyone cheered them. When the song ended, they passed them back again, and so on through carol after carol. The children, bless them, sang their little hearts out. It should have been a disaster and in the strictest sense it was. No one could hear the Christmas readings because of the noise. Once the wrong child got passed up onto the stage and stood there shouting that it wasn't her song. Then a small boy, seated in the middle of the crowded floor, threw up. No one could get to him to clean up the vomit and a couple of kids nearby began to finger it. When Santa Claus arrived he couldn't squeeze through the mass of people at the door and the parents passed his sack of sweets around for the children. And yet … And yet when the last song rang out, *Joy to the World*, and the domed ceiling echoed with over a hundred voices, it was as though joy truly was being born in that crowded little library.

There was a missed call on my phone when I got home. It was after midnight. The lolly papers and the vomit and everything else had taken a while to clear away. I looked at the number. Olivia. Five hours time difference in Los Angeles. They would just be getting up. 'How did the Carols Night go?' she asked.

'It was mayhem,' I said feelingly and paused as images of the night tumbled through my mind. 'No, not mayhem,' I corrected, 'more like creative chaos'.

'I can imagine!' I could hear the smile in her voice. 'Here they call it love under pressure.'

MARCHING ON CANBERRA

I was screwing my eyes up trying to make out the tiny figures in the monthly financial reports, wishing I had made the time to study the papers before the Board meeting. Maybe I was reading it wrongly but wasn't the government grant figure too low? We had been waiting for the special assistance distribution that came through the Catholic Schools Board; it was late and we needed the cash, especially with the new loan for the creative arts centre to service.

We had opened the completed building a couple of months before and we all loved it. It was light and airy and very flexible with movable walls in the main hall and sport, art, drama and food preparation rooms opening off it; glass and light everywhere. I dubbed the big hall The Possibility

Space. With the movable wall pulled across, we were able to have an all-season therapy area on one side with different sensory swings, beams and hammocks suspended from the reinforced ceiling as well as huge crash mats, soft shapes for climbing and falling and soft-shape mazes to strengthen co-ordination. On the other side of the wall we held our morning and afternoon gatherings and once a week a cafe, which the senior class ran for parents and other visitors.

Each Wednesday we held an afternoon assembly for parents. At first I ran it with a senior student chosen to say our version of the Lord's prayer but the staff were ahead of me now, fully imbued with the democratic spirit of Reggio Emilia, and at one staff meeting they urged me to let the children run the assembly, class by class, the non-verbal as well as the more verbal. I couldn't imagine how it would work and I was secretly sad to give up my role as the microphone woman, but what a vision! I had to embrace it. Week by week, a different class took on leading the prayers, announcing the songs and doing their best to read out the awards. My job was to give out the awards but often a child grabbed the certificate from me and bestowed it peremptorily on the recipient. And we always finished by singing 'Home Among the Gum Trees', a ritual so important to the children that I ignored the groans of staff and parents who after a time were more than over it.

Parents used to meet at a cafe for lunch on Wednesdays and then come along to assembly, knowing they'd have occasion to laugh, to cry and to praise the progress of each other's children. We could always count on something untoward happening, funny or surprising or heartwarming and often all three. Assembly was a community celebration second to none and for that alone, the cost of the new building was worth it. But the delayed quarterly instalment of the government grant jeopardised our cash flow and I had been sweating on it for some weeks. Now the grant had appeared in the monthly income figures but it seemed to be $15,000 less than I'd calculated. Surely that couldn't be right? A reduction of $15,000 a quarter would just about cost us a teacher's salary.

'Are you still with us, Jo?' It was Fergus, the new Board chair calling on me. Fergus had stepped into Gae's shoes when she and her husband moved north to Darwin. I saw his eyebrows were raised at me, a sizable censure from him, so I tried hard to concentrate on the discussion around the table but I couldn't take my mind off the grant money. I hoped the figure was a mistake but I was as restive as a pregnant cat for the rest of the meeting and that night lay awake for hours worrying about the implications. If governments could cut funding without notice like this, we and all the special schools were facing a precarious future.

The next morning I was at school early to hunt down the business manager, Razi and find out what she knew, but she was out on her regular constitutional and I hung about waiting impatiently. At last she appeared carrying a small bunch of flowers to place on Mary's statue as she did every morning. Brushing aside her ever-courteous greeting, I blurted out my worry about the special assistance grant and pressed her with questions about the figures in her accounts. With imperturbable calm she replied that the accounts were, as always, immaculately correct. 'The figure for the grant recorded in the accounts is the amount we have received.'

'And you didn't check?'

'No, no. You are the principal, I assumed you would know about it.' I called the Catholic Schools Board.

'Yes, that's the right figure,' they told me. 'The government has recalculated its special assistance grant to NSW schools and given the Catholic sector less. That means less special assistance for every Catholic school.'

'It means I'll have to sack a teacher,' I spluttered.

'It's up to you how you manage the cut.' So smooth, these officials. 'You shouldn't be relying on the special assistance grant anyway. It's meant to be an extra. It's meant for exceptional provisions.'

'That's us,' I said tersely. 'Exceptional is us. We need that money to keep going.'

'We tried. That's why the grant was late. We delayed signing up to the government's package because it was too low, but schools needed the money so in the end we had to accept the lower figure.'

'Isn't there something that can be done? What if we all

went to Canberra to make our case to the government?'

'That's the worst thing you could do. We have our lobbyists working for us and you will undo all their good work if you try talking to government yourself.'

I was stymied. There seemed no answer but to cut back on what we were doing for the children. Suddenly the costly new building and the loan repayments we faced each month looked like foolish risks. What was I thinking? I had been so confident that if we had a dream, somehow we'd find the means to fulfill it. But now I was brought up short against the reality of a society in which bureaucrats and governments blithely slash funding without a care for the effect. So when Talieh, who was originally from Iran, came excitedly to tell me she had been asked to go to Qatar as a special education consultant to the government there, I surprised her by giving in without a fight. Yes, she could have indefinite leave. No, we wouldn't replace her. The play programme she had set up would have to be abandoned. We had to be realistic.

In the same defeated and resigned mood, I reported the funding cut to the regular P&F meeting a couple of weeks later. 'How can they do that? Just take away $60,000?' Jenny, the president asked angrily. She was a single parent, new to the school, who oversaw a big retail outlet's operating budget in her day job. Her blonde ponytail swished about. 'Aren't they supposed to give you notice of any change to funding?'

'If they cut $60,000 this year, how much will it be next

year?' put in Conall's Dad. We had framed Conall's latest painting of furiously speeding cars and I had given it to him just before the meeting. Now he was outraged.

'Who is it anyway? Is it the government or is it Catholic Education?' asked a mother who worked for the Department of Education.

'The Catholic Schools Board says it's the government,' I replied. 'It seems they cut the whole NSW special assistance grant and head office shared the pain out amongst us all.'

'That's so not fair,' said Michelle, who had three older children in Catholic schools. 'They should take the money from those schools that can afford it, like my other kids' school.' I looked around at their angry faces, completely taken aback by the heat of their reaction. This was something new. Gae used to speak to me about the passivity of the parents, how easily they fell into helplessness and how we needed to do something to empower them. In our 2006 strategic plan she had set me a goal of developing parents' skills as advocates for their children. I had organised some workshops with a mother who was a professional lobbyist; our local Member of Parliament had come as guest speaker a couple of times but the turnout was always poor. Those who fronted were only there out of duty.

'It's just not me,' one in my workshop group had said. 'I couldn't go to my local MP. I don't even know what electorate I'm in. It's all I can do to get through the day. If things go wrong, I just grit my teeth and tough it out. I don't have time or energy for anything more than surviving.' Now however the parents' indignant voices were rising to a crescendo.

'Quiet, everyone!' Jenny shouted, asserting herself over the noise. 'Let's find out what Jo wants us to do.' As the hubbub quietened she turned and, emphatically crossing her arms, demanded to know what I thought would help.

'I don't know there is anything,' I said doubtfully. 'I did think of marching on Canberra but the people at the Catholic Schools Board said that would muddy the political waters.'

'They couldn't be more muddy, could they?' asked Conall's Dad. 'They've taken money away from kids with the greatest needs.' There was another babble of voices, each talking furiously over the other.

'I'd march on Canberra for this.'

'So would Greg and me and Mum too. We'd all come.'

'How can they do this, with no warning or anything.'

'We can get a bus and take the whole school. Let the kids loose in Parliament, see how they like it.' As I listened to them I felt torn. The appeal of a march on Canberra, against official advice, when we had only just finished the new buildings and I had a hundred neglected tasks to attend to, was underwhelming. But they were animated and keen and I didn't want to disappoint or fail them, not now they'd at last got the motivation to stand up for their children.

'We could take the school bus,' I offered doubtfully, 'but

how many people would be able to come? It would have to be a working day and could your kids manage it? It's a four hour trip. They'll go berserk.'

'We could go overnight – make an excursion of it,' suggested Jenny.

'That's right,' agreed someone else. 'Lots of schools go on excursion to Parliament. What better way for our kids to learn about democracy?'

'I suppose we could do it, if you're all up for it.' I looked at Jenny for guidance. 'Is this a serious decision Madam President?'

'You bet it is,' said Jenny. 'I for one don't want to be walked over. We've had to fight for our kids all their lives and mostly we get nowhere because we're just one voice. We get beaten down and we feel hopeless. You've just pulled off this amazing building, created a fantastic place for our kids with the best opportunities and straight up someone's trying to take it away from us. Well, we're not going to let it happen. I vote we go to Canberra.' A burst of clapping and over it Conall's Dad called out, 'Carried unanimously.' I looked around at their eager faces, feeling the thrill of a shared cause.

I found out the next sitting of Parliament was in two months time. The parents had confidently handed all the planning over to me. Since the meeting, my enthusiasm, such as it was, had begun to wane. I feared we'd look ridiculous, a little special school marching on the Houses of Parliament in the country's capital, a mouse roaring at a lion. I had little hope we could command attention for our cause or that anyone would care. I tried to swell our numbers by appealing to other special schools that had lost funding. The principals were sympathetic but sceptical. 'Our parents aren't like yours, Jo. They don't have the confidence your parents have,' Frank Pitt, the principal from Mater Dei said to me. I understood very well. Our parents hadn't had the confidence before now.

'I'm really stuck,' I said anxiously to Zandra as we indulged in our old habit of throwing creative ideas around in the gloom of the local pub. 'We might only get a couple of dozen families there. A straggly little bunch trying to look like a march.'

'Then we need a panorama-sized visual splash. Let's get t-shirts made for everyone with slogans on them and red balloons and banners for them to carry. At least we can look good on the television cameras if we all bunch up. And if we have the TV cameras then we can get the politicians out to meet the children, make our point that way.' So I asked all the relevant politicians and got courteous 'maybe' responses from the Liberal Opposition but not even a nibble from the government of the day. I wrote to the Hon. Julia Gillard, then Minister for Education, and told her what had happened to our funding, how much I admired her and asked to meet her in person. There was no response.

'You need to get the media involved,' Christina my daughter said to me. 'To prod her out.'

'But I don't know how!' I looked at her pleadingly. She had been a journalist before Alex's birth and I knew she had the skills to help, but more than that, I was in a blue funk and wanted her with me. She and my son Michael had both shunned helping out at the school, saying employing in-laws was bad enough. Now Christina gave me one of her long, blank looks I could never read, and relented.

'OK,' she said with a sigh, 'just this once, though.' It gave me heart, knowing she'd be alongside. I was able to get my panic under control. As she climbed into my Subaru for the trip south, the night before the march, she said, 'You have an interview with Julia Gillard at 10 'o'clock tomorrow morning.'

'What? How come? What happened?'

'I managed to get a radio interview for you on the ABC's AM programme tomorrow morning and then I rang Julia Gillard's personal assistant and told her you'd be interviewed about the 100 disabled children and parents travelling to Canberra to plead with her. She called back half an hour ago and said the Minister wants to meet with you.'

It was nearly midnight by the time we reached the Canberra motel. I was exhausted, too tired to eat and with no idea how many families were there or who would be taking part the next day. I slept fitfully and staggered bleary eyed and faintly nauseous into the breakfast room the next morning to find that at every table there was a family from our school. Little Jillian Jones sitting solemnly with her mother, a pink plastic handbag hanging over her shoulder and a doll on the table; Conall drawing cars on a napkin as he sat companionably with his father; Lachlan small and solemn with his sister and parents. Everywhere were families who had done days of difficult preparations, got time off work, put themselves through a testing drive with fractious children. Now they were filling the breakfast room, cheerfully calling out to each other. 'Never thought I'd be part of a protest march,' Conall's father joked as I passed his table.

'I hope we achieve something.'

'I don't know,' he said cheerfully. 'It feels good, whatever happens.' Back in my motel room I did the radio interview and then Christina and I drove to the gathering place at old Parliament House. It wasn't hard to find. Zandra was already there and unmissable. She had erected the banners and laid out trestle tables with t-shirts of every size for the marchers and packs of water bottles. Above the tables floated clouds of red helium balloons donated by the Balloon Lady in Sydney. The school bus bringing Pia and a load of children from school hadn't arrived yet but already there were large numbers of children and adults dressed in the white t-shirts with the slogan *Are We Part of the Education Revolution?* emblazoned in red. I saw Doug there, the principal of Boys Town, and several parents from other special schools. A Canberra friend who I'd known since Kindergarten and last seen at Costi's funeral turned up with a load of lemonade ice blocks for the children and best of all, a colleague who headed up one of Canberra's prestigious boys' schools appeared with a dozen boys, members of the school's drum band. Berenice had brought Selina and Abbey's mother Faye was there. Abbey was flourishing in her second year of high school and Faye had become a fervent advocate for special schools. I asked her to come with me to the interview with the Minister, so she could speak from the heart as a parent.

The press began to arrive, local and Sydney radio and TV journalists. Christina had done well and for the next hour she was busy briefing them and grabbing children and parents for comments. I looked nervously at my watch. 9.30. Just about time to leave the scene here and go meet with the Minister. It was hard to pull away from the buzzing, excited families with the school bus due to arrive any minute, but in fact the march was not due to take off until 12.00 so there was plenty of time for me to speak to the Minister and get back to be part of it all.

When Faye and I reached the green marble foyer of Australia's parliament house, we had to press through a crowd of school children to give our details to the official in charge. Then we had to stand about waiting for more than half an hour in the noisy, congested lobby before the Minister's executive assistant finally appeared to take us to her office. There we were told that the Minister had ducked out to speak to one of the teachers' unions in town and no one knew when she'd be back. Her advisor sat talking politely to us, drawing Faye out on her experiences with Abbey, while I fidgeted and fretted. Over an hour had passed and I had to get back.

A flurry at the door and the Minister entered, her red hair and energy making her unmistakable. She uttered a cheerful 'be with you in a minute' and disappeared into her office. When she came back, ten minutes later, I cleared my throat ready to launch into my carefully prepared castigation of our cut in funding when I felt a tickle on my vocal chords, the familiar warning that I was about to have a coughing attack, the embarrassing kind that overtook me sometimes when I was under stress. My throat swelled, my chest heaved and with ugly wheezing gasps I struggled for breath, tears running down my face, unable to speak, sitting there hot and helpless. And the Minister became suddenly solicitous, sent her aide off for a glass of water and told a funny story of having a coughing attack during a radio interview to give me time to recover. When I finally stammered out our reason for being there, she was understanding itself. She pinpointed the critical issues, she asked questions about the children's disabilities, she drew me out on our finances and she got Faye to relate bragging stories of Abbey. Finally, with a glance at her watch, she leaned back in her chair.

'You know, your problem is not with government. It is with your Catholic Education people. They're the ones you should be talking to.' Then she rose to her feet and signalled that the interview was over.

As she shepherded us considerately towards the door, she turned to me and asked in a conversational tone whether our school had benefitted from the Building the Education Revolution funding that was receiving a very mixed press at the time. 'Oh yes,' I replied eagerly, keen to repay the kindness she had shown us and babbled on about our new specially fitted bathrooms and wheelchair lift and what a difference they had made. Suddenly the Minister had gone and Faye and I looked at each other.

'That went well,' we said to each other, pleased. I floated down the marble staircase and out onto the steps of Parliament House and it was only there, as I looked out across the expanse of green lawn that spread all the way up to the steps that I remembered with a sudden return to reality that the march was due to start at 12.00. I looked at my watch and could have howled. Twelve o'clock! Where had the time vanished? It would take me ages to get across the acres of grass to where the families were waiting for me and then more time to get them assembled. That clever red head, I thought, blaming her in my dismay. Had she delayed us deliberately? Was it because she knew the TV crews and news journalists wouldn't wait, that they'd go off to their next assignment and there'd be no footage of the children's march on people's television sets that night? Probably the Opposition members wouldn't hang around either once the media had left. What a naive idiot I was, I thought as I stood dumbly on the steps in the hot glaring sun, numbed by my own culpability. To have let the families down like that after they had come so far; to have let myself be so charmed by a politician's attention that I forgot the time.

Then I heard very faintly the distant sound of drumming. Staring through the shimmering haze of heat, I could just discern movement beyond the trees in the far distance. Something red. Was it balloons? The drumming grew louder and now I could see children, parents, a whole mass of red and white that seemed to grow and grow, moving forward to the pulsing drum beat. On and on they came, a jubilant crowd advancing through the trees and onto the huge stretch of lawn that led up to Parliament House. And the TV cameras and radio microphones were there and a group of Opposition members were coming down the steps. Then the sound of singing as the crowd surged forward and came to a stop in front of the seat of government, the children's piping voices leading their parents in their favourite song: *'We are one, but we are many, and from all the lands on earth we come. We share a dream and speak with one voice, we are Australian.'*

As the Opposition leader began a fulsome speech about the need for more funding for special schools, I walked down towards the mass of children and parents, emotional with pride and relief. They hadn't needed me. This was their work, this was them. They were a community. I went through the mechanics of greeting the politicians and acting as the spokesperson but all the while I was in a euphoric daze. 'Your eyes are leaking,' young Conall said curiously and gave me his red balloon.

It was hot and Christina and I lay motionless in the shade of the now empty trestle tables, desultorily filling each other in on our part of the morning's events. Zandra had arranged a special experience for the children and families at Questacon, the science museum in Canberra, for the afternoon but I was too tired to join them. Some eager parents had gone to the public gallery for Question Time to hear the Opposition challenge the government on the cuts to our school's funding but I no longer had a stomach for politics. A number of families had stayed to picnic on the lawns and in a little while I moved among them chatting and thanking them. Suddenly there was a posse of parents surrounding me, vociferous and angry. 'What's that you said to the Minister?' they clamoured to know.

'Why, what's happened? What was said in Question Time?'

'Well, the Shadow Minister got up and challenged the government about our funding and Julia Gillard said that oh yes, she'd met with Mrs Karaolis this morning and Mrs

Karaolis was thrilled with the building grant the school had got through the Education Revolution money! Is that right? Is that what you talked about? She never even mentioned the cut in funding!' I felt suddenly sick. What an astute and clever politician. The parents told me she had been jubilant in Parliament as she threw my words about the new bathrooms and wheelchair lift back at the Opposition members, deflecting their efforts to argue for a reinstatement of our funding. I was terribly upset to have let them all down. She had won the battle on the floor of the House and I'd given her the bullets to fire.

But later, when I'd had time to reflect, I decided that after all, we had had the more significant victory that day. Nothing could beat that amazing moment when the parents, from their own inner strength and without need of me, had walked the distance from voicelessness to activism. 'It's the best demonstration I've seen here,' one of Parliament's security guards had said to me as I stood in the sun watching. 'They're all so happy and full of life, proud really. I hope you get your funding back.'

Two months later, without any heralding, we did. No notice, no letter of explanation. But there on the special assistance grants line of Razi's accounts was a large sum, restoring all that had been taken away and adding a bit more. I never knew to whom we owed the reversal. Was it the Minister? Did the government restore funding to the Catholic Schools Board or did the Catholic Schools

Board redistribute funding to the special schools? We never found out. But that year marked a turning point. After it came new initiatives from the government: the Gonski review of school funding which explicitly included children with disabilities in its mandate and later, at Julia Gillard's personal behest in her now role of Prime Minister, additional interim funding for children with special needs. I liked to think that the Minister's kindly sympathy for Faye's and my stories of the children had been genuine; that her clever political game-playing was only one part of what happened at Parliament House that day.

Back home, the parents formed a lobby group. It was Carolyn, one of the mothers who'd been to Canberra, who set it up. 'We need to make sure our funding can't be cut again,' she told them, but I think it was more than that. Now six months pregnant with bad morning sickness, riddled with anxiety over her frequently hospitalised son, she had nonetheless discovered a power in herself and others she did not want to let go. She worked like a terrier let loose in a burrow of ferrets, researching the federal and state members of parliament for every child in the school until she had run every one of them to ground. She trained parents in how to approach their local MP and wrote material for them to hand out when they visited, including the shocking participation rates of people with disabilities in homelessness, mental health problems and imprisonment statistics. 'They knocked us down once too often,' Carolyn said. 'It taught us justice only happens if you fight for it. Besides, it gives me energy, knowing I'm part of something, belonging, contributing.'

GOING OUTBACK

We were back in the conference room at the Catholic Schools Board and my old friend the Director was in full flight. 'It's all very well for you special schools in Sydney,' he was saying as I doodled on my printed meeting agenda, drawing his long trousers and sharp black shoes and beginning on his manicured hands so as to distract myself from the exasperation in his rising tones. 'The country dioceses don't see why you special schools get favoured treatment,' he went on, 'when they have to put their kids with disabilities into their ordinary schools. You get terribly precious, you principals. Out bush they don't have speech therapists and psychologists on hand like you do. And then there are the indigenous issues.' I drew an arrow straight through the white shirt front of my cartoon figure but in fact Mr Grey Suit had a point. The excellent facilities and services that we now had were only possible because we were in a big city where we could tap generous philanthropists for help and there were readily accessible services. Out in the far regions of New South Wales even money couldn't buy expert intervention for children with disabilities and wealthy philanthropists were thin on the ground.

I scribbled out the doodle and leaned back in my chair to stare blankly at the wall behind the speaker's head. The wind was whipping around my legs and the wild crash of waves was in my ears. I was eight years old and on holiday with my sister not far from my uncle's cattle station at Temma on the barren west coast of Tasmania. Left to our own devices while the men were away fishing, we'd come across a huge stretch of middens, far more than we'd ever seen before. They ran for miles and miles along the beach line, no end that we could see, the shells packed in tight layers where they'd been undisturbed for several lifetimes. 'How many people there must have been, to leave all these,' my sister said. Where were they now, I wondered, the women and children who had layered the shellfish there?

'You drove them to their death, you exterminated them all!' Our proudly British social studies teacher, Miss Curtis, stood at the front of our Year 7 class, red in the face, baying in a caustic English accent. I hated her. But I borrowed a book from the Launceston library and read how George Arthur Robinson, Tasmania's official Protector of Aboriginals, puffed up with good intentions, in 1834 resettled on Flinders Island the last known 150 Tasmanian Aboriginals who had escaped disease and death. And how they died anyway of sickness and heartache, wrested from their land and their customs.

'It was inevitable,' my mother said. 'Don't make such a meal of it. The strong survive, that's how life is.' I looked at her, not feeling strong at all. Later at Melbourne University I learned that anyone from Tasmania was a joke. 'It's all that in-breeding,' the mainlanders said. 'It spawns extra digits and fewer brains. And anyway, you killed all your Aborigines.' I carried the guilt of my island past for years until I started teaching history at a Sydney school from the brave new 1970's textbooks and discovered how many parts of Australia had their ugly history of black massacres.

At St Catherine's in the 1990's it was a different age. The Chairman of the Council cared about what happened to Aboriginal people and together we set up a scholarship scheme. Most of the children came from La Perouse or other parts of Sydney but I wanted to reach country areas too. That's how I connected with the all-black community of Mugajaa Rock Hole, eighty kilometres south of Alice Springs and Carina became our first boarder.

Carina's parents asked me to be her guardian which meant responsibility for everything from getting her the right glasses to staring down uppity sales clerks who hovered watchfully behind her in Sydney's classy department stores. She teased me for my ambitions for her and joked through the homework help I tried to give her and I loved her. She said that she was going to have a baby as soon as she got out of school and I thought she was teasing but it was what she wanted and what she did after she got her HSC and went home. Other Aboriginal girls who had scholarships with us at the same time as Carina went on to university; one studied medicine at King's College, Cambridge. I had watched them grow, I had seen them learn. I knew first hand how Aboriginal kids gained opportunity and confidence from good schooling.

But there were no students at our special school who identified as Aboriginal. When Mr Grey Suit had finished his harangue and the meeting was breaking up, I went to ask him how I could connect with regional Aboriginal students with disabilities and he referred me to the head of parent services. Before I left the building, I had made an appointment to speak at the next meeting with Aboriginal parents and education workers. 'I'm only giving you a time slot to speak,' the coordinator of parent services said. 'It will be up to them whether they take up your offer.' The next meeting was three months away. Three months to find funding for the partnership I had in mind. With Zandra's help, I was eventually successful with the James N. Kirby Foundation which included Aboriginal projects in its grants profile.

The quarterly meeting of Aboriginal parents and education workers was held in the Catholic School Board conference room but the atmosphere was very different from one of our meetings: noisy chatter and loud guffaws mingled with the clink of cups and the dark faces of twenty or thirty Aboriginal women chatting together or calling jokingly across the room. An awkward silence fell when I was introduced as the principal of a special school. I began with a PowerPoint I'd prepared but the women didn't pretend to watch it. They sat back, arms folded across their chests, eyes to the floor or staring at the ceiling. After ten minutes, I abandoned the presentation and asked them outright if they knew why we had no Aboriginal students coming to our school.

'Cos we don't have kids with disabilities,' a woman sitting near me said.

'You don't?'

'Nah, we just have kids. Them's all just kids, is what.'

'But don't any of them need a bit of extra help? I'm wanting to offer some extra help to those kids who struggle with their class work.' A large woman in a bright blue top sitting at the back of the room got noisily to her feet. 'We know your kind of help,' she scoffed, leaning against the wall. 'You white fellers come out with your tests and assessments and then you sends us reports on our kids. 'N the reports say horrible things about the kids, how they're behind in this and can't do that and how they have to have speech therapy 'n whatever. And then nothin' happens. Cos there ain't therapists around 'n the waiting list is six months' long. So nah, we don't want y' help, no thanks.' There were a few nods. I looked around the unyielding faces and realised I'd made a mistake thinking that getting the grant would be the hard part.

I shut down the offending PowerPoint and bent low to switch off the computer. As I did, Carina's teasing voice came into my head, laughing at me and I suddenly saw me as I looked to these women, a citified professional know-it-all expert, standing out the front and telling them their business. I shoved the computer to one side and sat on the table and did what I should have done at the beginning. I told them about my mob, about Costi and the kids and Alex and about Carina. 'We all love our kids. We all want the best for them. I'm not here to tell you what to do. I'm asking to be a sister school and to share our stuff.' As I spoke, I could feel the tension slacken and a murmuring of voices begin. The woman in blue up the back got slowly to her feet. Those near turned to look at her expectantly and I took a breath.

'D'ya mean that?' she said, hand on hip and head cocked to one side, 'bout bein' a sister school? Cause I reckon that's OK, if yer come in and get on with helpin' the kids and bringin' resources they can use and stuff. If that's what yer mean, I reckon yer can come out 'n talk to us.' She paused and then added, 'I'm from the diocese out west.'

The sprawling western diocese was part of the Australian outback; sparsely populated and very isolated, it covered half of NSW. I was elated by the invitation but I'd have to go through the local Director of Education who might, I knew, take offence at my interference. After the meeting I emailed the diocesan education office and requested a meeting with the Director. I received a positive reply and I set about booking flights, juggling appointments in my diary and negotiating dates with Pippa, the new young speech therapist who I wanted to come with me. There was just one thing I forgot. 'You're kidding!' Pippa exclaimed, staring at me in polite disbelief as we sat in the airport waiting lounge at six o'clock in the morning. 'They don't know we're coming?' I nodded, feeling sick, then buried my head in the free newspaper and prayed for a miracle.

'You couldn't have come on a worse day,' was the Director's flustered greeting when we finally got to meet her at one o'clock in the afternoon, after being sent off by the secretary to fill in time at the Parkes radio telescope nearby. The spring-tight curls on the Director's small fair head shook reprovingly as she made sure I understood the enormity of my presumption. I smiled as placatingly as I could but she went on to explain that this was the day they had brought all their principals in from their scattered distant schools to plan the new school halls they were able to build under the recently announced Building the Education Revolution. The government had introduced the BER scheme at the time of the GFC (Global Financial Crisis of 2008) to boost the economy by building school halls across the country, a boon everywhere but especially in remote NSW.

'It's our only day,' the agitated Director went on. 'We have architects and builders here to advise the principals and it's a big deal.' She shook her head at me and I had a sinking feeling that my thoughtlessness had lost us the partnership I hoped for. 'We do have another session this afternoon, with a consultant psychologist. I can ask her to give you a few minutes but her time is short so I don't know what she'll say.' She went off and Pippa smiled encouragingly at me.

'It's actually a great opportunity, having all the principals here,' she said, 'I bet if you'd remembered to ask for a date, they'd have said today wasn't an option.' I wished I had her young person's optimism. I was expecting a no. We sat for a while and eventually the Director reappeared.

'You didn't tell me you know Joy Cummings.' It sounded like a reprimand. I shook my head. 'Well, she knows you and she says it's a miracle that you've turned up today. She's the psychologist who has been doing the assessments in our schools. She's especially worried about Nicawinna, outback of Broken Hill. Says the kids' language skills are so low the whole lot need special education and that the methods you use at your school will help.' I'd never heard of Joy Cummings but I wasn't about to say so. Instead I seized her suggestion that I speak to the gathered principals and by the end of the day we had a partnership with the Catholic infants' school at Nicawinna. Over a celebratory drink at the Parkes' pub, I discovered that Joy was best friends with the special needs co-ordinator at St Cath's.

'It's a bit uncanny,' Pippa said as we waited on a windy tarmac for the plane home. 'How you stuff up and yet it all works out.'

Two months later she and I were sitting on the community bus on our first journey to the erstwhile mission school of Nicawinna. We had flown to Broken Hill and caught this small bus alongside a handful of Aboriginal women laden with their shopping. Through the bus window were endless stretches of red desert soil sparsely dotted with spinifex and mallee scrub and occasional rocky outcrops. A shimmer of heat lay above the black bitumen road and from time to time, stretches of bone-shaking red gravel. I looked at my watch. We'd been on the bus more than two hours; Nicawinna could only be twenty minutes away now.

'Do they know we're coming?' Pippa asked, grinning at me. I made a face. I liked Pippa. In the two months since our visit to the western diocese, I had given her an increasingly free hand and she'd risen to the challenge with a maturity and insight way beyond her years. But what I loved most was her excitement at this adventure, something she'd dreamed about as a student, taking her knowledge and skills – and a borrowed audiometer – out to where they were needed most. I wished I was young like her, not prey to anxiety about what we would find and whether the Aboriginal community would be open to us working with their kids.

'Must be something happening at the bridge,' the driver said as we got our first glimpse of the Darling River lying shallow and sluggish within its high red banks. I peered ahead but couldn't see anything except the towering steel truss of the old lift mechanism as the bus trundled across the bridge. Minutes later we pulled up alongside a large sign announcing the Catholic Community School. Pippa and I swung our bags onto our backs and made our way through neatly tended vegetable and flower beds to the pleasant red brick house whose door stood invitingly open. Fenced in alongside the garden were three demountable classrooms sitting in bare red dirt with some brightly coloured play equipment visible out the back.

The house was empty. A note on the kitchen bench from Sister Patricia said she'd had to go out unexpectedly and could we put the vegetables on for dinner. It was dark by the time she turned up and the strain in her face and body, as she wearily dropped into a chair, made me see with a start that she was much older than I'd thought when I met her at the conference at the diocese. One of those sterling women who seem ageless – until something happens and suddenly years are added. She had spent the last couple of hours, she said, talking a woman out of jumping from the bridge. 'They always send for Loreto or me,' she said. 'But Loreto's in Adelaide just now. We've known most of the people in town since they were kids you see. Loreto's the one who sits by them when they're dying.'

Patricia and Loreto were both Sisters of Mercy and had been at the former Mission school long enough to see a generation of students grow up and send their own children to them to begin their schooling. There were twenty-seven children on the school's books, Sister Patricia told us, but they didn't all turn up, even though the school bus did the rounds, house by house, each morning to collect them.

Pippa settled quickly to work the next day, testing each child's hearing and language. The task ended up taking her the whole time we were there and she loved every minute, working with children more vocal and more confident than at our school at home and quite irrepressible. As for me, Sister Patricia gave me free run of the school so I could assess what it needed and put together a schedule of what we could offer.

There were two classes, one of kindergarteners and one a composite of Years 1 and 2. For their later years the children went on to the government-run Central School. There were signs of money spent on facilities. The latest in electronic whiteboards in both classrooms which unfortunately couldn't be used because no one knew how to adjust them. Plenty of books in the library, all but two of them being of white children in cities or farmyards or at the beach. A good collection of teacher resources but most missing pieces. Three computers for the older children to use when they finished their work. Sister Patricia wasn't a trained teacher: her job as principal was to run the school which included preparing the children's breakfast and lunch and doing the administration. There were Aboriginal Education Workers (AEWs) helping in each room but getting teachers was Sister Patricia's biggest headache, she told me and the next biggest was keeping them, in a town where there was nothing for young people to do and few white people to socialise with.

When Pippa and I conferred at the end of that first day, we'd both formed the same conclusion. These children were of normal ability with a few very bright ones and a few strugglers. Only one showed up on Pippa's audiometer tests as having a hearing impairment but the language tests assessed most as having a severe language disability. 'This is why they scored so badly on the IQ test that Joy Cummings gave them,' Pippa said. 'Their language deficits and the fact that they can't sit still and can't concentrate for more than a few minutes.'

We sat up late that night discussing what help we could give that would make the most difference. Pippa was keen to come up for a week each term and develop language programmes for children and teachers, and she thought it was urgent to have an occupational therapist come with her to build a programme of integrated body and brain activities into the school day to help the children spend longer at their desks. I wanted to get Marta up to get all their technology working for them. After that she could provide IT support by phone from back in Sydney. I longed to relieve the dullness of their schoolroom days with art and drama lessons. They were such bubbly, lively kids and the creativity oozed out of them, but only in the playground and down at the community swimming pool. And I was on fire to do something about the Anglocentric curriculum and resources in the school. The children's first learning should draw on their own experiences here in the bush. Sister Patricia had shown me notes that a teacher at the school had made years before recording local language, stories and traditional knowledge of the elders and I itched to turn it into learning resources for the children.

In the years that followed we did all that we planned that night. The James N Kirby Foundation funded the costly air fares for two staff to visit Nicawinna each term of every year. Mostly it was the speech and occupational therapists. Pia and Mab, our art and drama teachers, ran lessons from our school via Skype for the Nicawinna children to share in. I worked with three local elders to re-write curriculum using traditional fish traps, earth ovens and bush medicine to teach principles of science and technology, local dreamtime and folk stories as part of their literature and for history, the stories, funny and terrible, of early encounters with white folk and the horror of massacres retained in living memory. It took me a couple of summers before I had it all done. I hesitated over the massacres. 'Are you sure you want them to know this?' I asked one of the elders. 'They're only little remember, only six or seven.'

'I don't want them to be scared,' he said. 'But I want them to know we didn't just stand by and let the land be taken. We were carers of the land and we owed hospitality to the strangers. The white people took advantage of that, then they attacked us. We didn't stand a chance. I want the kids to know that.'

In the third year of our sister-school arrangement, Sister Patricia retired and Sister Loreto reluctantly left with her. I was dismayed and despondent. I couldn't see how anyone could replace them, not the way they had stuck around for years supporting the community through heartbreak and despair. But then a new young principal was appointed who had done his first years of teaching at Nicawinna and made friends in the town and been married in the Nicawinna church. Brandan was ambitious for the school and to my delight, was ready to call on us for the help he couldn't get outback. I got used to hearing his voice on the phone asking, 'Jo do you think you could …'

All that came later. On this first visit it was just castles in the air. We were outsiders from a big city far away. We had no authority to impose our ideas and vision. Getting the money to make it happen was less of a problem, to my mind, than winning the support of the local people. Sister Patricia, who was enthusiastic about our proposals, seemed to think me over-fastidious but there was no way I was going ahead without local agreement. I kept asking her how I could meet the children's parents or speak to their Aunties and Uncles but it was not until our last day, after I insisted, that Sister Patricia asked Aunty Grace, one of the Aboriginal Education Workers to take me down town. I could see Aunty Grace wasn't happy about it. With her head down, she kept on chopping apples for a while, then, on Sister Patricia's third prompt, wiped her hands, took off her apron, lifted the keys off the nail near the door and disappeared without saying a word. 'Better hurry or she'll go without you,' Sister Patricia said grinning.

It was the hottest day we'd had since we arrived and the main street lay deserted in the white glare of the sun. Most of the shops and businesses had been boarded up but there was an IGA store and Aunty Grace pulled the bus up outside it. In the shock of the dark inside I couldn't at first see the dark figure of an Aboriginal woman behind the counter. There seemed to be no customers. I introduced myself and stumbled through an awkward explanation that I was in town to help up at the school. Silence. 'Do you have children at the school?' I asked. 'Nah,' the woman said. Back in the bus, Aunty Grace drove slowly across the wide street and swerved into the town's service station where a van was parked. A woman, a man and a couple of kids sat inside it. I got out and poked my head through the car window. A bare two minutes of explaining what I was doing up at the school. 'Good oh,' the man said opening the car door in my face and going off into the service station. I climbed back into the bus. 'The streets are so empty. Where is everyone?'

'Pay day,' Aunty Grace mumbled. I looked at her uncomprehendingly.

'Thursday. Pay day,' she said again, staring straight ahead. 'People come to town for their pay,' and when I still looked blank she said dully, 'They're at the pub.'

'Then let's go there,' I said reaching for the door handle. 'That'd be just the thing.'

'No!' she said loudly, and then with control, 'no, we can't go there.'

'It's all right, I'm all right to go.' I jumped down from the bus.

'You can't go in there, not alone,' she said, 'and I'm not going with you.'

I sighed and gave up on the pub. But on the opposite corner of the street a group of Aboriginal men and women lounged, talking and laughing. This seemed like a go. I crossed over and as I got close, saw a store of bottles near their feet and some broken glass. Ribald laughter and a few curious looks. I felt nervous but it was my last day and I had to get some kind of okay from the local people. 'I wonder if I can have a few words with you?' I asked from a few metres away, uncomfortably conscious of my plummy vowels.

'Ya wanna speak with us love? Then just you go ahead and do it!' laughed one of the men, adding 'Ya wanna beer?' I shook my head. I was so hot and flustered I'd have liked to have said yes, except that Aunty Grace was watching from the bus.

'Let 'er speak,' a woman standing near me said and I launched into my story again. She peered closely into my face all the while I was talking. 'I got grandkids at the school,' she said. 'Tibby and Donald. D'ya know 'em?' That was easy. Tibby was a smart little will o' the wisp who flitted between chairs and practised cartwheels. Donald was plump and struggled with reading.

'They're great kids,' I said, 'but they could do with some one-on-one help. That's what I want to do, bring people to the school who can help.'

'Are you gonna be a blow-in?' she asked with sudden seriousness, leaning close into my face and breathing beer over me. 'Cos we've had a stomach full of 'em. Come up here and promise the earth. They're gonna do this and they're gonna do that. And then they blow off and we never see nor hear of 'em again.'

'No, that's just the point,' I said earnestly. 'We want to be a sister school.'

'Oh, a sister school,' she said. 'Youse'd be sisters to our kids, would yer? Yeah, I reckon that'd be the go. Wadda ya reckon?' she said to the others though they seemed to have stopped listening. 'Ya reckon we're OK with her school being sisters with the Mission school, helpin' our kids? Wadda ya say?'

'Oh yeah, love. Good on yer! Have a beer?' There was a chorus of voices and I shook hands with them all as though we'd made a deal. Aunty Grace said nothing when I climbed back into the bus but the squeal of tires as she pressed her foot to the accelerator was comment enough.

Trivia Night on Thursdays at the bowling club was a big deal. The Mission School and the Central School were fierce rivals and Sister Patricia was counting on Pippa and me to ensure a victory. I hoped Pippa's cool head would be up to it because I was flat exhausted after the morning's expedition and saying goodbye to the children in the afternoon. There was an Aboriginal crowd standing in the street light at the entrance to the bowling club when Sister Patricia pulled up in the bus. I thought at first they were queuing up to go in but Sister Patricia strode past them and belatedly I saw they had slabs of beer on the roofs of a couple of cars and seemed to be camped in for the night. A woman's slurred voice called out from the dark. 'Hey there, aren't you the lady's gonna help our kids?' I stopped. It was the woman from the morning. She was grinning and reeked of ale. 'Yer goin' back on the bus tonight, ain't yer?' I nodded.

'An' yer comin' back, right?'

'Yes, yes I am. We are.'

She leaned forward and pulled me into a beery hug. For a moment time slipped away. I was a child again, mourning over the middens of shells on a windswept beach, the generations of dispossession of a people. She hugged me close. 'See yer when you come back, Sis,' she said.

HARRY

Harry had been away a long time. He was still away when Sister Clare, whose term on the Board had expired, became pastoral carer at the school. We heard that the Starlight Foundation had granted Harry a wish, a wish for all the family to be together in Tasmania for Christmas. Then in January a parent said Harry had been rushed back from Tasmania to Westmead hospital in Sydney. Later we learned he had been moved to Bear Cottage, the children's hospice at Manly. Kelly, his teacher for that year, resolutely displayed his photo with the rest of the class and his name was printed above his empty bag peg, but there was no Harry.

And then one day he did come back. He was taller

and thinner and one side of his face was stiff but he had great wheels: a big black Whomobile with fifteen different positions that turned on a fifty cent piece, so Harry said. He was surprised and rather miffed when he came to his first morning song to find a strange woman talking to his teacher like she belonged. He zoomed his wheelchair away and stared balefully at her from the other side of the worship space. Sister Clare ignored him, which was new to him. He had to whiz his chair back to get her attention. Sister Clare had a way of smiling through to your soul. 'I don't know who you are,' he said grudgingly, 'and I don't know what you're doing here. But I'm Harry. And I like you.'

'I like you too, Harry.'

'Then you can wheel me to class if you like.' There Harry got a huge reception. They were making a film for our inaugural film festival and Kelly appointed Harry the director and camera man. The high vantage point of his Whomobile gave him the perfect angle for the tripod and camera and years of dictating to his father, Lyell, the terms on which he would live each day had prepared him well to be a peremptory and decisive director. And Kelly could relax since a film made by Harry would be sure to win accolades.

The rest of the staff resented my insistence that they all make a film but I persisted. The camera offered the children a voice, I believed. Their eyes, their laughter, the things they were able to say, gave hints of so much more than they had words for. From my first chats with Pia about the creative arts, I had wanted to put a camera into every child's hand, the way in other schools you put a pencil and then a pen. At first I tried to convince staff by presenting them with research showing the importance of visual communication for children with language delay and Zandra got cameras donated for each classroom. But they led a checkered life, those cameras, often found at the bottom of a fish tank or dismembered against a wall. 'Pencils are easier to hand out,' was Marta's answer when I questioned why the staff weren't taking to film and photography as another language for the kids.

'The teachers are stuck in an old paradigm of learning; they don't get visual communication,' was Pia's answer. I resorted to compulsion. Each class teacher was to produce a class video for an inaugural film festival and all the children and families would be invited to submit photographs to a companion photography exhibition to be held the same night.

'I'm not creative,' wailed some; 'I'm rubbish with a camera,' complained another.

'She can whistle for it,' Sybil said loftily. But they did it anyway and as they experimented with the medium they grew ambitious and competitive. I loved the way the culture of the school had become a life force, a faith of its own. Though some staff had moved on and new ones had come, the spirit of the place carried us forward together, even into paths we didn't choose. Anything became possible. Eight year old Theo's film was about ants. His camera followed them from small cracks across the face of a red brick wall to other cracks and down, and along and in and from, the journeying of ants. I couldn't wait for Ernesto to see his son George's class film: George was starring in it as the boy who stole the pie. It was a comic triumph and I assured Pia that the climax when George pulled off the old pie-in-the-face routine would give Ernesto more of a boost than a 200 point rise in the All Ordinaries.

We held the film festival in the new creative arts centre and set up the photography exhibition in the gallery where we were also serving drinks before the festival. The photographs were extraordinary: a glimpse of the world through the eyes of the children. Numerous photos of feet; a geometric study of car tyres; portraits of teachers; a photo of a fly on a peeled banana.

By 6.30 pm the gallery was crowded with parents and I wove my way between them, warm greetings on all sides, anxiously seeking Seth's parents. Only half an hour before the film showing began and I wanted to watch their faces when they saw his photographs. They'd been dismayed when I first told them Seth was learning photography. 'But he's blind!' they protested. It had been Marta's idea. She thought Seth was rather isolated, especially when Harry was away. She saw photography as a way for him to share with others what he heard and felt. She taught him to listen for sounds and train the camera to where they were coming from; to track after smells and zoom the lens to where they were strongest, and when he felt the warmth of the sun on his skin, to aim the camera towards it. Then she described for him what he had captured, giving him visual images to put with what he knew through his other senses.

Now here were his photographs, the gleam of silver sun rays through cloud, a late gardenia nestled in a floret of dark green leaves, the thick branch of a tree against an expanse of blue sky. And next to them, photographs that Seth took of himself using a tripod with a remote control cable. I noticed that the milling, moving crowd of parents fell silent in front of those self-portraits. Seth, concentrating mightily to stay still and in position while he pressed the button on the remote, had caught on his unseeing soulful face with its huge brown eyes, an iconic image of solitariness.

Ah, there were Seth's parents near the door, deep in conversation with long-haired Lori, young Scott's mother. I was surprised to see Scott's father Hugh was there too, his big arm around Lori. A busy engineer who travelled a lot, Hugh rarely made it to school events. I pushed as hard as I politely could through the press of backs, bursting to take Seth's parents to see his photographs, but when I got close, a stillness about the group stayed me. Lori turned and with a tremulous smile reached her hand out to me. 'I've just come from the hospital,' she said. 'They say I've got cancer.

It's in the pancreas.' Now she was laughing, dabbing at her eyes and apologising for being emotional in public, she who never drew attention to herself. She leaned into Hugh's sheltering shoulder. 'We're going to fight it,' she said. 'We're going to win.' Pia's voice in upbeat mode burst from the microphone to summon us into the Possibility Space for the Inaugural Film Festival. In the surge of parents towards the door, Lori drew me aside and whispered, 'I can't see Lyell. Is Harry all right?' I shrugged, unable to speak. Not Lori too. I felt as though the Apocolypse's white horseman, bringer of pestilence, was attacking the walls and I couldn't keep him out. Lori and I clung to each other for a moment.

Cancer was everywhere. Sister Clare who'd been free of it for many years was in chemotherapy again for secondaries, though she kept turning up at school. 'Don't look like that, Jo,' she said when she told me. 'I've had a wonderful life.' But I couldn't help it. After Costi, my husband, died, I had developed a chronic hypersensitivity to the pain and grief that come with death. So when a vibrant, freckle-faced young woman called Morgan replied to our advertisement for casual teachers and said she was recovering from cancer, I shrank a little.

'What do you mean, recovering?' I asked tentatively.

'Well, they told me I had the most rampant form of breast cancer there is and that I would die, but that was ages ago and here I am.' She giggled. I couldn't say no; after all, we had advertised. And I thought a casual teacher who came and went spasmodically wouldn't get into everyone's hearts as much as someone like Sister Clare or Harry or Scott's mother Lori. But in fact Morgan did; she was the most positive person I had ever known. She volunteered for everything, she had answers to every difficulty. She was effervescent in the classroom. So when the teacher who had replaced Robyn Thomas was in turn head-hunted by Ronald MacDonald House, Morgan was the obvious replacement and I talked down my fear. 'It's the living that matters,' Lyell had said. 'The dying takes care of itself.' Morgan was committed to living.

Harry did not come back to school after the film festival. Shelagh our new secretary and registrar who had taken on Bev's job when she retired, also took on her close friendship with the parents and children: but with Harry it was more than friendship. Lyell claimed it was Shelagh's shoulder length blonde hair that Harry couldn't resist. 'He's always had a thing for blondes,' he confided as we watched the two of them exchange compliments and insults in equal measure across the high black reception counter. As soon as Harry wheeled off in his chair, I'd see Shelagh surreptitiously reach under the counter for her tissues. Now when Shelagh rang to see why they had missed the big night and the showing of Harry's film, Lyell told her that Harry had had a bad turn and was back in hospital.

He was sent home a few weeks later and we hoped for the best but Lyell rang one damp grey day and said we'd better come and see Harry now if we wanted to say goodbye. Shelagh, Zandra and I went together, slipping on the wet pavers of the steep drive at their house and holding on to each other so we wouldn't be propelled precipitously down the hill. The front door was open and I could hear the TV. 'Let yourselves in,' shouted Lyell's voice. 'The maid's busy.'

Harry was lying on his black Whomobile, his face swollen and puffy, his skin waxy. Even his eyes seemed pale. 'Glad you're here,' Lyell said loudly and jovially. 'You can make Harry eat his lunch. Harry, the Principal's here'.

'No carrot', Harry said faintly with a frown of distaste. Lyell stared with mock dismay at the small bowl of pureed carrot.

'You break my heart. I cooked it all myself. Who's the best cook in the world?;

'Not you', breathed Harry with barely a smile. We sat while Lyell cajoled and Harry took a few small mouthfuls of the carrot puree. What do I say? I thought. How do you say goodbye to an eight year old? I reached out to rest my hand on his right arm.

'Nah', said Lyell. 'Harry's in a lot of pain.' I jerked my hand back and crossed my arms over my chest, holding the helpless, aching grief. The silly prattle of the children's TV show pushed me to my feet. The others stood too. I looked at Harry, drinking him in, remembering the bright eyes and cheeky spirit of his better days.

'We'll be going, Harry', I said.

'Good!' he said, forcing the words out on his limited breath. 'I'll – be able – to see – the TV!'

But weeks went by and Harry held on. Months passed and it was Christmas, the season of joy, the end of another year. At the Dominican Christmas party, Sister Clare told me she had declined any further treatment. She was spooning fruit salad from a large dish into my bowl at the time and I could only look dumbly at the rising heap of pineapple and watermelon. 'Cream?' she asked.

Morgan's routine check-up with her oncologist showed her cancer markers were up. 'Don't put off the things that are important to you,' the oncologist advised. While at school we tried to hide our dismay, Morgan responded in typical upbeat fashion and she and her partner, Tas, decided they would marry. Instead of a traditional wedding with family and friends and all the trimmings that Morgan's parents would have wanted, they planned a fantasy wedding day on their own in Las Vegas without tears or fears. They were leaving as soon as the school year ended and the staff held a roof-raising hens' party for Morgan the night before the final liturgy of the year. A lot of sore heads the next morning, but no one called in sick because it was the Christmas liturgy and that was big in our families' calendar these days. Those of us who were not hung-over worked to deck out the Possibility Space with tinsel and holly and decorate the Christmas tree near the altar.

'Lyell telephoned!' Shelagh's face at the door was pale.

I grabbed for the glass angel that almost slipped from my hand. 'No, no, it's not that,' she said. 'He's bringing Harry to the liturgy this afternoon.'

They didn't come though. I delayed the start of the liturgy until the kids were restless and the audience of parents were beginning to look at their watches and then reluctantly took the microphone to welcome everyone. We were half way through the first carol when there was a noise and commotion at the door and it was Lyell manoevering Harry's now recumbent Whomobile, Shelagh hovering alongside.

Harry lay still in the black wheeled bed, his head propped on a pillow and his eyes staring upward. The carol faded to a close and there was a silence. It was as though the old reaper himself had entered with Harry, he lay so wasted and still. I wanted to welcome him, to speak words of pleasure that they were with us again, but I couldn't find my voice. And then the rascal Theo from Harry's class stepped forward. I flinched. Theo's stream of colourful swearing daily penetrated my office when he came for his medication and on some days words were not enough and he'd lash out at whoever was near. Out of all Harry's friends it was Theo who stood by Harry's bed. As he looked down at Harry's thin, still body, I tensed, ready to intervene. Theo leaned as far forward as he could and laid his head on Harry's pillow, next to his friend's face and Harry smiled at him. After a long moment Theo straightened and turned around to face the crowd and announced in a voice of wonder, 'Harry's here, Harry's here.' Everyone broke into applause and shouts of welcome and seized the moment with such full-hearted celebration it became the best Christmas liturgy in the history of the world.

And then at last it was holidays, seven weeks of summer break. I spent a lot of time alone camping rough in the bush near Bullaburra in the Blue Mountains where I had bought my bit of land on the edge of the national park. I would trundle up there in my old campervan and calm my mind by messing about with ropes and shovels amidst the new scrub and old blackened trunks of burnt out gum trees until the day heated up and I'd sit silent and thoughtful atop massive old boulders until the mosquitoes moved in with the evening cool. On the way up the mountains I'd stop off to see Sister Clare who was now in a hospice in Strathfield and find her sitting with her prayer book and rosary. 'You look sad, Jo,' she said one day.

'Defeated, Clare. I work and work, thinking I can fix things, make things better and it all ... There's too much death.' I broke off suddenly, shocked that I could be so tactless.

'Death doesn't defeat life,' Sister Clare said with her comforting chuckle. 'Life has many enemies but death isn't one of them, Jo. Cynicism is, and despair. They're what you have to fight, not death.'

'It feels useless, the little I can do.'

'Nonsense. Just sit here a while and hold my hand.' I sat there until she drifted into sleep, and then I left. She died soon after, on a day when the sky in the mountains was red from bush fire.

The new school year began with its usual inevitability. New staff, new parents, new children. I now had an executive assistant, a New Zealander called Dix who was getting me organised along with my office. Morgan was back from Las Vegas and we practised calling her Mrs Davis. 'You know it's Morgan's birthday in a couple of weeks?' Gabby the new sports teacher reminded me, bounding into my office with her usual casual disregard of my appointment book. Dix had trained everyone else to make an appointment but Gabby acted as though she had special rights.

Gabby and I had not known each other when I'd advertised for a new sports teacher the previous year. I had already interviewed four others when Gabby came loping in, her basketballer's height and bounce overwhelming the small room. She had less experience than the others and on paper was the least promising applicant; she was also hung over she told me later, but I didn't see that. What I saw was a free spirit with a grasp on the heart of life that would fit her well to break through our children's physical challenges. Without fuss she told me her life story, promised to get her driver's licence, talked about her mother who was sick with cancer and signed on the dotted line. But the day she was due to start, there was no sign of her and eventually she sent a text to say sorry but her mother had just died. I feared we might not see her again but two weeks later a broken-winged and drooping Gabby took up her job as sports teacher. We were both grieving, she for her mother and me for everyone.

I felt responsible to Gabby's mother. I could imagine what it must be like to lie on your deathbed and think about the young adult daughter you were leaving behind. Gabby said her mother had been thrilled when she got the job working with special needs children. I thought about that. Gabby lived for the day, still a heedless party girl and I wondered if her mother had hoped we would draw from her daughter the depths that as a mother she knew were there. Consequently I nudged and worried and nagged at the girl and she maneuvered and managed me. The moment I saw her strapping figure at my door, I'd start smiling and this day was no different.

'I think Morgan would like us to have a party for her, to celebrate her birthday.'

'But Gabby, we can't. It would feel like a wake; we'd all be standing around trying not to show her we thought it was probably her last.'

'Morgan needs a party.' I shook my head. It was too much; I could already feel what the forced gaiety would cost. Gabby pulled a face, looking stubborn and I had another thought.

'What say we get a male stripper?' Gabby's mouth

opened a little and stayed that way for a couple of seconds before a slow smile broke across her face.

'Oh my God, you mean it, don't you?'

'Yes, but you'd have to organise it. I'll pay. Could you get a fireman, d'you think?' We went on the internet and started to search for stripper sites. Gabby was almost wetting herself. 'I can't wait to let people know. They won't believe it.'

'It has to be a total surprise. I want everyone to be laughing too much to remember that Kirsty is dying.'

I had never actually seen a stripper perform and I was surprised at how little it cost. Poor young man, I thought. I spread the word that we were having a celebration for Morgan after the staff meeting and, knowing I had an obligation not to expose staff to sexual experiences involuntarily, I added cryptically that there would be a demonstration after the staff meeting that might cause offence to some viewers and they were free to leave. I was really surprised how many did scramble out as soon as the formal meeting ended. Morgan seemed to be a bit baffled too, having expected they'd all stay on and share birthday drinks with her into the wee hours. But then she saw the fireman at the door. Morgan loved firemen. Whenever we had one of our many false alarms, the rest of the staff moaned and complained that we never seemed to get the wiring fixed as they evacuated their class for the umpteenth time, but not Morgan. She was out there with her class, unapologetically gawking and eager. Now though, she screamed.

Gabby had told the young man Morgan's story and he got his act just right. He was funny, tender, outrageous and comical and we watchers giggled and screamed as Morgan first hid her eyes then opened them wider and wider. I didn't notice a couple of the younger staff take their phones out to film. I was too taken with watching the hilarity in Morgan's face, the laughter shaking her whole body, how the shadows had disappeared from around her. And then as the young man turned and started to walk purposefully towards me, I realised too late that of course Gabby wouldn't miss an opportunity like this. I was blushing to my roots by the time the young man left.

Oh gosh, it was late and I was due to have dinner with the Dominican Sisters at Strathfield. Our eager new chairman, Fergus was going and that meant I'd be in trouble for my tardiness. I hugged Morgan and told Gabby to behave herself and left them all drinking and laughing and toasting Morgan as I hurried to make the forty-five minute drive to Strathfield. It was a very different mood I walked into when I finally got there, a sad and sombre affair, the Sisters still grieving for their loved Sister Clare. By the end of the main course I felt sorry for the Prioress, Sister Agnes, when she got to her feet to say a few words, obviously trying to lift the mood. She asked if any of us had a story from our week we'd like to share. No one volunteered. 'Something heartwarming?' she said, 'or something to make us smile?' Well, I could do that. I got to my feet and launched into the story of Morgan's birthday. When I finished the tables of diners were silent. 'What did she say?' one of the nuns whispered loudly into the void. 'Did she say *stripper?*' The silence continued as I sat down and then the sound of solitary clapping arose from one of the tables, and went on into the silence until slowly another joined in and another.

'I think you've broken new ground,' Fergus said, giving me a rudimentary Chairman's frown as he joined me at the coffee percolator. 'I suppose you can reconcile it with Dominican values?'

'Oh yes,' I said. 'Joy. It's one of their values. The triumph of life over despair,' and I had the satisfaction of seeing Fergus smile. As it turned out, I was lucky that the Sisters heard my version of the story first. A couple of staff put the photos they had taken up on their Facebook sites and our devout accountant Razi, shocked by my disregard of proper standards, took it on herself to email the link to the Prioress, and to Fergus for good measure. 'Some free advice for you Miss Joy,' Fergus said when he rang to pass on the complaint. 'Not every one sees the world the way you do. Get those photos wiped into oblivion, quickly.'

Two months after Morgan's birthday, Lyell phoned Shelagh with the news that Harry had died during the night. Harry had known something, Lyell reckoned. He wouldn't go to bed until he'd spoken to his grandparents on the phone and then he'd asked if he could sleep with Lyell that night. Lyell woke to the sound of Harry choking in the early hours of the morning and that was it, the long journey was over. 'Jo and I want to come round for a chat,' Lyell said. 'Got some things to do first and then we'll be round.' I had met Jo, Harry's mother, only once or twice before. Her grief-stained face was marked with the years she had endured. Family breadwinner, going to work each day, leaving the child of her loins to live his days out in the glow of Lyell's love. Now they sat side by side, the bond between them almost a visible cord .

'We've come because we want Harry's friends to sing at his funeral,' Lyell said after recounting Harry's last hours in his quiet, matey way. 'The Rainbow song. It was always his favourite.' I had said we would help in any way we could but I hadn't expected this. I tried to hide the panic in my mind. I wasn't sure what the children would make of Harry's dying and now to ask them to stand by his coffin and sing? But Lyell and Jo sat there, stripped of their child.

'Of course. Leave it with me.'

'And we want everyone in red. His favourite colour. Red everywhere.'

'We can organise red balloons.'

Zandra got the balloons, a towering red archway of balloons at the entrance to the chapel at the crematorium. The Balloon Woman who'd donated for our march on Canberra donated these too. There was a huge crowd including a mass of families from the school. I was slow to recognise Lyell when he got up to give the eulogy: he had shaved off his beard. Harry used to complain that it tickled and Lyell retorted that he was working his butt off for Harry and didn't have time to shave. 'I'll shave it off when you're dead!' he'd say. And he had. The boys of Harry's class gathered alongside their friend's coffin, solemn and quiet. 'Red and yellow and blue and green', they sang for him, staring puzzled as they saw the adults start to cry. 'I can sing a rainbow, sing a rainbow too.' Afterwards no one wanted to leave and go home but the man from the crematorium had another funeral and he came to ask me to take out the red archway of balloons. I hadn't planned for this and didn't know what to do with them. 'Would you like me to bring them to your place?' I asked Harry's younger brother Jake who as usual seemed to be standing on the edge of things.

'Ooh, yes,' he said, his eyes brightening.

'Thanks Jo,' Lyell said. 'We'll be home in a while.'

I hadn't realised how hard it would be to squash a hundred or more balloons into the boot of my car. I drove back to school and fiddled with paper work until I calculated the family would be back home. It was nearly dark and there was a light rain falling as I went back out to my car to do my last task for Harry. Zandra's small red Corolla was parked at the exit and her blonde head peered out the window. 'I thought I'd come with you.' The sweetest words. We drove in convoy the short distance to the vicinity where Harry lived and I pulled up and walked back to Zandra.

'Do you know the address?'

'No. I thought you did.'

'Well, I think it's around here somewhere.'

I soon saw the place. I could recognise it from the steep drive we'd walked down the day we went to say goodbye to Harry. The balloons were stuck in my boot and a couple burst as I tugged at them. Frantic that they'd all pop before I got them out, I nudged and yanked and swore and some moments later the great archway of red balloons came away free and soared up above my head. It was difficult negotiating that drive in the gathering dark, slipping on the rain-wet pavers with Zandra, stumbling noisily on her high-heeled shoes behind me, but finally we made it and Zandra fussed a while at the festive arch before she would let me knock on the door. It was a long while until I heard the sound of approaching footsteps and a man I'd never seen before stood in the doorway in his pyjamas. He took in the archway of balloons and the two wet bedraggled women standing there. 'I think you've got the wrong place,' he said with an apologetic grin.

Back up the drive. Impossible to think of fighting the balloons back into the boot. 'It must be somewhere near here,' Zandra said. 'I'll drive ahead of you and find it.' I walked blindly along the dark street, catching the floating balloons on low hanging branches and stumbling over roots of trees, despairingly counting the pops as one after another burst. Would there be any left? Rain was falling steadily now and my face was streaming. I kept on walking. Car lights and Zandra's voice. 'Cooee … Next turn to the right and down the hill. Second on the left. I'll wait at the top.' My arms aching, I got to the bottom of another steep paved drive and once more lowered the two black foil balloon weights to the ground. Despite the scattering of burst balloon skins, there was still joy in the soar of the red arch that sprang upwards. Through the open door I could hear laughter and voices, a party in full swing. Suddenly Jake burst out of wherever he had been hiding. 'My balloons, my balloons!' he shouted and circling his small arms around those he could reach he tugged the great red edifice through the door, excitedly calling for Lyell as he went. I stood there in the dark and wet until a man I didn't know came and closed the door.

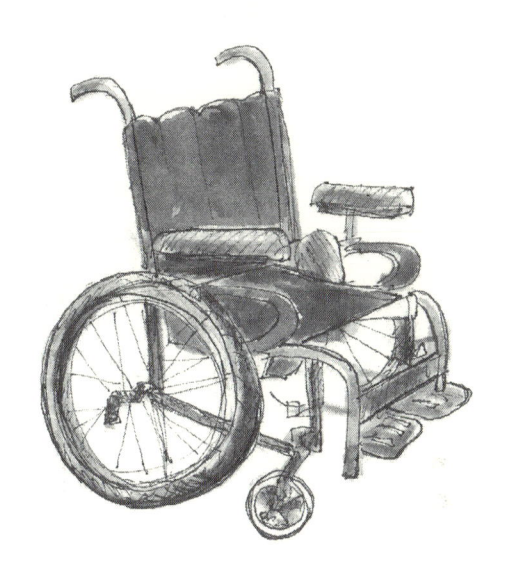

MOMENT OF TRUTH

It was January, 2011 and I had been at the school for eight years. My second contract finished the previous December and I had decided to sign on for two more years. The school had been through challenging changes and great heartache as well as joy and it felt like we needed two years of gentle consolidation. And there was lots to be done. I wanted to revisit the whole school curriculum and make our assessment programme more consistent. I was keen to integrate the therapists' work into the classrooms better and start to train our army of volunteers. We now had well over a hundred very competent volunteers and they were hungry to be taught professional skills in the tasks we assigned them. It was an opportunity to give the children the one-to-one teaching of reading and other skilled interventions that only very high fee special schools could afford.

I felt relaxed and happy as I drew up the strategic plan for my last two years. We had an outstanding new deputy, Sarah Williams, who I hoped would become the next principal. Under Pia Lombardi and the artistic Mab's direction, the children's talents in drama and art were gaining recognition with performances and exhibitions of their work in a range of public venues and galleries in Sydney. Students from surrounding schools came over each week to train our children in soccer, join in their art and drama classes and act as 'play buddies' to encourage sharing and turn taking or perhaps stimulate initiative or simply to be a conversation partner. The staff were stable and enthusiastic, our deficit was comfortably covered by donations and earnings; we had all the buildings and facilities we needed. We even had a new charismatic local priest, Father David, who understood and cherished the children as well as their parents. It was a cheerful prospect. I could happily tie up loose ends for the next two years while the staff harvested the fruits of what we had put in place.

'We don't have a diagnosis for our daughter. No one can tell us what the future holds for her.' The striking face of the round Argentinian woman was marked not by despair but resolute purpose. Her husband sat quietly alongside. 'She was a beautiful baby. We were so proud of her, weren't we Franco?' she said, glancing at him.

'We're still proud of her,' her husband said softly. 'Constanza is everything to us.'

'Oh yes.' Sofia turned back to me. 'You have to understand Constanza is our life. All we do is for her. Occupational therapy, speech therapy, conductive therapy, physiotherapy. Hours of every day. And now they say she has to go to school. It's a disaster. She'll go backwards. After all our work.' Her lovely face flushed, large dark eyes made huge by tears.

'Going to school can support her development in other ways,' I said but quickly added, seeing the hasty anger rise, 'but we can talk about that later. Why don't I start entering her information on the application form and we can have a chat about things after that?'

This was the one part of my job I had never gotten used to. The annual interviews of parents. I loved meeting them but it was always with the terrible knowledge that we had places for fewer than half the children who applied each year, even though I had doubled the number of classes. I would listen to their stories and write down all their details and then would face the painful job of deciding who to accept and who to refuse. Shelagh found it as hard as I did because she made friends with them all but she didn't have to make the decision. I found it so troubling I always ended up at the counsellor's each May. 'You can't take them all,' she'd say, much as Sister Clare used to do.

Now, while Sofia and her husband answered my questions with a halting recital of milestones not achieved, my fingers like automatons tapped their pain into the computer.

'Walking?'

'No.'

'Standing up unaided?'

'No.'

'Sitting up?'

'No.'

'Language?'

'No.'

'Self-feeding with spoon?'

'No.' It was here that I stopped. There were still two more pages of the form to fill in but it would be a pretence. I took my hands from the keyboard and swung round. Deep breath. This was going to be very hard.

'I don't want to mislead you,' I told them regretfully. 'From what you have told me, your daughter has a level of disability that we have never provided for. We don't have experience or expertise in the interventions she needs.' Sofia's body jerked back as though I had leaned across the desk and slapped her. I tried to explain, to let her down gently 'All of our students are able to walk, at least with assistance. They can all sit up and they all feed themselves independently. We are a school; the day here is taken up with reading and writing and numeracy. We just aren't the right place for your daughter.' Sofia looked at her husband whose pleasant face had crumpled a little. I shuffled uncomfortably in my chair, sharply aware of the grief and despair I was fueling, feeling helpless and guilty. But Sofia straightened suddenly, became erect and proud in her seat, her chin up and defiant.

'I expected you would say that. We had to try but I didn't really expect any different. I've visited the school the government says she's to go to. The children just lie there in their wheelchairs in the sun. I said to Franco, if she has to go to school, I want that she goes to a school where there are children running around and children talking. We can't give her a brother or sister. We don't dare risk another child. At least at school she can have other children to learn from. But not if all the other kids are in wheelchairs too.' She paused and reached her hand out to Franco, then leaned forward as though sharing a confidence.

'We are both Catholic. I don't think we would have got through the past six years if we didn't feel God is with us, that this is what he has called us to do, to love Constanza with all our hearts. So I said, she will go to a Catholic school.' She straightened up, letting go of Franco's hand to smooth her uncreased skirt. 'But don't concern yourself. I expected you to say no.' And with that, she picked up her handbag from the floor. 'Come Franco,' she said, and rising to her feet, swept out of the room. Franco followed with an apologetic nod at me as he went. I hurried out after them.

'I am so sorry, Sofia,' I said from behind her in the corridor. She turned and her face was streaked with tears. 'I am not angry with you,' she said. 'She is not your child. Not your worry.'

But I worried all that night. I always felt uncomfortable that from the surplus of children who applied each year, I selected those who would fit in best. We now had two classes in most years. One was a stream of children we were preparing to integrate into mainstream schools and the other was a stream of children we expected would stay with us until Year 6. Over the years I had accepted more and more children with very challenging needs, but I continued to exclude the ones who had profound disabilities. If I accepted Sofia's daughter, there'd be more like her, more and more over time. Our creative arts would be increasingly irrelevant, we'd become a therapy centre and the life-giving vibrant community that we had become would change to something different. And I didn't want it to change. Not after all our work, not with only two years to go.

All the other special schools selected their preferred students just as I did but I couldn't hide behind that, not that night. The radical Jew in whose name we served said otherwise. 'What you do for the least of these my children, you do for me.' I spent the night tossed between my conscience and the cherished vision of the school for which I had worked so hard. The sky above the dark trees was growing light when I finally fell asleep.

'What do you think, Sybil?' She sat with her back to me, eyes still on her computer, sipping her early morning coffee. Sybil had pulled out of the school executive. She said she didn't find it fun now that I'd invited others in.

'Let the young ones have their day,' she said but I suspected the real reason was her frustration at the time we took reaching a consensus. There was only ever one truth, as far as Sybil was concerned and right now her single-minded clarity was what I needed.

'I think it's obvious,' she said bluntly. 'We are here for kids with special needs, aren't we? From what you say this kid's needs are pretty special.'

'But we're a school. What she needs is intensive physical care and support, not education.'

'Education's not reading and Maths, like you think it is. The most basic learning is to connect with another human being. Can we do that for her? Can we get her to be curious about something? That's education. Can we teach her to make choices, to go after what she wants?' She swung around to face me full on and I saw in the pinkness of her cheeks a rising excitement. 'You don't know how I'd love the chance to teach her!'

'You've got it,' I said, 'and I just hope neither of us regrets it.'

I had expected Sofia to be overjoyed when I rang but her voice was quite flat. In fact, she didn't turn up the day we'd agreed Constanza would start, nor the day after. I remembered then that sending Constanza to school was not her choice; keeping her at home was. I rang Franco and asked what was happening and he and Sofia brought Constanza to school the next day. Up until now I had not seen her. I had been thrashing around in the abstract depths of an existential dilemma about the nature of the school and now here in front of me was the concrete, living child lying strapped into a stroller, her arms and legs flailing, her head rolling involuntarily from side to side. Her hands scratched at her face as she tried to get them in her mouth but fell helplessly away again. Her eyes rolled about in her head resting on nothing, connecting with nothing.

'What will you do with her?' I whispered to Sybil after they left. I felt appalled by the enormity of her needs.

'Take her out of this stroller and lie her on the floor for a start,' she said. I felt very doubtful. She seemed so fragile, so defenceless.

'But is it safe? Won't she hurt herself? What about the other children? What if one of them bites her?'

'Why don't you go and get some work done,' Sybil said.

Less than an hour later I was back peering through the glass wall of her classroom. Dark-eyed Constanza lay on a blanket on the floor, her body twisting and her legs flailing as before with her hands restlessly reaching for her mouth. But her beautiful dark head was cocked a little. Near her Matthew, a little boy with cerebral palsy, stood holding out a blue plastic duck. When Constanza didn't take it, Matthew moved cautiously out of the way of her randomly jerking legs and bent down and placed the duck next to her head. He watched a moment as Constanza continued her threshing and then staggered off, looking around for another toy. Sybil waved me into the room. 'Did you see that?' she asked excitedly, 'Did you see how Constanza's jerking stopped when Matthew came near?' I shook my head. I hadn't seen it; I didn't like to trust it, not when I knew how much we both hoped. But two weeks later Constanza rolled onto her stomach and a month later she rolled across the classroom to where Matthew was playing.

Sybil got Mick our maintenance fellow to attach a leather strap to Constanza's chair and by the end of the year when I visited the classroom, it would take me a few moments to pick out Constanza, sitting up like the others in their morning circle. She was held up only by the strap, her arms and legs still moved uncontrollably and I couldn't tell how much she understood but she was in the circle, part of the class. The physiotherapist who had worked with Constanza for years was awed by her progress. 'I've not seen her alert like this; it's being with other children that's done it.' And then she added, 'You know you've opened the floodgates though?'

Next to come through the so-called floodgates was Lexie, a little girl with Rett syndrome. Anne her mother was an athletic, determined young sportswoman who never questioned that we would accept her fourth child. She was angry with the Catholic school her other children attended because they had felt unable to take her youngest who had a problem with vomiting attacks, could not speak, could not sit up unaided, had uncontrolled seizures and a prognosis of further deterioration. 'Lexie adores her brothers and sister,' Anne said sadly. 'She would have loved going off to school with them each day.' This time I remembered to invite Anne to bring Lexie to the school before we accepted her, to let staff meet her. I was nervous that they would object to another child with profound needs, but I hadn't counted on Lexie.

I was in a meeting when Anne arrived with her daughter in a wheelchair and so Shelagh took them straight out onto the playground. By the time I got out there, I could hardly get near for the huddle of clucking teachers and I had to poke my head between their shoulders to get a glimpse of her. Her mittened hands were tied down to the arms of the wheelchair to stop them from jerking. Her body was propped up on cushions, her legs lay immobile – and yet a vital incandescent spirit shone from her bright blue eyes and lit the upturned corners of the sweetest of smiles as she looked around in delight at these new, attentive faces. You couldn't miss that this was a child who knew only love; nor fail to be awed by the light that shone from her, rising unfiltered from deep well-springs that source life itself. The teachers noticing me behind them turned at once with a chorus of voices.

'Can she be in my class?'

'What a darling!'

'Please, I'd love to have her. Can she be in mine?'

In the end though, I placed her with Constanza in Sybil's class so I could concentrate the additional assistance and supervision they both needed in the one room. Sybil took the changes in her brisk stride but I continued to worry. At our annual Open Day, a visiting parent had queried publicly the number of children with severe disabilities we seemed to be taking and suggested that this school was no longer the right place for little ones like hers who had only mild disabilities. I flared up and said that all children flourished where there was enough love, whatever their needs, but she had touched a raw nerve.

It was true that our school days were often more chaotic than they used to be. Morning song was noisier these days, there were more non-verbal children using electronic devices to speak the prayer for them, more severely affected children running out to escape the noise of the music. To take a class out on an excursion now required a two-page risk assessment and a troop of volunteers. Our staff meetings devoted more time to discussing therapy than education. It felt right in principle to accept more children with severe and profound needs but there was a cost. We had created a school so special that even brothers and sisters wanted to come to it and often complained they didn't have as much fun at their own school. I wasn't sure we could hold onto that kind of fun. For a little while I lost confidence, so mired I became in the challenges accompanying unrestricted enrolment.

It was therefore with a troubled mind and heart that I went along to the Possibility Space for the once-a-term Friday Mass for families. Father David, who was now our parish priest, had early on structured it to consist mostly of the children's God songs to keep the children engaged and free their parents to enjoy the Mass. The worship space was set up with bright yellow and purple soft seats and benches and on the rugs in the middle were piled big, plump cushions where children were already gathering, jostling and rolling. Banners of St Dominic attended by his faithful dog hung on each wall and out the front was the long narrow altar set with the silver chalice and the paten for the Communion bread and wine. I could see the tall figure of Father David bending down to talk to the acolytes in their cream surplices. One of them, Nathan, was in some sort of fluster. As I watched, Whitney turned to him with the severity of a parent. 'You know what to do, Nathan. Stop fussing. Sit down.' The room was quickly filling with parents and children, and before long the first strains of *Come Together Let's Celebrate* sounded for the start of the Mass.

Father David had placed a glass baptismal font, rather like a huge glass bowl, on a low table next to the altar.

Tonight Conall was being baptised and his family had turned out in force. Near them sat the Johnstone parents with their two girls, Gretel and Gigi, beautiful girls with severe autism. Gigi was restless tonight and her father Sol was holding her firmly as the prayers of intercession began. Suddenly she pushed away from him and escaped his long arms as he reached out belatedly to grab at her dress. With a vague air that belied the purposefulness of her steps, she made her way forward to the altar, bent her head over the glass font and began to drink noisily. She must have been thirsty for she drank and drank while an awed silence fell over the room. 'Good, Gigi,' said Father David with his comfortable smile and spoke to the gathered crowd. 'Everyone, Gigi has just demonstrated to us the gift that water is for us all. Now let us baptise Conall with it.'

Later in the Mass as children carried forward the gifts of bread and wine to the priest, ten year old Bill brought from the kitchen a large bowl heaped high with popcorn that his mother had left there for the supper. Father David lifted the bread high for its consecration and Bill stood in front of him with his bowl of popcorn. A crowd of children quickly gathered and Bill had them sit around him as he doled it out. Father David imperturbably completed the consecration and distributed the host to the parents. 'Doesn't it bother you?' I asked him afterwards, conscious that the children had just goofed up a ceremony consecrated through two thousand years of practice, to which as a priest he had given his life.

'Not at all,' he said with a relaxed smile. 'It is a privilege. Each time I celebrate the Mass here with the children, I feel the Spirit of God overflow with delight and laughter. He is their unseen partner.'

His serene acceptance floored me with its contrast to my own overwrought and fretful misgivings. His love for the children shamed my overriding concern for the school. I decided that I too would trust that whatever was beautiful and true and good would endure. My job was just to open the door and care for whomever came through it with the best strategies and resources we could provide.

Amazingly it was then that Julia Gillard, recently appointed Prime Minister, announced she was giving more support to children with disabilities. We would receive funding for additional speech and occupational therapy hours, which made all the difference to enabling us to meet the extra needs the children presented. Pumped up with this, I suggested to Rhoda that she bring her daughter Isabella to be part of the school.

Isabella was ten and had been coming once a term to our Family Mass. I would see her sitting demurely next to her mother and be amused by the exaggerated solemnity of her expression. She was 'doing holy'. Like so many children with Down syndrome, she threw herself into life and drank up its possibilities as though it was a feast to which she had been invited. I wondered why Rhoda, her mother, didn't send her to school with us instead of just bringing her to Mass once a term. I knew she was very religious and very Catholic; she had once proudly shown me a photo of a great-aunt who had been beatified by the Pope. When I asked her, she blushed and shook her head vehemently.

'Oh no. Isabella's not right for here.'

'Why ever not?'

'She's not as clever as your children,' she said in an apologetic way. 'I wouldn't want to give you the trouble.'

'Come on! You can't know us very well if you think that.'

'Actually I applied here when she was starting school but I was told then that her disability was too severe.'

'I don't remember that.'

'It was your secretary. She rang me when she saw Isabella's papers.'

'Oh well, we've learned a lot since then. Isabella would be very welcome.'

She just shook her head and I shrugged, wondering at her reluctance. A few weeks later though, she rang and asked if she could come and talk and eventually after a lot of uncertain changes of mind, she allowed me to persuade her. I put Isabella into the irrepressible Morgan's class knowing she'd be enthusiastic about her. On her first day, Isabella behaved like an angel. On her second, Morgan rushed through my door with her eyes wide. 'Isabella's taken all her clothes off. She is at the top of the climbing spider and she won't come down.'

'OK, I'll come straight away.'

'Sarah's already gone. She said to let you know.'

Once again I gave thanks for the unflappable Sarah Williams. I had first met her when she was an Inspector with the Board of Studies and gave us a rigorous and professional doing over. I was more than a little chuffed that she thought well enough of us to accept the role of Deputy. I had quickly realised what a treasure we had found in her, especially for situations like this.

Out in the playground, I spied Sarah coming through the Oval gate. No sign of Isabella and Sarah looked a bit dishevelled. She stretched out her shirt. 'Look at me. She peed on me! I was climbing up to get her. It was so deliberate.' Sarah was laughing but Morgan rocketed past her through the gate and I could hear her shouting in fury at Isabella. The two of them appeared a moment later, bare little Isabella looking like nothing so much as a round and pink teddy bear with plump little arms and legs and a contrite face.

'She was already down,' Morgan said. 'And very ashamed. What do you say to Mrs Williams, Isabella?'

'Sorry, Williams.'

For the next few weeks we were at our wits' end with Isabella who continued to take off her clothes at the slightest provocation, getting the attention she wanted every time. 'I can't just ignore it,' Morgan said. 'She's too well-developed. And I can't find a motivator that works with her.' I gladly passed the problem on to Sarah who shortly discovered the one reward that Isabella hankered for – leading the whole school in prayer. Morgan would appear at my side in morning exercises with Isabella in tow, and say, 'Mrs Karaolis, Isabella has been very good for two days now. Could she say the prayer today?' And a demure Isabella would come out and with a saintly face make her way through the words she could manage. 'God our Maker and Friend, we love you and we thank you for loving us.' She still turned on histrionic tantrums, sulky fits and did the occasional strip but generally a reminder that she could lose the privilege of leading the prayer was enough to settle her. A few months later I received an email in my inbox.

'Dear Jo,

Today I did something I have not been able to do since Isabella was born. I went to a cafe with Isabella and had a cappuccino and she was fine. I can't tell you what it means to be able to go out in public with my daughter. I never thought I would see this day.

Rhoda

I was very moved by that letter and I guess it influenced what happened next. I had needed a hair cut for some time and never seemed to fit it in, so one afternoon I headed off to the nearest shopping centre to a Just Cuts salon. I'd not been before but I wanted somewhere quick. 'Where do you work?' The woman deftly snipping hair away from my ears was politely making conversation but I wanted to get back and make a few phone calls before the business day ended.

'At a school. You wouldn't know it. A small place.'

'What's it's name?' I told her.

'The special school? Is that what you mean?' She stood up, put her scissors down and leaned back with arms crossed, staring at me. 'There's someone here you have to meet,' she said. She called out a name and a woman with dark sunken eyes came from a back room. 'Here, Vida,' my hairdresser said, 'this woman works at the special school. Why don't you talk to her, tell her what's happened.'

'Oh, I don't know. It's …'

'Tell her. See what she thinks.'

The other woman kept her eyes on the ground as she began a faltering story in a heavily accented voice I struggled to understand. It seemed she had brought her son as a two year old to Australia with her husband when they emigrated from Iran. Soon after their arrival he had been diagnosed with cancer. 'It was terrible,' she said. 'I was so afraid. I prayed and prayed. I prayed to the God. I prayed to the Jesus.' During his long stay in hospital one of the doctors had asked whether she had ever considered that her son might be autistic; it didn't seem important, just make him better. God had been good – and the doctors. An operation got rid of the cancer and it had not come back.

On the doctor's advice she sent the boy to a special school. But one day she called in unannounced at the school and she heard shouting as she passed the toilets. She went over to the cubicles and saw two women with her son, aides who worked in his class. 'They were screaming so loud at him,' she said. 'It was terrible. I could see him. They had him, no clothes, and then I saw one, she hit him. I went quick. I said, Stop, stop, it's my boy. What are you doing? They said, your son is bad, very bad. He soil himself. I took him out of there and I not go back. But the Department, they say he has to go back, that he has to be at school. I don't know what to do. I write a report and send it to the Department and they do an investigation. But I not send Karim back.' She looked at me then and I looked away, unnerved by the pain in her eyes. I gave her my card.

'Um, well, he's ...' Shelagh, whose big heart went out to anyone who walked through the door, seemed uncharacteristically troubled. I had told her Vida's story when I got back so late from my hair cut and Shelagh had pointed out very sensibly that since the boy was already eleven, it was a bit late for him to come to us. 'He'll have to move on to high school in a year anyway,' she reminded me.

'Well, they may not come,' I had said, 'and anyway, it's only to have a look around.' But now they were here and given the look on Shelagh's face, the boy must be bad. I remembered the pain in his mother's eyes. Like all of us, she had dreamed of a happy healthy baby who would grow into a son to be proud of, as we do. Instead he had autism and intellectual impairment and had been through cancer and suffered abuse and she was at her wits' end. But I could only do this if I had a teacher willing to take him on. 'Ask Rob to come down,' I said.

Rob had a class of older kids with a lot of idiosyncratic abilities and disabilities, who did well under his unorthodox methods and if we were to take this boy, that's where he would have to go. Rob thought rather differently from the other staff, probably because he was a sculptor by calling and studied each of his students with great care before setting to work to draw out the person he saw within. Shelagh was still showing the mother around the school when Rob brought Karim back to my office, a firm hold on his arm. 'I've spent some time with your boy,' he said with a grin.

'Would he fit into your class?'

'Not sure about that. If he needs us, then we'll work it out somehow. It's what we're here for.'

HIGH SCHOOL

Karim turned out to be more of a challenge than I had expected. Rob took his time as he always did, watching, listening, analysing everything the tall, strange boy did, trying to find out what his fears were, what pleasures motivated him – but he was flummoxed. If Karim wanted to pee, he did, right wherever he was at the time. If he felt bothered by anyone, he pinched them. If he was hungry, he ate whatever was near. He appeared to have no social awareness at all. 'Give him time,' Sarah the Deputy said, 'he's a gentle boy. He'll learn.' But time was something we didn't have, not with Karim. In twelve months he would have to go to high school. His mother, Vida, didn't want him to leave.

'Oh no,' she said, 'Not now I see how happy he is here, how you all love him. He is a different boy. Much less anxious. No, no, he has to be where he is loved.' A light glowed from her face as she spoke. The dark, dejected woman I had first met was gone. She was lighter now, full of laughter and warmth and with new friends. A few days before she had left a note for me. 'Since Karim came to your school, love is revived in my heart again.'

Vida was not alone in wanting her child to stay on with us past Year 6. It had become an increasing problem now the school had grown so big and we had more students finishing primary school each year. Once upon a time most would go on to the Catholic special secondary school round the corner but now we had many more students to be placed and besides, that school had gone in the opposite direction from us and narrowed its selection of students to the more capable and least disruptive. The stakes were high for our Year 6 parents. Their children stood to lose the strong friendships they had formed with their classmates and they themselves would fall out of the tight social net that had supported them since their child had started school here six years before. They all applied to the school around the corner and then spent months swinging between hope and dread, feeding each other's anxiety and waiting in trepidation for the letter that would deliver their child's fate.

The parents had come up with the solution to all this

stress some years before. They proposed to the Board that we add a high school. The Board brushed off the suggestion. I was in two minds myself. I felt for their need but I shrank from the work and trouble of a high school. Each year though the call from the parents became more vociferous and their arguments more irresistible. There was no chance of a Catholic high school place for the children with severe and profound disabilities we were now accepting. Not unless we provided it. But I was less than two years from retirement and it seemed reasonable to let the new principal worry about it. I had enough to do in making the school shipshape for my successor.

But then I had a call from Alice Foster. Her gentle-faced son Cole had been at school with us for a few years. He was very withdrawn when he first came, silent, unresponsive, unable to sit at a desk, ceaselessly circuiting the classroom. But then he started having solo art lessons with Mab. We knew he had made the leap into life the day Pia Lombardi circulated a photo she had taken of Cole with his face alight with laughter as he reached towards the puppet she called Beast. The contrast with the sad, lost boy of the past was so striking I forwarded it to all the Board members. It was graphic proof of the power of the creative arts with our students. We'd have liked to have more years to work with Cole but when he turned 13 he had to go to high school and he didn't get a place at the school around the corner. Alice had wept a little when she got the rejection letter and then got on with it, as she always did. Now the sound of her bright, positive voice on the phone made my spirits rise.

'Hi, Alice, how's Cole going?'

'He has been suspended for a week. He hit a teacher. Oh it's all right, they're taking him back.' Her comfortable laugh belied the anxiety she must be feeling. 'It's not why I'm ringing,' she went on. 'I'm ringing because I just bought a ticket in Oz Lotto. There's a $21 million draw this Saturday. I want you to know that when it wins I'm donating it for starting the high school.'

'It's not working out for Cole, then?'

'Look, they're good people and they do their best. But they don't think Cole has any capacity, they don't teach him things the way he needs them taught and he's anxious and bored. They don't do art the way you do. It's not an education. It's as if they just mind him through the day. I don't want him to have a lifetime of being minded. I want him to have a life.' The lottery ticked didn't win but Alice let me know every few weeks that she had bought another. 'We're going to get that high school, Jo.'

After one of her calls, I told Sarah Williams about the lottery tickets. She looked at me quizzically. 'We can't wait for a lottery win, you know,' she said. 'We have to do it anyway.' I wriggled uncomfortably. 'I know you say the school will change if you add big strapping adolescents stuffed with hormones,' she said. 'But think of it the other way; what sense does it make to move our students on just when puberty strikes and they need us more than ever.'

'But Sarah, I can't start a high school. I'm sixty eight. I've only got eighteen months left.'

'Then there's no time to waste, is there?' But I didn't want to lose my dream of a calm, smooth closure. With a sheepish smile, I hurried out of her office. Then some time afterwards, one of the mothers rang with bad news about Lori, the parent with pancreatic cancer. She said she didn't think Lori had long to go and asked would I like to accompany her and her friend the next time they went to the hospital. 'Hugh is clinging to hope,' she said, 'but it looks bad to us.'

At the door of the hospital room, I hung back awkwardly, shocked by the ominous looking tubes and medical paraphernalia and by how thin and wasted Lori looked lying back on the deathly white sheets. Her face lit up at the sight of her friends but then her eyes moved to me and in a fluster she fumbled for her wig and tried ineffectually to get it straight on her head. Sorry to cause her embarrassment, I hurried over and took her hand. Her fingers felt very small. She looked at me then and whispered a few words of apology for her appearance and fell silent without letting go of my hand. Something in her eyes seemed to struggle for expression. In a flash I guessed what it was.

'You're worried about Scotty, are you Lori?' She nodded and a tear escaped down her cheek.

'What will happen to him? Can he stay?'

'Yes, of course.'

'No, I mean, well, for high school? Will there be a high school?'

'I'll do my best,' I said gripping her hand tighter.

It was terrible to see Scotty's confusion and insecurity now his mother was always away in hospital. Several times his teacher Kelly had to call down for help because Scotty was in a panic and screaming or throwing things. One day in morning song I noticed his eyes fixed across the room on Mrs Stell, an occupational therapist who was the mother of one of our boys and volunteered with us for a few hours each week. She was an excellent therapist, not least because she'd learned so much from her own son, but it didn't explain why Scotty's eyes seemed never to leave her. 'I think it's her long brown hair,' Kelly murmured. 'It probably reminds him of his mother.' When morning song ended, Scotty seemed in no mood to leave with the rest of his class but stayed watching Mrs Stell until she disappeared from the worship space. Kelly took his hand to pull him to his feet but Scotty threw himself down onto the floor and curled up into a tight ball, his face hidden.

'Leave him with me for a moment,' I said. 'I'll bring him up when he has settled.' Once he knew his class had safely gone, Scotty got up and moved to one of the banana coloured benches and sat drumming his heels on the floor. Keeping an eye on him, I went through to the phone in the next room and watched through the glass walls as I waited for Susan Stell to pick up. It took only a couple of minutes to explain to her what I wanted but when I put down the phone, there was an empty bench where Scotty had been sitting. Where could he have gone? There'd been no time and anyway, everything was locked. I rushed to the only open door, the one to the kitchen, and with relief saw Scotty standing at the bench. He had a large coffee tin open and was helping himself to it with a hefty spoon.

'Scotty, put that down at once!' He looked around and gave me the smile of an angel before shoving the laden spoon into his mouth. Quickly grabbing it from him, I started frantically scraping inside his mouth with a wooden stirrer while his mischievous eyes laughed up at me.

'Need a hand?,' an amused voice called from the door and Susan Stell moved to my side. Scotty stared at her, eyes large, his coffee stained mouth fixed open. 'Here, Scotty,' she said. 'Do you know how to spit?' and helped him to a mouthful of water. 'I'll take him now,' she said, 'and let you know how we get on.'

Perhaps Kelly was right and Scotty identified her with his mother, or perhaps Mrs Stell had particular skills, but it took just a few days before all of us could see the difference in Scotty. Often he was happy just to play with her, but there were days when he needed the swings and trampoline to oust his devils. The funding the Prime Minister, Julia Gillard, had promised for therapy had now come through and I was able to use it to put Mrs Stell on staff as an additional occupational therapist. In addition to Scotty, she also worked extensively with Lexie and Constanza in Sybil's class, giving Constanza regular workouts on the walking frame and teaching Lexie to use the big 'cause and effect' switch to turn music on and off.

By luck Mrs Stell was in the classroom a few weeks later when Lexie went into a kind of choking seizure and started to turn blue. Sybil hurried to the emergency button to call for help but before Shelagh and I could arrive with the first aid box, Mrs Stell had already calmly put Lexie over her knees and massaged her until with a hiccup she started to breathe again. 'Thank God she was there,' Sybil said to me with a shudder at the thought of what could have been. She had come to my office to debrief at the end of the day and we talked for a while before she felt ready to go off home. After she left I didn't feel like settling to work. I sat musing on the chances of life and how lucky we were to have Mrs Stell just when we needed her. That's when my mind turned to the Prime Minister. She was having a particularly hard time, the target of some very bitter politicking, attacked by opponents in her own party as well as by the Opposition and vociferous sections of the media.

I remembered the sympathetic way she'd listened when I'd talked to her on the day of our march on Parliament House. I wondered how she was feeling this night and whether she had any idea what a difference her initiative for special needs children made, here on the ground, where it actually mattered but was never reported. So leaving my in-tray untouched, I wrote a letter to her, about Scotty and Lexie and how we were able to employ Mrs Stell only because of the extra funding she had introduced to give therapy to children with disabilities. I wasn't sure the letter would get past the Prime Minister's minders but I addressed the envelope and dropped it in a letter box on my way home.

I had been thinking a lot about politics recently: Board politics. I had given up fighting against the high school. Lori had brought home to me my responsibility for children like Scotty. I had opened our doors to them, knowing that their needs were exceptional. We had put our hand to the plough. Now we had to make sure they weren't put out into the cold at the end of Year 6. With the knowledge and connections I had built up, I was in the best position to get a project like that under way. A new principal wouldn't have time to do the groundwork. I should move it ahead as far as I could in the remaining time I had.

My problem was how to convince the Board. Fergus was sympathetic because he often spoke to parents and understood why they wanted it so badly. Other Board members tended to be less aware. They came up to the school only rarely and drew their information more from the financial figures than from anecdotal stories about the children. Of these, the strongest nay-sayer was Carl, a senior solicitor with a major city law firm blessed with a daunting analytical mind and a nature averse to risk. At the Board planning day when I tried to persuade the Board of the importance of a high school, it was Carl who convinced them to defer consideration of the risky venture.

'Then let's debate it at the staff night with the Board,' Sarah Williams suggested. 'It won't just be you grinding on about it, they'll hear it from the staff too.'

'But are you sure all the staff are in favour?' I asked.

'I don't know, but if they come up with something to prove it's not viable, then none of us should touch it,' she countered. 'It's a win no matter how the debate turns out.'

Each year we had a cocktail party so that Board members could mix and talk freely with staff. Usually we made it an opportunity for particular staff members to describe their work and challenges but this year it would be the debate. After the opening drinks and nibbles, Pia Lombardi got discussion underway by asking hypothetical questions about the high school and handing the microphone to staff or Board members to answer. She kept the jokes running as she moved the microphone around the room. When after half an hour or so, she handed it to Sybil, I caught Sarah's eye. You could never be sure what Sybil would say. She was loud in her complaints about what an imposition these nights with the Board were, but she always came. She said she hated speaking in public and in staff meetings preferred to whisper to her neighbour behind her hand, but now she actually stood up and the expression on her face made me sit back in expectation. Sybil was in for the fight.

'This school isn't a business,' she said, standing as tall as I'd ever seen her and staring at the Board members one by one. 'It's a mission. That's what it says on the school logo. You talk about Dominican values but you tot up the dollars and weigh the risks. Well, this school wouldn't be here if the early Dominican sisters had thought like you. They'd not have set out in a leaky boat from Ireland. They'd not have loaded up a cart and gone off to start a school for the blind when all they knew about was teaching the deaf. You don't want the risk and the trouble. Well, you don't have to want it; you just have to do it. Because these children and these parents need a high school.' She went to sit down but changed her mind and taking back the microphone, said loudly into it. 'And don't you dare say we can't do it, because we can. God knows I'm not very religious but even I know that the money will come if you have the faith.' The atmosphere was electric and feeling it, Pia cut short the debate and put the question to the vote. A mass of hands went up in favour.

When the next Board meeting came round, Carl proposed that I should undertake a thorough feasibility study to be completed in six months. Excited and determined, Sarah and I divided the work between us: she doing the curriculum and investigating registration with the Board of Studies and

I doing the property, finances and compliance.

If I could have, I'd have planned a high school on acreage that would give big, restless kids the chance to roam, where they could learn practical tasks like nursery gardening, animal husbandry, wood working and technology and could swim and climb and jump. But we had to start small and make the concept of a high school as readily digestible as possible to all the stakeholders. This meant somehow getting hold of land adjacent to the school. It should have been impossible, given the cost of the neighbouring properties but Sybil had been right about having faith and things unfold. First the Prioress, Sister Agnes, promised us the cottage next door when the Sisters were ready to move out of it. Then Hilary, the lady who lived in the next house up, decided to downsize and gave us first option to buy. It was an offer too good for the Board to refuse and suddenly we had enough land to start a high school.

Jonathan, the architect who had designed our creative arts centre sketched out plans that met our brief and fitted onto the two blocks. Sarah, for her part, gained approval in principle from the Board of Studies for the high school, the curriculum and the building plans. It had taken only a few months and all our ducks were lined up. Only the finances remained to be dealt with. I was confident we would raise the capital cost of building. We had done it for the creative arts centre and a high school would be an easier cause to win support for, especially among parents.

But there was a real risk that the high school would blow the annual operating budget beyond our capacity to pay, to a degree that would put the whole school at risk. Unless, that was, the government introduced a more realistic level of funding for students with severe and profound needs. This I knew to be under discussion. The Gonski review had specifically recommended that special students be funded according to the severity of their needs. But for months now progress had stalled for lack of agreement between the States over how to define different levels and types of disability. Without an assurance that there'd be a substantial increase in funding for the kind of student we'd be enrolling in the high school, I couldn't give the Board an assurance that it wouldn't be a drain on the existing school.

Then out of the blue I had a call from my old sparring partner at the Catholic Schools Board. With a lot of hurumphing and throat clearing, he told me that the Parliamentary Secretary for Education was touring Catholic schools for two days as part of her visit to NSW. 'I don't know why,' he said, 'but she has specifically asked to visit your school.' He sounded rather put out, I thought, but I was too pleased to care. This was our chance to ask about money. A quick ring-around and I had parents and key staff lined up and planned a tour that would make the biggest impression we could in the ninety minutes allocated.

The Senator was warm and gracious and seemed comfortably ordinary as she strode into the foyer and greeted us all but when I quickly outlined what I had planned for her visit, she demurred. 'I don't have a lot of time,' she said, 'and I'd like to meet Lexie and Scotty first.' Lexie and Scotty? So it was the letter I had sent to the Prime Minister after Lexie's near-death seizure that had brought her here. I quickly dropped my planned tour and let her spend her time with the children. Lexie was only recently back from hospital and rather weak but the radiance of her smile was undimmed and the Senator lingered by her wheelchair. Mrs Stell brought Scotty down and he shyly reached out his hand to shake the Senator's. In Morgan's class, Nathan boasted that he was up to level 9 in maths and Aislin introduced herself to the Senator and then introduced herself again, and would have done it again but the Senator got in first. We visited Isabella's class and Karim who was already beginning to relax and respond to Rob's patient teaching, smiled and let the Senator take his hand. Then she called a halt and said, 'Where can we talk?'

We joined the parents around the table in the kitchen where they had gathered with Sarah and Pia. 'Your principal tells me you need a high school,' the Senator said as she sat down. The parents talked eagerly over each other, explaining their children and their hopes and fears for their future while she nodded and I poured the tea and passed the biscuits. When the ninety minutes were nearly up, the Senator rose to her feet. As we walked to the door she muttered quietly in my ear, 'I can't say anything you know'.

'Of course not,' I replied, moving to open the door for her.

'But I think you should go ahead with your high school.'

'You do? You think the funding will be enough for what we want to do?'

'Of course not. But our modelling will give much more than you've been getting, for students like Isabella and Karim and the others you're thinking of.' She was now through the door and she put a quick hand on my arm. 'Build the high school,' she said. It was the reassurance we needed.

I went to work like a tiger. I drew up an exemplar budget, created a business model, added a detailed financial analysis, mapped out a project plan with a schedule of deliverables and finished it all off with a comprehensive risk analysis. Dix, my executive assistant, was determined to make it look totally professional and utterly convincing and obtained special folders which she boldly labelled High School and in which she carefully laid out the whole proposal including Sarah's unimpeachable six year curriculum, ready for the next Board meeting. I couldn't see how the Board would say no, because, with the proposed funding for students with severe disabilities, the financial figures were very encouraging.

But I overlooked something. I assumed the Dominican Sisters would embrace the high school because of their commitment to social justice and their activism on behalf of the disadvantaged. But they had not been at the meetings with parents, they did not know the children like Scotty and little Jillian and Lexie, they hadn't heard Sybil's impassioned speech. Instead of answering Jesus' call to serve the most marginalised, they got out their economic slide rule and weighed the costs against the benefits. A high school was risky, they said and the Board should put in safeguards. Carl seized on their cautious advice and proposed to the Board that the high school should be seen as a pilot and a review held after three years. 'If there is no harm to the existing school, then we can go ahead,' he said.

'But what about the children already in the high school. What will happen to them if we don't go ahead?' asked another lawyer on the Board.

'We'll have committed to them,' Fergus interposed firmly. 'They'll stay on with us until they have finished high school.' I felt crushed. I had no doubt the pilot would be a great success and that after three years no one would think of winding it back. But this grudging approval was not the whole-hearted embrace of students with the greatest needs that I had anticipated.

At least we had good news for the parents. Year after year they had come along to the annual meeting with the Board to put forward their argument for a high school and been brushed off. This year would be different. I could hardly hide my smiles as I went along the corridor to the Possibility Space from where floated the happy sounds of a party getting under way. Rhoda grabbed me as soon as I walked in. 'I've got something for you, Jo,' she said, pressing a small tissue-wrapped parcel into my hands. 'It's my mother's rosary beads.'

'I can't take these, Rhoda,' I protested as I glimpsed the shine of gold and pink pearl. 'You need to save them for Isabella.'

'No, I want you to have them. I've a feeling you need them.'

'Just wait,' I whispered in her ear as I gave her a hug, 'I think you'll find everything is OK.' She blinked and looked away and as I glanced around I saw that other parents were looking tense too. They laughed but their faces quickly fell back into worry creases; a few were not attempting sociability but sat in anxious silence and I glimpsed Jillian's parents holding hands under the table. Thankfully Fergus wasted no time in taking the microphone and getting up to speak. He smiled around at the uneasy gathering. 'I think you've waited a long time to hear this,' he said and there was an expectant murmur. The parents liked Fergus and it wasn't just his shy, boyish charm: he often was up at the school, spending time in classes and attending all the major events. I saw Hugh bend over and say something to Theo's parents and I felt a pang for Lori lying pinned by tubes to her hospital bed. Vida was at the next table, and Carolyn with Angus whispering to little Jillian's parents – so many to whom this decision meant the end of worry. 'I won't keep you in suspense. The Board has decided to extend the school into the post-primary years and the first Year 7 will be in 2013.' He started to explain about it being a pilot and that the Board had committed to providing for their own children until the end of their schooling, but Michelle interrupted him.

'I don't get it,' she said, on her feet with anxiety. 'Are you saying you are starting a high school?'

'Yes, that's what I'm saying,' Fergus nodded, smiling. I looked across at Hugh; his face, weary with anxiety, showed no emotion. Jillian's father, Herb Jones got to his feet. He had always appeared urbane and smooth to me but now he struggled to keep his voice even. 'It has been hard for us as lifetime Catholics to have our children rejected from Catholic schools. What you have taken on will be difficult but it is right and we will all help. This school will be a witness that Jesus did not die for just some of us: that his love includes these little ones who did not ask for the disabilities that have until now excluded them.' He sat down abruptly into a long silence.

'But that's over!' Rhoda cried out. 'Now they'll have their own high school.' Somebody cheered and others clapped and the meeting broke up in a cacophony of laughter. Rhoda and Vida were hugging each other and I squeezed the rosary beads in my pocket. Later that night as I went around the school locking up, turning off lights, shutting doors, setting alarms, I decided that after all, my work was complete. The high school would be built. There would be a welcome for every child. Isabella and Karim would have the time they needed. How often had Sister Clare said to me, 'You can't fix everything Jo'? But for one euphoric night I thought I had. The next day I rang Lori. 'We have a high school for Scotty.' I said.

'I know. Hugh rang me when he got home last night.' Her voice was weak but there was a smile in it. A few weeks later she was gone.

FINAL YEAR

Up and down, Stephanie's tanned calves went, up and down relentlessly. My eyes were fixed on them, my foot ready to touch the brake when she lost speed, to accelerate when her pace picked up. I was terrified I'd lose concentration and run into her. For six days now I had been driving my old campervan at twenty five kilometers per hour, something I'd have shuddered at normally but with Stephanie busting heart and sinew just metres ahead, my mind had settled to the rhythm of her legs, up and down.

Brandon, the young principal of the Catholic school

at Nicawinna, had asked us to help them raise money to bring Grade 2 children and their families to Sydney in the holidays. 'I want them to experience a bigger world than Nicawinna,' he said. 'But it will cost a lot.' What we should do, I suggested in a fit of inspired enthusiasm, was get sponsorship to cycle the thousand kilometres out west from Sydney to Nicawinna. It would be a message to everyone about the isolation of outback schools.

'You're going to cycle?'

'No, Brandon. We're principals. We delegate.'

When I spruiked the proposal at our staff day at the start of 2012, hoping the staff would indulge my last bright idea, they jeered. 'You've played that card too often already, Jo,' Sarah Williams laughed. 'It's over.' But at the morning tea break, Stephanie, one of the teachers from the satellite class on the coast, came to me and said she and her teaching partner, Jeremy, would like to do it.

Stephanie was a gem of a teacher who gave the lie to the negative profiling of Gen Y. She was dedicated and passionate and drove herself and others tirelessly. But she was also physically slight and her fine boned frame made me wonder if it was fair to let her volunteer for a 1000 kilometre ride into the outback. I didn't know Jeremy, her teaching partner, as well as Steph. Everyone teased him for his New Zealand accent. 'Say Six, Jeremy!' He struck me as a courteous, laid back, humorous kind of person who took most things in his stride. His big news, coming back to work after summer, was that his wife was pregnant and he was still grinningly accepting congratulations from a small knot of staff when I caught up with him after morning tea. 'Yes, glad to,' he said when I checked that he was really up for the Nicawinna ride. 'I need to get fit now I'm going to be a dad. And don't worry about Steph. She's tougher than she looks.'

Somewhere ahead of us in the shimmering heat, Mick was shadowing Jeremy, driving his 4WD that he'd ingeniously converted into an escort vehicle by building a storage and sleeping cabin on top. Mick, the maintenance man at school, was mechanic, purser and cook on this trip and I wouldn't have dared take it on without his know-how and commonsense, not to mention the hearty meals that he cooked en route.

I had a lot to think about during the long slow hours of driving. In only a few months I'd be leaving. I had thought I was ready for my retirement this time and that I had my succession plan neatly secured at the school. But one by one during the last few months my keystones had become dislodged. First Zandra handed in her resignation, saying her work with us was finished and she was off to find a new struggling cause she could turn into a success. Then Sarah confided that she and her partner had decided to start a family and though she knew I had her tagged to replace me, she would not be applying for the role of principal. Pia Lombardi then warned me she would be applying for maternity leave and, worst of all, Fergus announced he was stepping down as Chair and leaving the Board because his company needed him to give more time to his job.

'What's wrong with God, Gertie?' I complained. 'I was so pleased at having everything covered, knowing the school would roll on from strength to strength, the high school would unfold, all the children and parents would be safe. It was all in place, and now look at the mess.'

'Seems to me it's your plan that's gone awry, not God's.' Sister Gertrude was not smiling and I looked at her closely. I had come to join her under the lilly pilly tree, seeking a little commiseration in my disappointments, expecting to be teased and hoping to be cheered, but there was no fun. I saw that her eyes were sunken with deep shadows and as the sun caught her frizzy black hair, there were streaks of iron grey. Even the redoubtable Sister Gertrude was getting old.

'Are you OK, Gertie?'

'Yes, I'm fine. Only thing is, I'm losing my hearing. I had no idea how much I needed it to find my way around. It's awful. And people too. I used to know them by their voices. Now I don't know who's speaking or where they are. I don't s'pose it matters because I don't know what they're saying either.'

'But you knew me just now and heard me.'

'Oh that! Even God heard you complaining, Jo.' There was an uncommon edge to her voice despite the laugh, but I thought it only too understandable. She had given her life to God and to teaching the blind and this is what she had for it. It certainly put my disappointment into perspective.

Just before we left on our momentous cycling adventure, Gertie had placed in my hands as a gift for the trip a beautiful copy of the prayer commonly attributed to the martyred Archbishop Oscar Romero. Now as my eyes stayed glued on Stephanie's relentless legs, I said over and over to myself so as to memorise the words: *This is what we are about ... planting seeds that one day will grow ... laying foundations we won't build upon ... We accomplish in our lives only a tiny fraction ... nothing we do is ever complete ... no programme accomplishes all its mission ...*

Ahead of me, Stephanie pulled in to the side of the road and leaned exhaustedly over her bike. I stopped the van and reached behind the seat to pull out another bottle of the hydrating sports drink with which I'd filled the van. I wished Steph would just shove her bike in the back and let me drive her to the next stop. But to her it would be giving in and also letting down all her enthusiastic sponsors, not to ride every single one of those painful kilometres. The harder the ride got, and the longer it went on, the more deeply she drew on her inner reserves until it seemed that she herself was on test out there. I understood all too well but it was troubling to watch.

'The heat is really building, Steph. It must be close to forty degrees. It's not realistic to think you can keep this up.'

'How far to the truck stop?'

'Twenty five kilometres.'

'I'll start again in five minutes.'

'No, Steph. You can't do it. Hop into the van and let's drive there. It's not far and once we meet up with Jeremy and Mick we can decide where to stay the night.'

'Jeremy won't sleep over tonight. He's too worried about his wife. He's going to ride through to Nicawinna today, I know it.'

'But Steph you can't do that. You know you can't.'

'I have to. I'm all right, really.' She handed me the now empty drink bottle and swinging her leg over her bike, gave me a wave and rode off. I got back into the van very troubled. I thought Jeremy probably could ride through without stopping. His legs were amazing and each day of this trip they seemed to get stronger. When he'd stripped off at our first stop-over, sleeping in the school hall at Bathurst, I'd seen the Maori tattoos on his chest and realised where his extraordinary strength had its roots. And the slight and valiant Steph was attempting to match him.

Our plan had been to break the 260 km stretch from Cobar to Nicawinna at a truck stop and camp the night. But when we had reached Cobar the night before, Jeremy found a text from his wife saying she was bleeding and afraid for her baby, who was not due for another three months. Jeremy had gone pale beneath his week-old tan. We discussed abandoning the trip and heading back for Sydney but he didn't want to let the kids down. He knew they'd be waiting at Nicawinna.

'Let's see what the news is in the morning,' he had said. Early the next day, his wife rang to say she was in hospital and the doctors thought the chances were good that she'd go full term. 'We'll keep on to Nicawinna,' Jeremy decided.

When we pulled into the truck stop twenty five kilometers and over an hour later, Mick and Jeremy were just finishing their lunch. Steph was very quiet. She slid into the seat alongside Jeremy and didn't answer when Mick joked about their being ready to go. I went to order her a hamburger and as I brought it back, I saw Jeremy was up and stretching his hamstrings. That meant he was going to ride on.

'I've rung through to Brandon and told him we'll be there in five hours,' he said, straightening up. 'The kids are all terribly excited, he says and they'll be at the school to welcome us in.'

'It's over forty degrees, Jeremy,' I protested. 'You look as fresh as a daisy but Steph isn't up to a five hour ride in this temperature.'

'Of course not. Put your cycle in the van and drive there, Steph.' he urged. She nodded and with a wave, Jeremy set off with Mick towards the car park. A few minutes later he rode past, Mick's 4WD following soon after. I looked at Steph, knowing how devastated she'd feel, giving up her goal. But she was smiling.

'Come on,' she said. 'Five hours to go and we have to get there by dark.'

She had her leg over her bike and was off, already on the road by the time I had reversed the van and driven out of the car park. The sun was baking down and creating mirages on the bitumen. As I sweated in the cabin of the campervan and watched Steph push herself towards oblivion in the oppressive heat outside, I knew why she couldn't let go. She was just one of those people driven to putting the world to rights and this ride for the children of Nicawinna was her way of defying the wrongness of things. What she could do was small but she would give her whole self to it, to obliterate by effort the paradox that no effort is ever enough. And I was letting her push herself on to her goal because I secretly identified with her. Because I couldn't deal with letting go of my own fading dream. But it was over forty degrees and she had been cycling for six days and was now running only on will power.

Four hours later the shadows were growing long on the road; it would soon be dark. Steph had slowed to below ten kilometres an hour and we were still fifty kilometres out of Nicawinna. Then I saw her, with a shrug of defeat, pull to a stop and lean heavily over her handlebars. I braked quickly and stumbled hastily out of the van. Steph had grabbed the drink bottle from the side of her bike and was drinking slowly from it. She didn't look at me. 'I can't do any more,' she said in a flat voice. 'It's all I wanted, to ride all the way, but I'm done.' She let me take her cycle from her and stow it in the back of the van as she dejectedly levered herself into the passenger seat as though she was climbing into a paddy wagon. Her face was set grimly and although I ached for her, I couldn't think of a consoling word. I turned my attention to getting us to the school before the party ended. But although I kept my foot flat to the floor and got every bit of speed from the old van that it could give, when in the gathering dark we finally pulled up at the school there was only Brandon and his wife Vivienne, with a fresh-looking Jeremy and smiling Mick, sitting at a table covered with empty plates under a welcome banner and a dozen slightly deflated balloons.

'Sorry, the kids couldn't wait,' said Brandon standing up. 'We weren't sure how long you'd be. But we kept some cake for you.' He poured us a glass of red cordial as he described how the children and parents had made a guard of honour for Jeremy as he rode in. 'You should have seen their faces when Jeremy handed over the cheque for $7000. Now they know that getting to Sydney is for real. They were terribly excited. Really I don't know how you did it, you guys. Cycling 1000 kilometres from Sydney to here. The kids feel terribly special, knowing you did it for them. They think they're kings.'

Steph didn't sit down. I watched her hang uncertainly by the table, exchange a few words with Brandon and Vivienne and then walk off out of sight behind the girls' toilets. When I got to her she was sitting on the grass with her head between her knees. 'I forgot it wasn't about me,' she said raising a face blank of emotion. 'It was about getting the kids to Sydney. And I wasn't here to see them. I got it wrong.' I wanted to protest, to say she had achieved a marathon of the human spirit against the odds, but I was silent before her despair and she got tiredly to her feet and walked off. I hardly slept that night. Whenever I closed my eyes, I saw the back wheel of Steph's bike and the flash of white socks as her muscled calves made a rhythm in my head: *I should have made her stop sooner, I should have got her here on time.*

Steph was young though. The next morning she got up early full of excited plans. She'd make up for not getting to the party by giving the children the best possible time while they were in Sydney. 'We'll take them to Manly, Jeremy. We'll go with our class. It'll be their first taste of the sea. Imagine it! Imagine how our kids will love taking them into the surf and teaching them to catch a wave.' Her eyes were shining, her disappointment buried.

We drove in convoy through the night on the trip home, eating up the miles at a pace which mocked Steph and Jeremy's pain doing it by bike. As the two of them slept through unawares in Mick's 4WD, I drove behind, thinking about what it was that brought the best of teachers to work at a small special school. For it wasn't just Steph and Jeremy, the other staff were the same, people any principal would prize having on staff, resilient, self-giving, dedicated to the children, refusing to take time off, endlessly patient and inventive. We paid less than other non-government schools and we asked longer unpaid hours, yet they came to work brimming over with laughter and optimism. Most stayed with us for years and years, through their youth, through their baby rearing years, through their menopause. Still they stayed. What was our secret?

It was not just teachers but the volunteers too. When I caught one volunteer at the end of her long day to thank her, she said, 'Oh no, don't thank me. This is the highlight of my week. It's the children. I love them.' And that was it, I thought. It's the children. Funny that people don't see their beauty, not until they get close up and personal. It had taken me a while. And yet, I thought as I drove along, it is because of our children that we keep such amazing people at the school. It's because through the children our lives become joy-filled, surprising and meaningful.

By now we were rolling downhill towards Lithgow, the valley almost black apart from the few streetlights at its major crossroads. It wasn't just what we found in the children, I thought, changing gear as the old van started the steep climb out of Little Hartley and up Mt Victoria. It was also what the children found in us, and brought out of us. We were at our best when we were with them. They were honest and funny and they loved us without agenda, but they were also confusing, confronting and pushed us to the limits of our being. We none of us wanted to leave because we didn't want to lose touch with the deeper self the children drew from us, nor give up that experience of shining they evoked somewhere between our hearts and our souls. Afar off, I glimpsed the pin-point lights of Sydney spread across the plain. Less than an hour to home.

Two months after our marathon trip, the Nicawinna children and their families and teachers made their trip to Sydney. We were agog with anticipation when the dust-covered bus offloaded its gaggle of excited, gesticulating little brown children in red t-shirts who shouted and giggled and then fell silent as they looked around at the watching white children. I had not thought about this. To eyes not used to them, our children were a miscellany of shapes and aberrations and while they smiled eagerly at their new friends who'd landed among them, the Nicawinna children shrank a little. It was an awkward moment. Seeing it, Steph and Jeremy quickly stepped forward and with cheerful encouragement moved everyone through to the playground where the visitors got over the shock of the first encounter by clambering onto the climbing spider and sharing a rope, whirling round in a group on the super fast carousel and lining up together to use the flying fox.

At the end of a day of art and drama and dance and giggling, all the children gathered in the worship space for the Goodbye Song and I went along to farewell the Nicawinna mob. It was the usual babble of voices and mass of squirming movement only I noticed that red t-shirts were mingled with our stripy school tops and I saw Athena holding hands with one of the Nicawinna twins.

I thought of the awkward, faltering assemblies we used to have in the early days in the old gym. Now our children's energy filled the room as they confidently ran the end-of-day ceremony themselves. Tomasz, a clever boy with autism in Year 5, had the microphone.

'We have to say goodbye to our special visitors. Sit down. Be quiet,' he began. And as the chatter continued, he called over to me, 'Come and do cross, Karaolis.'

Once I had everyone seated and as silent as they could manage, I handed the microphone back to Tomasz. He put on his public smile and launched into a prepared speech. 'Our visitors are from Nicawinna. They came by bus. The bus went on the Newell Highway, then the Mitchell Highway, then the Barrier Highway and the Great Western Highway and lots more highways until they got to Cleveland Street, Wahroonga which is our place. Now it's time to sing. Everybody come out the front and sing.'

As the children crowded out the front and I watched little Jimmy Grady push himself between Tibby and Donald from Nicawinna and hold their hands, Steph slipped up behind me. 'This is everything you've worked for, isn't it?' she whispered into my ear. 'They are so alive. Everyone different and all mixed in together.'

The music had started and the children's voices rang out in loud enthusiasm, the song they all loved, *'We share a dream, we sing with one voice, we are Australian.*' With Tomasz vigorously conducting, slightly after the beat, the children who had never travelled beyond their *'dusty red soil plains'* before, joined in loudly with the city children who had no idea they were different, not even in colour. I turned and smiled at Steph.

'It's grace, isn't it?' I said. 'Grace. That's what it is.' It was in the energy that rose from the children as they gave themselves full-heartedly to the moment. It was in the smile she gave back to me.

The parents had put together a book for me as a farewell gift. On every page were portraits of their children, photographs and self-portraits and scribbles, with words from the parents and over and over they said the same thing. 'Maggie loves school', 'Jesse never wants to miss a day of school', 'Sam always says as we drive away, Goodbye Happy School'. This life force didn't depend on me or Sarah or Pia or the Chair of the Board. It sprang from the children and was kept alive by them.

I could see Logan sitting at the back, now a member of the class who would be going off to high school next year. His unshakable friendship with his invisible dragon had come to a tragic end a few weeks before. His teacher found him sobbing in the playground because Joshua had killed the dragon. 'Did he say sorry?' the teacher asked. 'Yes', replied Logan in a voice of doom, 'but it was too late'. And as he stood there, inconsolable, little Jillian had walked over and handed him the pretty leaf she had been twirling in her hand. There was a quality of innocence in this place left over as it were from the time before humans ate the apple of knowledge and lost paradise. It was grace. I had been lucky to have it in my care for a time and now it was passing into the care of other hands.

In October the school held a Changing of the Guard ceremony, just before the new principal was to begin her induction period. I sat up on the stage next to the Governor, Professor Marie Bashir, who had been a good friend to us, as to so many, over the years, and Fergus of course, who was now the outgoing Chair and Father David. Everyone seemed to be there, even those whose children had left years before. I picked out parents from all through the years and marvellous patrons of the school, like the architects and other donors who had given us so much, and Gae who had come down from Darwin sitting with Zandra. And then I saw Lyell, Harry's Dad and there were tears on his face and I stopped looking. I had to hold it together. There was so much I wanted to say today of the lessons that I had learnt from the children: to give myself up to the joy, or the grief, or the humour of the moment; to know that a life worth living comes in many forms and that all lives flourish where there is enough love.

First though, young Richard was to lead everyone in the school's version of the creed. He had rehearsed it over and over with Pia but now when he stood and looked out at the hundreds of people in front of him, he froze. A few seconds of awful silence as everyone held their breath and then, his face red and blotched with distress, he rushed from the stage. The audience covered for him by loudly reciting the words of the creed from the programme and then it was time for my speech.

I was just getting started on the official welcome to the Governor and distinguished guests when I saw Pia Lombardi out of the corner of my eye, signalling urgently, with Richard beside her. At first I shook my head: it was too late, we'd already done the creed, but she went on nodding and pointing at Richard. Of course, I thought, what was important here? I beckoned him up on to the stage and with his chest out and his chin up, he proudly said the words he had practised so hard. *I believe in God who out of love created the world.* And everyone in that huge audience repeated after him as though they had not just said those very same words. *I believe in Jesus who out of love came to live on earth. I believe in the Holy Spirit who out of love breathes life through us.* Then they loudly clapped him as he walked proudly from the stage. I had a quick look at my watch. The buses would be here for the children soon.

Never mind: it would take a book to say all that was in my heart. I gave away my prepared speech and made a simple acknowledgement of my gratitude to them all. Then I took off my shoes. 'People say my successor has big shoes to fill.' I held them up and then crossed the dais and placed, in the hands of the very tall new principal, the very small shoes of a short seventy year old woman whose day was done. Then I stood in my stockinged feet and felt my cheeks grow wet as I looked out at the mass of friends who rose to acknowledge the journey we had travelled together, with clapping that went on, and on, and on.

GOODBYE

Shortly before the year ended, as I was sorting through my personal files for papers I should leave for the new principal, Morgan came to tell me she had an appointment with her oncologist. 'Tas doesn't want me to have the tests,' she confided. 'He says they won't change anything and why do we have to know?' I understood how he felt. I didn't want to know either. But Morgan gave a rueful smile. 'I can see his point,' she said, 'but I'm restless. I have to find out.' I made her promise to call as soon as she could with the results. I hung around near my phone all afternoon and stayed at my desk for anxious hours into the night but no call came. It could only mean that the results were bad. I sat in the gloom of my desk lamp and thought about those others who had died: mischievous Harry and wise Sister Clare, and so recently, beautiful Lori: all those prayers unanswered and now another. Next morning there was still no word from Morgan and small huddles of whispering staff gathered in corridors and corners, all pretence of optimism gone.

Then just before the Recess bell at eleven 'o' clock I heard Shelagh's voice shout out in the foyer and Morgan walked into my office. Her wide open eyes were staring as though in shock. She stood hesitantly in the doorway, her hand over her mouth, and peered at me in silence. Then, dropping her hand, she said, 'Get this. You won't believe it.' She moved across the room to flop into my visitor's chair. 'The cancer has gone. The oncologist couldn't find a trace of it. They did the tests twice. It went so late I couldn't ring and then I didn't know what to say. I've been preparing to die for so long, I don't know how to talk about living.'

At last, a miracle, the one most prayed for. Word ran around the school faster than fire: people emerged from their rooms and shouted down the corridors asking each other, *is it true?* Children caught the carnival atmosphere and wanting to be part of it, were let loose on the playground to dance about with their teachers. It transformed the last few weeks at school for all of us. I was euphoric. Nothing mattered now, everything was perfect. I waved off the children, I hugged all the staff, I archived my files and prepared for my last Board meeting.

I had planned a gift for the children as my farewell signature but it arrived only after they left for the summer holidays. I needed a ceremony so I resolved to unveil it at my final meeting with the Board. It was a statement of a kind. A prayer that the children would always be cherished and kept safe, an acknowledgement of St Dominic who inspired this school, a concession to the Catholic way of communicating faith through sculptures and statues. Two Sydney sculptors, Gillie and Marc, had created it for me and I had asked Father David to come over before the Board meeting and unveil it. I invited a few of the Dominicans too: Sister Agnes and of course, Sister Gertrude. Dear Shelagh, Pia and Sarah had stayed back to join the Board members who were sitting uncomfortably on metal chairs in gently falling rain, just outside the front entrance, and even Jorge was there, leaning on his long mop.

Father David said a prayer of blessing and then carefully and painstakingly tugged at the blanket covering the robust, bulky shape to reveal ... a dog, a beautiful, big bronze sculpted dog. Dominic's dog, his eternal symbol. A labrador in tribute to the school's many years as a school for the blind. A friendly, eager dog with large compassionate eyes standing on watch. I imagined generations of children to come, rushing to hug their friend the dog as they arrived at school. I looked to the Sisters to see if they found it a subversive gesture from someone with no taste for religious icons, but they were smiling. I could hardly contain the grin spreading across my face. I was leaving, but the dog would remain.

Two weeks later I gave my office its final clearing out, emptied my desk drawers into boxes and packed away the photos and mementoes from ten years at this special place. It took several trips out to my car before I had the last carton stowed in place. I set the alarms and pulled the big front doors closed behind me. Dominic's dog sat on the front steps, solid and very present. I leaned down and reached my arms around his cold bronze neck. 'Take care of them for me,' I whispered. Then I went to my car and drove out the gates for the last time.

ACKNOWLEDGEMENTS

The journey that culminated in this book was inspired by encounters at an early time with three exceptional young people. Stephen Nancarrow was the son of our local minister, a young boy with cerebral palsy and a loving, sensitive heart. Jill Suggate was a fellow-student at Janet Clarke Hall, Melbourne University who dealt with her lack of physical control with immense courage and humour. Jordana Goodman was in my first class at SCEGGS Darlinghurst. It was in company with these three young people that I grew to look beyond the impairments that fate or genetics can dispose to recognise nobility of heart greater than most of us can attain.

From my St Catherine's years I wish to acknowledge all my beautiful students and pay special tribute to Michelle Mallet, Alex Toohey, Alexandra Robinson and Joanna Garvin.

A throng of children from St Lucy's School have inspired this book. Their shining spirits, their honest forthright perception, their deep abiding love for life and for others are now part of who I am. I hope I have captured something of their special quality in this book. The teachers and staff of St Lucy's, as in any vibrant school, are at the core of what is best in our society. The tolerance and friendship they so freely gave me are among my dearest treasures. To the parents I offer my humble admiration and gratitude for the gifts of courage and joy that life has drawn from them.

The publication of this book gives me the opportunity to acknowledge the many corporate and professional people who helped us in our goal of providing the best possible environment and opportunities for children who might otherwise have missed out. I am thinking of those who awarded us seed grants, especially the Telstra Foundation and Westpac Foundation who launched our creative arts programme and the James N. Kirby Foundation who financed our support for St Therese's, Wilcannia. Special thanks too to John McBain at Centurion, the IT and HR staff of Westfield and to Cathy Sertori whose interest in our students led to the Farrell Family scholarship programme.

I owe much to special friends like Alec Tzannes and Jonathon, Eleanor and Derek from Tzannes and Associates; the inimitable Robert Burton who gave us our uniform; and the many individuals who gave generously to playground, buildings, teaching programmes and equipment: too many to name unfortunately.

Then there are the psychologists, social workers, paediatricians and lawywers who gave advice freely when

Acknowledgements

we or our parents needed it, and of course the political representatives who gave advice and assistance including Barry O'Farrell, Mitch Fifield, Paul Fletcher, Brendan Nelson, Alex Hawke, Jacinta Collins and not least, Julia Gillard.

I wish to acknowledge the unfailing support of the St Lucy's School Board even in times when things, and I, were most difficult, especially Beth Gilligan and Tim Horvat; also the members of the St Lucy's Foundation and its Chair, Anton Tagliaferro. Anton's support and assistance in every aspect of St Lucy's development was pivotal.

Special thanks also to Andrew Bird and David Goodrich and to the indomitable Gailene Keen whose work is celebrated in these pages. My deep thanks to the Dominican Sisters who founded St Lucy's and laid the foundations of the special place it is today and who gently shaped their non-Catholic recruit.

Thank you to the staff of the Broken Bay Diocese and the Catholic Education Office and to Anne Duncan and other principals of Narraweena and Narrabeen; to my fellow-principals of the seven Catholic special schools, thanks for your comradeship, and to Patrick Ellis and Sister Margaret at St Therese's, Wilcannia, I salute you.

I wish in particular to acknowledge the spiritual leadership provided to staff and parents, and to myself in particular, by Fr David Ranson, and the personal support of my professional supervisor, Ann Mulheron.

The writing, editing and publishing of this book is the fruit of much labour not my own. It began in the Memoir writing classes of Faber & Faber and owes much therefore to the guidance of Patti Miller but also to the friendly critique, encouragement and companionship of my fellow writers, especially Penny, Jayne, Rebecca, Ann, Therese, Camilla and Jessica.

Thank you to Anthony Reeder for editing and to Janet Grundy for her painstaking copy editing and her generous advice and assistance as monitoring angel. Thank you to all who have read the manuscript in its different stages and given advice or permission, with especial gratitude to Terry Williamson. I wish to thank the wonderful people at Captain Honey publishers, Roz and Natalie, and Stieve at Reputation Australia, and the two very generous donors who enabled me to take advantage of their services, Guy Fowler and Anton Tagliaferro.

Very importantly, I wish to thank those who have read the book and written endorsements for it, especially Prof Robyn Ewing, Prof Gordon Stanley, Hugh Mackay, Prof Mary Foley and David Gonski. It was a special privilege and delight to have Professor the Honourable Dame Marie Bashir, with her extensive knowledge and experience of children's needs, accept my invitation to write a Foreword.

Most of all I am indebted to my friend Robyn Chadwick for her generosity in providing delightful drawings to enhance every chapter and to her wonderful art protégée

Acknowledgements

Clare Hooper for permission to use her painting in the cover.

In conclusion I wish to thank the people most precious to me for the part they played in the journey and for letting me include them in these pages, my children Christina and Michael, Guillaume and Olivia, and my very special grandchildren Alexi, Won Bhin, Dan and Rose.

Printed in Great Britain
by Amazon